SCIENCE AND INTEGRATED RURAL DEVELOPMENT

M.S. SWAMINATHAN

CONCEPT PUBLISHING COMPANY, NEW DELHI 110059

First Published 1982
Reprinted 1991

Published and Printed by
Ashok Kumar Mittal
Concept Publishing Company
A/15-16, Commercial Block, Mohan Garden
New Delhi 110059

PREFACE

WHEN I was approached by the Concept Publishing Company for permission to bring together some of the lectures I had delivered during the past ten years, I readily agreed in the hope that such a compilation may be of some value to students and scholars interested in ending the divorce between intellect and labour in rural India, which Mahatma Gandhi identified about 50 years ago as the major cause of rural poverty. It is now widely agreed that unless the drain of brains and resources from the village to the town is arrested, India will never derive benefit from its real blessings—soil, water, sunshine, plants, animals and vast numbers of hardworking and honest rural women and men. In my view the pathway for achieving a reversal of current trends is a mass movement designed to foster a blend of brain, brawn and bank in rural professions. Brain power provides us with location specific, economically viable and culturally compatible technologies which help to convert the natural endowments of each area into wealth meaningful to the people. Brawn or hard work involving physical labour helps to promote labour intensive technologies and foster production by masses. Bank or financial and other resources are essential for achieving modernisation of agriculture, industry and services since modernisation involves the use of cash inputs, in addition to non-monetary ones.

The data cited in the various lectures are largely from the publications of our Agricultural Universities, Research Institutes of the Indian Council of Agricultural Research and the Economics and Statistics Directorate of the Ministry of Agriculture. I owe a deep debt of gratitude to them. The data relate to the time when the lecture was delivered and have not been updated. My sincere thanks are due to many colleagues and students who from time to time have helped me in collecting references and information.

M.S. SWAMINATHAN

CONTENTS

GLOSSARY OF TERMS USED

arhar : Pigeon pea (*Cajanus cajan* Milsp.)

bajra : Pearl millet (*Pennisetum typhoides* L.)

balwadis : Child care centres

ber : *Zizyphus jujuba*

catla : Indian common carp

diara : Riverine land (along major rivers)

grampanchayat : Village council

gram sabha : Village assembly

gram sevak : Village level worker

gram sevika : Village level worker (female)

gur : Jaggery

jamun : *Eugenia jambulana*

jhumming : Shifting cultivation

jowar : Sorghum (*Sorghum vulgare* Pers.)

kalitur : Variety of soy-bean with black skin colour

Kankar : Small pebble

khadir : Bowl like land system on either side of the river bank

kharif : South-west monsoon season (May to September)

krishi melas : Farmers' fairs

Krishi Vigyan Kendras : Farm Science Centres

moong : Green gram (*Phaseoulus aureus* Roxb.)

mrigal :	Indian common carp
phalsa :	*Grewia subinaequalis*
rabi :	Winter season (October to March)
regur :	Deep black soil (vertisols)
rohu :	Indian common carp
til :	Sesame (*Sesamum indicum* L.)
urad :	Black gram (*phaseous mungo* Var. *radiatus* Lin.)
warabandi (system) :	Rotational distribution of water

ABBREVIATIONS

ARDC : Agricultural Refinance and Development Corporation
ARIMA : Auto Regressive Integrated Moving Averages
BHC : Benzene Hexachloride
CAD : Command Area Development
CADA : Command Area Development Authority
CAZRI : Central Arid Zone Research Institute
CCA : Culturable Command Area
CGWB : Central Ground Water Board
DNA : Deoxyribonucleic acid
DPAP : Drought Prone Areas Programme
DRDA : District Rural Development Agency
ESD : Economics and Statistics Directorate
ETO : Exploratory Tubewells Organisation
FAO : Food and Agricultural Organisation
GDP : Gross Domestic Product
GMF : Grow More Food
GNP : Gross National Product
GSI : Geological Survey of India
GWP : Gross World Product
HYVP : High-Yielding Varieties Programmes
IADP : Intensive Agriculture Development Programme
IARI : Indian Agricultural Research Institute
ICAR : Indian Council of Agricultural Research
INSAT : Indian National Geostationary Satellite
IRD : Integrated Rural Development
KVK : Krishi Vigyan Kendra
LPM : Litres Per Minute
MCM : Milliard Cubic Metre
MFA : Most Favourable Area
MIT : Massachusetts Institute of Technology
MSA : Most Seriously Affected

NCA	:	National Commission on Agriculture
NCAER	:	National Council of Applied Economic Research
NCPB	:	National Crop Planning Board
NCST	:	National Committee on Science and Technology
NREP	:	National Rural Employment Project
OFD	:	On Farm Development
PEO	:	Programme Evaluation Organisation
REC	:	Rural Electrification Corporation
SFDA	:	Small Farmers Development Agency
TRYSEM	:	Training Rural Youth for Self-Employment
UNDP	:	United Nations Development Programme

OUR AGRICULTURAL FUTURE 1

FOOD is a basic requirement in the hierarchical needs of man. The successful domestication of plants, animals, soil and water by settled human communities has hence been the starting point for the evolution of culture and orderly government. Ironically, the very centres of civilisation, where the domestication of plants and animals took place in the past, are the areas which are struggling today to find an honourable equation between population growth and food supply on the one hand, and population growth and opportunities for productive and remunerative employment, on the other. The secondary and tertiary centres of origin of agriculture have, in contrast, more than enough to eat and constitute the developed or rich nations of the world.

It has been estimated that in the poor nations, which have contributed most of the domesticated plants and animals to the world, nearly 800 million individuals live under conditions of absolute poverty, resulting in protein-calorie malnutrition, squalor, illiteracy and disease. Again, ironically, the lands of the poor have often greater biological assets, the most important of which is abundance of sunlight throughout the year, rendering the historic concept of cereal inapplicable. This word refers to crops which grow during only part of the year, being derived from the myth of Ceres' happy seasonal reunion with her daughter. On our earth, appropriately compared to a spaceship by Buckminister Fuller, the first class compartment which the rich nations as well as the rich of the poor nations occupy, is consuming a greater and greater proportion of the available resources, thereby making life for those living in absolute poverty more and more hard. Those living in the first class compartment of the spaceship have forgotten the meaning of the prayer 'God, give us our daily bread', while for the vast majority of humanity squeezed into the small second class compartment, 'God is bread', to use the words of Mahatma Gandhi. Why are we in this state of paradox ? Why do plants seem to be unhappy and hence not so productive in their historic native homes ?

Contrasting trends

The state of food and agriculture in the world shows two contrasting trends. In one kind of agriculture, larger and larger farms are being farmed by fewer and fewer cultivators. Such farms are highly automated and capital-intensive. To cite an illustration : A recent article on computerised farming in California tells how a firm called Superior Farming Company, owned by a Texas oil company, raises 26 different crops on about 6,000 hectares,with land and equipment worth about Rs 30 crores. In this agri-business, an irrigation system, called the drip method, brings individually piped water to every fruit tree and regulates the flow to a trickle, supplying exactly what each tree needs and no more. Under such systems of farming, not only is the efficiency of use of inputs such as water and fertiliser high, but labour productivity also is very high. In one study conducted during the mid-1950s it was found that while in many countries of Asia and Africa about 2.5 to 10 work days were needed to produce one quintal of grain, the extent of labour time needed to produce the same quantity of grain was about 3 hours in parts of France and only 6-12 minutes in parts of the U.S.A. The gap in the relative productivity of farm labour was therefore about 1 to 800 even over 15 years ago and this gap, which also represents the relative earning and purchasing power of farm labour, has been growing ever since.

In many of the poor nations, including our own, smaller and smaller farms have to be cultivated by the same or even larger number of farmers. The percentage of work force employed in farming in India was 72.1 in 1971 and it is anticipated that this percentage will remain practically unaltered in 1981. The relative productivity of small farms, however, varies widely in the world. McNamara (1973) recently pointed out that 'if Japan could produce 6,720 kg of grain per hectare on very small farms in 1970, then Africa with its 1,270 kg, Asia with 1,750 kg and Latin America with 2,060 kg per hectare have an enormous potential for expanding productivity.

Agricultural growth

Besides farm size and land and labour productivity, the other two major differences in the agriculture of the rich nations as compared to the poor ones, are in the pattern of agricultural growth and the nature of the food chain. The mechanised and low-labour consuming agriculture has achieved increased productivity largely on the basis of a high consumption of energy derived from the non-renewable resources of the earth. Thus, while in 1964, about 286 kilocalories of energy were needed in countries like India and Indonesia to produce one kg of rice protein, 2,860 kilocalories of energy were needed to produce one kg of wheat protein and over 65,000 kilocalories to produce one kg of beef protein in the U.S.A. Such a situation has now resulted in a widespread awareness of the simple truth that any finite resource, if exploited in an exponential manner on the assumption that the resource is infinite, will some day or the other get exhausted, thereby bringing the pattern of growth based on its consumption to ruin.

It has also become clear that the tools of modernisation of agriculture, such as pesticide, fertiliser, farm power and water, if indiscriminately used and excessively, based on non-renewable resources, will end in crises now referred to as 'ecological crises', 'energy crises' and so on. For example, 96 per cent of the energy input in the U.S.A. in 1970 came from oil, gas and coal, while in the same year non-commercial fuels namely, dung, firewood and wastes provided 52 per cent of our energy needs. The reserves of the fossil fuels are expected to decline rapidly in the next 30 years and even now, we have started witnessing some shortages of the most desirable fuels. Our agricultural production process is still predominantly based on the use of renewable resources but our current productivity is very low. Hence, there is urgent need for the development of technologies where the productivity of land can be continuously increased with diminishing dependence on non-renewable components of energy, by deploying recycling processes more and more effectively. A consequence of the agriculture of the high-energy-consumption and low-labour-input pattern is the diversion of labour from agriculture to more industrial pursuits and a close linkage between farm and factory. Diversification of labour use, leading to a reduction in the number of people employed in the physical operations of farming has historically been associated with a rise in the standard of living.

Contrasting food chains

A biological consequence of affluence has been a rise in the consumption of animal products. The poor and rich nations are hence characterised today by the former depending largely on the plant-to-man food chain and the latter on the plant-animal-man food chain. Consequently, the average per capita consumption of grain is about one tonne per year in the developed nations, out of which only about 70 kg are consumed directly in the form of bread, biscuits, cakes and other products made from flour. The remaining 930 kg are used to feed animals whose products like meat, milk and eggs are consumed by man. In contrast, the per capita consumption of grain per year in the developing countries is about 190 kg, most of which is directly consumed.

To summarise, the two major contrasting systems of agriculture we see today differ in the size of farm, the proportion of work force employed in agriculture, the types of linkages developed between farm and factory, the extent of consumption of non-renewable resources of energy, management efficiency, per capita productivity and income, and the extent of use of animal products in daily diet. Our need is an agricultural system where the benefits of a large human and animal population, robust soils, abundant sunlight, rich ecological diversity, availability of large quantities of organic wastes and a fairly extensive irrigation network are optimised in a manner that productivity is continuously increased without damage to the long term production potential of the soil, stability is imparted to the production as well as prices of foodgrains and labour and land use diversified, so as to increase real income and purchasing power.

About 10 years ago, some foreign experts believed that India could never become self-sufficient in its food requirements. They predicted the outbreak of widespread famine and hunger in India on the basis of theoretical calculations of the year when the food needs of the poor nations would exceed the capacity of the rich nations to meet them. William and Paul Paddock (1967) for example fixed this year as 1975. Some others felt that such a contingency would arise only in 1985. Our failure to achieve the anticipated results with the community development and the intensive agricultural district programmes during the 1950s and early 1960s fanned the sentiments of the pessimists.

It was widely believed that in our rural areas developmental action and achievement were being impeded by the limited sights of our farming community. Experts wondered why we should find it so difficult to become self-reliant in our food needs, when there appeared to exist several easy pathways of attaining this goal. An expert on rodent control would thus advocate the control of rats to wipe out the deficit in our food budget, while the agronomist would plead for using good seeds and some fertiliser for achieving the same end. The fact remained, however, that progress in improving production was slow and largely took place through an increase in the cropped and irrigated area, rather than through any appreciable increase in productivity. The economic plight of the small farmer remained unchanged since his real income would rise only if productivity was improved and marketing organised so that the small producer got a fair share of the price paid by the consumer for a commodity. While the government was anxious to push up agricultural production, there was despair during the drought years of the mid-sixties concerning our agricultural destiny.

Famines and scarcities

Historically, famines and scarcities have been known in our country from the earliest times. They are mentioned in the Mahabharata and there is a Jain legend of a 12-year famine in the fourth century A.D. It is recorded by the official historian in the *Badshah Namah* that in the famine of 1630-32, the Emperor Shah Jehan opened soup kitchens, gave 1.5 lakhs to charity and remitted 1/11 of the land revenue in the affected area. Subsequently, there have been numerous famines but it was only during the famine of 1868-69, that it was clearly stated that 'the object of government was to save every life'. The birth of agricultural departments in our States and of Famine Codes took place as a result of the recommendations of the Famine Commission of 1878. The Scarcity Manuals currently used by several state governments are largely based on the Famine Codes of the last century. Verghese's penetrating articles (1967-1973) entitled Beyond the famine and A blessing code named famine on the droughts of Bihar and Maharashtra have highlighted the advantages conferred on the helpless rural population by famines, since it is only during such crises that at least some food and employment are assured to those living in absolute poverty.

Meanwhile, a silent revolution has been taking place in the minds of our farming community as a result of the new production technologies introduced through the high-yielding varieties programmes, intensive cotton district programme including hybrid cotton which was introduced into commercial cultivation for the first time in the world, and the cattle cross-breeding projects. Obsession with destructive criticism has blinded us to the meaning and implications of the increase in wheat production from a little over 12 million tonnes to over 27 million tonnes in just six crop seasons beginning from 1967-68. There has not been much interest in studying how a small government programme in wheat was converted into a mass movement by our farmers. It is not only in Punjab or Haryana that wheat production went up dramatically but also in non-traditional wheat areas, such as West Bengal. While in the past it was difficult to induce farmers to take to a rat control operation, farmers took pains, in the wheat belt, to see that rats did not migrate from sugarcane fields to wheat. While in the past everyone knew that farmers were sitting over a large underground water resource in the Indo-Gangetic plains, it was only the introduction of high-yielding varieties of wheat and rice that provided the necessary motivation for them to take to the construction of tube wells—whether made of metal or of bamboo—on a large scale. The truth of the saying 'necessity is the mother of invention' was proved to be true in the case of wheat cultivation, where farmers somehow managed to produce or get the seeds they needed, use diesel pumps if electricity was not available and get the requisite number of threshers and other implements as well as storage bins fabricated in record time.

That our farmers may not wait for research workers to produce perfect tools but will themselves innovate and find a solution to a pressing need was shown by the Bihar farmer, Ram Prasad Chaudhary Jaiswal of the village Lalpur who first put up a bamboo tube well in the Saharsa district. Farmers who learnt the economic value of good management in wheat also took to better practices in rice, potato and other crops, with the result that agriculture as a whole started moving forward in such areas. The sudden and steep spurt in fertiliser demand is an eloquent testimony to the credibility of the new varieties and techniques. The concept that agricultural advance in India would suffer owing to the limited vision of the farming community was thus disproved. The social tensions between those who had access to the inputs needed for adopting the new technology and those who did not have similar access, only underlined the fact that those who have not derived economic benefit from such technology are equally anxious to take to the technology. The desire to change farming methods thus fanned both joy and sorrow in our countryside. This in turn generated considerable thinking and action on the part of the government, resulting in programmes for marginal and small farmers, expansion of credit facilities and more recently, in integrated farmers' service societies on the lines recommended by the National Commission on Agriculture.

Assets and liabilities

Thus, starting from the mid-sixties we have gone through waves of pessimism and optimism. We have been happy over good seasons and more than alarmed by bad ones. It is probably time that we look at our agricultural assets and liabilities critically and scientifically and evolve a pattern of growth which would help us to take full advantage of good seasons, be prepared for the worst and make agricultural growth yield more income and more jobs, in addition to more food. This is an appropriate time (1973) to undertake such a review since, thanks to one of the best *kharif* harvests we have had so far, we can afford to stop concentrating on holding operations and divert our attention to constructive programmes. Complacency at this stage and any relaxation of relentless efforts to achieve agricultural advance would be disastrous.

Let us deal with our agricultural assets first.

ASSETS

Sunlight, soil, water, plants, animals and human beings constitute the basic resources of our agriculture. Fortunately, sunlight is abundant except during limited periods in the monsoon season and generally does not constitute a limiting factor in production. In arid and semi-arid areas, the intensity of solar energy is fairly high and exceeds 650 calories per cm^2 per day. Under such conditions evapo-transpiration rates become high. The average annual values of energies available in peninsular and north India are 473 and 460 calories per cm^2 per day, respectively. Apart from the use of sunlight by plants in the process of photosynthesis, solar energy is used in rural areas for purposes, such as drying of crops and grains, distillation, evaporation for salt production and heating. There is, however, considerable scope for improving the use of sunlight both by plants, through multiple cropping, and by converting solar energy into thermal energy.

Out of our total geographical area of 328.05 million hectares, the net area sown during 1969-70 was about 139 million hectares. Forests occupied about 65 million hectares and uncultivated land was about 101 million hectares. Thus, the net sown area under crops in 1969-70 was 45.5 per cent of the reporting area and the area under forests was 21.3 per cent. The net national product was Rs 34,253 crores during 1970-71 at current prices and Rs 18,876 crores at constant 1960-61 prices. At 1960-61 prices, the contribution of agriculture, forestry and fishing to net national product in 1970-71 was 44.4 per cent. The contribution of agricultural products to the total export earning in the same year was 37.1 per cent.

Diversity in physiography

The physiography of our country shows great diversity. On the one hand we have major mountain ranges with the Himalaya—at once one of the youngest as well as the mightiest of the world's mountain systems—in the north, and the Aravallis, the Vindhyas, the Satpuras, the eastern and western Ghats and the north-eastern ranges including the Garo, Khasi and Jaintia hills in the other parts of the country. Plateaus, ranging in elevation from 300m to 900m constitute a prominent feature of our topography, the well-known among them being the Malwa, the Vindhya, the Chhota-Nagpur, the Satpura, the Deccan, Ladakh and Meghalaya. A very large part of the country consists of extensive plains watered by great rivers where a considerable proportion of humanity live. In the rivers originating from the Himalaya, the dry weather flow is generally good because of water from melting snows and glaciers. The lean period for these rivers is the winter months, but at no time is the flow so reduced as in the peninsular rivers. The flow in the rivers of peninsular India undulates heavily, with big discharges during the monsoons followed by low discharges during the rainless months. Variations of the order of 1 to 300 in the mean monthly flows of these rivers are common.

Our climate shows equally great diversity, ranging from continental to oceanic, from extremes of heat to extremes of cold, from extreme aridity and negligible rainfall to excessive humidity and torrential rainfall. The Himalaya present a barrier to the influence of cold winds from Central Asia and give the subcontinent the elements of a tropical type of climate. The variations in rainfall, temperature and humidity caused by the incursion of comparatively cool currents from the Indian Ocean across the Bay of Bengal and the Arabian Sea and by the movement of shallow depressions which originate outside India to the west, lead to extremely complex weather patterns which prevail even over those areas which can be grouped climatologically under a single type. Thus, temperature, rainfall and the amount of vapour in the air which influence greatly the growth of crops show wide variation even within small areas.

An interesting feature of the wind system over the Indian Ocean and the adjoining sea and land areas is the seasonal reversal of the monsoon. During the late summer the winds flow from the south-west over the sea towards India and Burma, while during the winter the flow of currents is from India and Burma over the Bay of Bengal and the Arabian Sea towards the Equator. The south-west monsoon season is responsible for over 80 per cent of the total rainfall in most parts of the country.

On an average, we receive an annual rainfall of about 370 million hectare-metres. It has been estimated that about 80 million hectare-metres seep into the soil of which about 43 million hectare-metres remain in the top layers and contribute to soil moisture which supports crop-growth. The ground water recharge available for utilisation may be of the order of 26.75 million hectare-metres, while the current utilisation is about 10 million hectare-metres. As a result of the various major, medium and minor irrigation projects undertaken, the area under irrigation during 1969-70 was 30.3 million hectares. The Second Irrigation Commission has calculated that the ultimate potential for irrigation from conventional sources is t81.7 million hectares. It is premature to guess what the contribution of weather modification and desalination will be in the future to augment water availability in drought-prone areas. The States which have less than 15 per cent of the net cultivated area with irrigation facilities are Karnataka, Madhya Pradesh, Maharashtra, Gujarat and Rajasthan.

Much of the knowledge we have on ground water resources is confined to the alluvial and semi-consolidated areas, whereas 70 per cent of the total geographical area of the country is covered by hard rock. The geo-hydrological studies carried out by the Geological Survey of India as well as the studies carried out under the auspices of the Central Ground Water Board have revealed great opportunities for scientific ground water exploitation. Fresh ground water has been found in the heart of the great Indian desert near Jaisalmer, in the Narmada and Purna valleys, the Rajamundry and Tirupati sandstone areas of Andhra Pradesh and the Cuddalore sandstone and the Neyveli lignite areas of Tamil Nadu, in addition to the already well-known areas of Punjab, Haryana, Uttar Pradesh, Bihar, West Bengal and Assam. Opportunities for lift irrigation from perennial streams and rivulets are also yet to be fully utilised.

With the growth of vegetation and evolution of agriculture, what were once geological deposits got gradually converted into soils. The topography, biology, physics and chemistry of soils provide an interesting account of past history of that soil. In particular, they indicate the extent of interest taken by man in the care and maintenance of soil fertility and productivity. Examined by such criteria our record is dismal.

Our major soil groups

We have four major groups of soils, alluvial, black, red and laterite, several other types, such as forest, desert, alkaline, saline and acidic soils occurring in smaller areas. The red soils occupy 72 million hectares and are found in both high and low rainfall areas. The stored moisture of a saturated red soil profile is generally sufficient to support a standing crop only for 2-4 weeks, hence mostly *kharif* crops are raised in such soils. Red soils are generally low in nitrogen, low to medium in phosphorus, and medium to high in potash. Drainage is not usually a problem in such soils and therefore, they can be converted into irrigated land without difficulty if a water source is available.

Black soils which occur in about 64 million hectares are variable in depth and are generally found in regions with an annual rainfall ranging from 500 mm to 1200 mm. While in the shallow black soils only *kharif* crops are grown, *rabi* crops are raised in the deeper soils with residual moisture. Drainage and erosion are serious problems in such soils and hence there have to be appropriate arrangements for drainage and soil conservation when such soils are brought under irrigation. Black soils contain 40-60 per cent clay and are plastic and sticky when wet and very hard when dry. They contain a high proportion of calcium and organic matter, magnesium carbonate, considerable iron and fairly large quantities of magnesia, alumina and potash. In black soils derived from ferruginous schists, there is generally a layer rich in nodules of *kankar* formed by segregation of calcium carbonate at lower depths. The most important difference between the red and the black soil lies in the amount and type of clay mineral present. The montmorillinitic type of clay predominates in the black soil and this imparts the characteristic swelling and shrinking properties of these soils. On the other hand, the non-swelling kaolinitic clay predominates in the red soil. The black soils, also known as 'grumosol', *regur* and 'black cotton soils', have self-mulching properties, the repeated wetting and drying causing clods to crumble into small aggregates forming a surface mulch. These soils are also referred to as being 'self-swallowing', since the surface mulch falls into the deep cracks and thus becomes incorporated into the sub-soil. Thus, on the one hand the black soils have a good capacity for conserving soil moisture, and on the other they need proper tillage and management to overcome the handicaps of their bad structure.

Alluvial soils occupy an area of about 64 million hectares and are generally deep and variable in structure, ranging from drift sand to loams and from fine silts to stiff clays. The main characteristics of these soils are derived from their having been deposited as silt by the rivers particularly those of the Indo-Gangetic and the Brahmaputra systems. The physical characteristics and nutrients status of these soils vary considerably. In the south, for example, the Godavari alluvium is rich in lime, phosphates and potash, while the Cauvery alluvium is relatively poor in plant nutrients. In Assam the old alluvial soils are acidic, while the new alluvium is usually neutral or alkaline. In West Bengal the old alluvial areas are much less fertile and productive than the new alluvial soils.

Hard pans occur in the soil profile, particularly in the Indo-Gangetic alluvium of Uttar Pradesh, Punjab, and Delhi as a result of infiltration of silica or calcareous matter and the presence of *kankar*. Such hard layers impede root growth and percolation of water. In general, alluvial soils are ideal for irrigation and ground water exploitation.

In about 13 million hectares, we have laterite soils, generally associated with undulating topography in regions with annual rainfall ranging from 1,200 mm to 3000 mm. They are essentially composed of a mixture of the hydrated oxides of aluminium and iron with small quantities of manganese oxide and titanium. These soils are poor in lime and magnesium and deficient in nitrogen. Generally, they are poor in available phosphorus and calcium and have a relatively low organic matter content. Such soils are well-developed on the hills of the Deccan, Karnataka, Kerala, Tamil Nadu, Madhya Pradesh, Eastern Ghat region, Orissa, Maharashtra and parts of Assam. The high and low level laterites of Tamil Nadu and Kerala are rich in plant nutrients, supporting paddy in the low levels and tea, coffee, rubber and cinchona at the higher levels. The higher the altitude, the more acidic is the soil. There is a good potential for exploiting ground water in many lateritic areas.

In addition to these major groups of soils, we have problem soils suffering from salinity and alkalinity in about 7 million hectares. There are also peaty saline soils called *kari* soils which are heavy black soils, highly acidic and rich in organic matter. Marshy soils occur in the coastal tracts of Orissa, the Sunderbans and other areas of West Bengal, north Bihar, the Almora district of Uttar Pradesh (U.P.) and the south-east coast of Tamil Nadu. Forest soils containing a heavy deposition of organic matter derived from forest growth and desert soils occurring in parts of Rajasthan, Gujarat and Haryana, constitute the other important groups.

The main rivers of the Indo-Gangetic plains have extensive areas lying adjacent to them known as *khadir* in western and central U.P., *diara* in Bihar and eastern U.P. and *char* in West Bengal. The soils of these areas range from unconsolidated sand to silt and are rich in potash but low in phosphorus. Different management procedures are needed for the sandy, water-logged, saline and good areas of the riverine soils of Bihar, U.P. and West Bengal. In U.P. and Bihar alone, such area extends to about 2.4 million hectares and these are potentially high-production soils.

We have also rich rock phosphate deposits both in north and south India and phosphorus rich sands on the beaches of the Laccadive, Minicoy and related groups of islands in the Arabian Sea. Gypsum deposits are available in Rajasthan.

Floristic diversity

Because of our varied soil and climatic endowments, we have over 20,000 plant species occurring in our country, far higher in number than those found in countries with a larger land mass. Such a floristic diversity is obviously the consequence of the prevalence of tropical, subtropical, temperate and alpine areas, where the precise flora may vary depending on latitude, altitude, variation in mean annual day and night temperature and the severity of summer and winter. We have over 4,000 woody species of plants and among them about 50 are of major utility. The potential productivity of our forests (in 1973) has been estimated to be of the order of 490 million m^3 of wood. The current annual harvests comprising 12.9 million m^3 of fuel wood and 8.9 million m^3 of industrial wood are, however, extremely low, the gross revenue being only Rs 21.50 per hectare.

Our wild plant wealth, used in various forms by people in tribal areas, includes about 500 species mainly belonging to the families Gramineae, Orchidaceas, Papilionaceae, Rubiaceae, Euphorbiaceae, Moraceae, Compositae and Labiatae. If we total up plants under cultivation on some scale, their number comes to about 250, excluding the ornamental trees, shrubs and herbs. It is believed that about 35 of these species might have been first domesticated in India and our neighbouring countries. There is a large genetic variability in our country in crops such as rice, sugarcane, mustard, *arboreum* or asiatic cotton, *tossa* jute, various pulses, vegetables such as brinjal, cucumber, gourd, yam, black pepper, cinnamon, turmeric, mango, banana, citrus, jack fruit, *ber*, *phalsa*, *amla*, and *jamun*. Even in plants introduced from the New World, considerable variability appears to have been generated subsequent to arrival in India. A few examples are maize, chilli, potato and cucurbits. We have areas in the country, such as the north-eastern Himalaya which have very rich variability in crops, namely rice, maize and *citrus*. A unique type of *arboreum* cotton with long bolls occurs in the Garo hills. There are trees of mandarin oranges in the Jowai area of Meghalaya which have been productive for over a century. The Jeypore tract of Orissa is also a centre of considerable variability in rice, while in central India, there is vast variability in several pulse crops. It is only recently that serious attempts have been made to domesticate some of the medicinal plants which are otherwise directly collected from the wild state and used.

An example of such a recent domestication is the release for cultivation in the Bangalore area of strains of *Dioscorea floribunda*, a plant native to Central America and which contains diosgenin, a steroid used in oral contraceptive pills.

Impressive animal wealth

Equally impressive is our animal wealth. According to the livestock census of 1966, our total livestock population was 344 million including 176 million cattle and 53 million buffaloes. Both in cows and buffaloes, we have an impressive array of hardy and productive breeds. Exotic breeds such as Holstein, Brown Swiss and Jersey are being increasingly used in cattle-breeding programmes. More than 60 per cent of the total milk production comes from about 23.4 million buffalo cows. The best dairy animals in our country have, however, an average production efficiency of only 25 per cent of their counterparts in Europe and North America.

We have about 4.2 per cent of the world sheep population, numbering according to the 1966 census about 42.0 million. In addition to wool, mutton and milk, sheep contribute at present 15.5 million pieces of skins and 2.1 million tonnes of manure. Sheep abound in semi-arid and arid areas and both the hot desert of Rajasthan and the cold desert of Ladakh offer great scope for sheep and goat improvement. Our poultry population is equally high, having been estimated at 115 million in 1966.

Animals also contribute over 28 million horsepower of energy per day for agricultural operations. Good animals found in states such as Punjab, Haryana, Andhra Pradesh and Tamil Nadu may give about one horsepower per pair per day of 8 hours, while those in the eastern states may give only half as much. It has been calculated that to produce a yield of 2 tonnes per hectare, the average power requirement would be about 0.75 horsepower per day. The current power availability including those provided by man, animals, tractors and power tillers comes to only 0.30 horsepower per hectare. Thus, inadequacy of power is one of the basic causes for our inability to improve the efficiency of farming through timely agricultural operations.

Marine fisheries

Fisheries, both marine and fresh water, constitute one of our great assets. Over 3 million persons live on marine fisheries and the gross annual revenue to the country from fisheries is over 300 crores of rupees. Our marine fish catch has increased from about 4 lakh tonnes in 1947 to about 1.2 million tonnes in 1971. We are now (in 1973) the second biggest shrimp producing country in the world and the export of seafood during 1972 earned for the country over Rs 60 crores. The estimated potential catch from the western Indian Ocean is about 8.9 million tonnes consisting of 4.4 million tonnes of pelagic fishes and 4.5 million tonnes of demersal fish including prawns and other crustaceans. The potential catch from the eastern Indian ocean is about 5.5 million tonnes which includes 2.4 million tonnes of pelagic fish and 3.1 million tonnes of demersal fish. Another index of the untapped marine fish resources we have is provided by comparative figures on catch in different oceans. The yield per km^2 is about 233 kg in the Atlantic ocean and 196 kg in the Pacific ocean, in contrast to 37 kg in the Indian ocean. Even out of this low yield we catch very little. For example, the total tuna catch from the Indian ocean is about 175,000 tonnes, out of which our share is about 5,000 tonnes. The rest is caught mainly by Japanese, Korean and Taiwanese vessels.

Though the current contribution of inland fisheries, including both capture and culture fish is low and amounts only to about 690,000 tonnes per year, there is vast scope for improvement through modern aquaculture techniques. Water pollution and water weeds could become some of the greatest threats to fish culture and hence deserve serious attention. Domestic and municipal wastes contribute more to pollution in many areas than industrial effluents.

Any account of our agricultural assets will be incomplete without a reference to the excellent network of agricultural universities, research institutes and demonstration-cum-training centres which we fortunately have. A recent analysis at Yale University has shown that while investment in agricultural research has been very small in many parts of India in relation to other sectors of research, the gain from investment on agricultural research in our country has been one of the greatest in the world. Among factors which have contributed to the effectiveness of our agricultural research system is the development by the Indian Council of Agricultural Research (ICAR) of a national grid of co-operative experiments conducted by scientists belonging to all the relevant disciplines and institutions. Such all-India co-ordinated research projects cover all the major areas of crop, animal and fish improvement. The data collected in such projects are discussed at all-India workshops and decisions on recommendations to development agencies and farmers are made collectively by all the concerned scientists. Another important strength of our research system is the direct linkages which have been established between the research centres and the farmer through national and mini-kit demonstrations, *krishi melas* and travelling seminars. This feed-back relationship assists in the fine tuning of the research apparatus to the needs of its clients. Though impressive in terms of contributions, our research efforts are still very small in relation to the magnitude and diversity of problems facing us.

Now, let us turn to some of our major liabilities.

LIABILITIES

The low productivity of our agricultural systems is well-known and comparative statistics place our country in the bottom group with reference to the yield per hectare of many economic plants such as rice, wheat, jowar, maize, pulses, oilseeds and cotton. An important reason for our relatively poor average agricultural productivity is the vast area under the important crops, which includes considerable marginal lands. Historically, cropping systems have evolved, partially owing to ecological and pest and disease compulsions, but more importantly on the basis of the home needs of the farmer and his family. We now know that many low-yield environments for rice or wheat may constitute high yield environments for some pulse or oilseed crops. An effective food distribution machinery can pave the way for readjustments in crop planning based on considerations of ecology and economics. If this is not done, our agriculture will become increasingly inefficient and expensive and our cost of production will increase, since wages tend to rise with or without co-incident improvement in productivity. For example, our average rice yield now is about 1,170 kg per hectare and if the tentative fifth plan projection of productivity improvement is all that we can achieve, the average yield will be 1,375 kg per hectare by 1979. In contrast, the average yield of rice even in 1971 was over 5000 kg per hectare in the Arab Republic of Egypt, Japan, Italy, the U.S.A. and several other countries. Thus, after the inadequacy of farm power, a major handicap is defective land and water use resulting in low yields.

Probability estimates

It was mentioned earlier that one of our great natural assets is variability in weather and soil conditions which fostered the domestication of a wide range of economic plants and animals.

Aberrations in weather, however, also constitute a major handicap. The rainfall distribution is uneven about 80 per cent occurring during the south-west monsoon season. About 30 per cent of our geographical area receives annually less than 75 cm rainfall and the occurrence of drought, floods, breaks in monsoon, cyclonic storms, thunderstorms and duststorms are common in one part of the country or the other. Although the periodicity of such weather aberrations cannot be determined with precision, it is possible to work out anticipatory measures and cropping systems on the basis of probability estimates. This is yet be done systematically.

The next major handicap is the growing loss of soil and the damage that is being done to soil health and fertility. For reasons which are not clear there has been great neglect of the soil in our country in comparison with China or Japan. While it takes anywhere between 100 years to 400 years for one centimetre of top soil to be formed in nature, all this soil can be lost in just one year because of erosion. It has been estimated that nearly 80 million hectares out of the 139 million hectares under cultivation require attention from the soil conservation point of view. A wide range of factors, such as denudation of forests and vegetation cover, inappropriate tillage and cropping techniques, and practices, such as shifting cultivation are causing a considerable loss of valuable soil through water and wind erosion.

Shifting cultivation, known as *jhuming* in the north-eastern Himalayan region, involves cutting down all vegetation from hill slopes, use of fire to clear the debris, growing a crop like a hill paddy, millets, sweet potato or beans, abandoning the land after a few years and restarting the cycle at another place. According to a Food and Agricultural Organisation (FAO) estimate, this form of cultivation dates back to the Neolithic period. While this practice has gradually tended to disappear from States such as Bihar, Orissa, and Madhya Pradesh, the area cleared annually for *jhuming* may be about 100,000 hectares in Assam and Meghalaya. Observations in the Assam hills, indicate that at least 10 cm of soil may be washed away even from moderate slopes in each *jhuming* cycle. One of the factors influencing such indifference to soil care is the fact that the land cleared for *jhuming* is not owned by the cultivator, whose interest in the land ends with the cropping cycle. Shifting cultivation as well as growing one crop once in two to three years were two of the ancient methods of overcoming the implications of the law of the diminishing return of the soil in relation to crop-yield. In areas with settled cultivation, application of organic wastes and the cultivation of pulse crops and other legumes which can fix atmospheric nitrogen in the soil were the common methods of restoring soil fertility adopted in the past.

Soil conservation

Soil erosion leads to an enormous loss of nutrients. Some calculations show that the annual loss of soil owing to erosion is about 6,000 million tonnes and that of nutrients is 2.5 million tonnes of nitrogen, 3.3 million tonnes of phosphorus and 2.6 million tonnes of potash. A portion of these nutrients may get deposited elsewhere. In fact, such loss of nutrients may be the most important cause of water pollution in our country. A major approach to soil conservation has been the construction of contour bunds for the purpose of decreasing erosion, conserving water above the bund and increasing infiltration. We have so far treated, during the various plan periods, about 13.3 million hectares of agricultural land and 1.2 million hectares of non-agricultural land with various soil conservation measures. While these programmes have been very valuable both for diminishing erosion and providing employment, the agricultural benefits from such programmes have not been commensurate either with the effort or expenditure involved.

Often bunding has neither been followed up with other measures, such as providing a vegetation cover, nor has it been carried out with an understanding of crop production technology. For example, a recent survey by the Madhya Pradesh Department of Agriculture on the effectiveness of contour bunds in increasing *rabi* wheat yields has shown that on the whole, the effect of bunding was strongly negative. Similarly, a study on the effect of bunding on the yield of *kharif* crops in the Bellary area indicated that contour bunding decreased the yields of *jowar*, cotton and safflower both as a result of water stagnation and delay in cultural operations. It is obvious, therefore, that soil conservation measures need to be planned and implemented in a much more scientific manner taking into consideration not only the need to check erosion, but also the end purpose of promoting crop growth.

One has only to see how land is being used for brick-making and road-making in our country to understand the extent of indifference to the care of the soil. While planned use of land for brick-making could help in building up permanent assets, such as for example tanks, unplanned use results both in the loss of good agricultural land and in erosion. Similarly, there is always a danger that natural drains may be plugged if a total view on soil and water conservation is not taken while planning the construction of roads and railway lines. Closing natural drains leads to floods and thereby to considerable soil erosion. Thus, deforestation, shifting cultivation, overgrazing and improper cropping of undulating lands, bunding without vegetation cover, plugging of natural drains and other kinds of poor land management are causing increased run-off, reduced ground water recharge and severe erosion resulting in the deterioration of soil, loss of valuable nutrients, lower yields, flooding of lowland areas, sedimentation of small tanks and large reservoirs and the wastage of precious water to the ocean. Therefore, it is not surprising that in an article entitled 'The eleventh commandment', Lowdermilk (1966) stated a few years ago that 'the use of land is a down-to-earth index of a civilization, for land has been the silent partner in the rise and fall of civilizations'.

We can continue to neglect our soil only at the peril of our future. The authors of *The limits to growth* (Meadows *et al.* 1972) have calculated that every child born today would need 0.08 hectare of land for purposes like housing, roads, waste disposal, power supply and other uses and 0.4 hectare of land for producing the food he or she needs. On this formula, we will need at least 5 million hectares of additional land every year to cater to the needs of those added to our population. In contrast even in 1969-70 the availability of agricultural land was only 0.34 hectare per person. Obviously, it is time we woke up and spread a consciousness of the value of soil and the importance of scientific land use throughout the country.

Improper and inefficient water use, inadequate tapping of sunlight, poor utilisation of biological nitrogen fixation, wasteful disposal of wastes, lack of understanding of recycling processes, and poor integration of crop and animal husbandry on the one hand, and terrestrial and aquatic production systems on the other, are some of our other major liabilities.

The slow pace of progress in getting the best out of our water resources is evident both from the relative stagnation in *kharif* crop production and the low intensity of farming. During the *kharif* season, when much of the rainfall is received, the production of foodgrains was 65.6 and 62.0 million tonnes in 1964-65 and 1971-72, respectively. In contrast, the *rabi* production during these two years was, respectively, 23.7 and 42.7 million tonnes. Thus, our major grains in production have come from the non-rainy season. With the development of irrigation facilities it should have been possible to bring more area under double and multiple cropping, thereby raising the intensity of cropping. The intensity of cropping is, however, still low, and has risen from 114 per cent in 1965-66 to only 117 per cent in 1969-70.

A low intensity of cropping even when water is available also implies poor utilisation of sunlight, since in the tropics and subtropics green plants can be made to produce food, feed and fodder continuously by photosynthesis from water and atmospheric carbon dioxide. The cellulose produced by photosynthesis on the earth is not only the chief basis of all fossil fuels, but is also the most abundant renewable raw material currently available.

Nutrient supply

In the area of nutrient supply to crops organic manures, namely farmyard manure, compost, green manure, oil-cakes, and various waste products of animal origin, such as dried blood, bones, fish manure and urine, had been used in the past. With the growth in population farmyard manure and other organic wastes have increasingly been diverted to fuel purposes. Though some work has been done on the generation of gas from such wastes in order to obtain both fuel and manure from the same material, such techniques have not come into use on any significant scale. Much of the urban wastes, sewage water, cattle and human urine and human excreta are not recycled in a manner that will promote productivity.

A great marvel of nature is the way in which micro-organisms fix atmospheric nitrogen in the soil largely through leguminous plants. While synthetic nitrogen fertiliser production requires very high temperature and pressure for combining nitrogen, hydrogen and oxygen, the nitrogen-fixing organisms, namely Azotobactor, Rhizobium, and blue-green algae are able to do this at ordinary soil temperature and pressure with the help of the enzyme nitrogenase. Nitrogen is now being introduced into the earth in a fixed form at the rate of about 92 million tonnes per year, whereas the total amount being denitrified and returned to the atmosphere is only about 83 million tonnes per year. The difference of 9 million tonnes per year may represent the rate at which fixed nitrogen is building up in the soil, ground water, rivers, lakes and oceans. Unfortunately, studies show that while Australia, the United States and the Soviet Union are adding substantial nitrogen to their soils every year, we have a negative nitrogen balance to the extent of 8.2 lakh tonnes per year.

Before ending this discussion on our agricultural assets and liabilities, it would be pertinent to refer to the most important factor which will determine our agricultural future, namely, our human population. The principal characteristic of our population are the predominance of youth, poverty, under-nutrition and illiteracy. According to the projections of the Registrar General, we will have about 657 million people by 1981, over 40 per cent of them will be below the age of 18. Nearly 80 per cent of our population lived in villages during 1971. We are thus mainly a land of youth and of rural people. Impressive statistics on poverty are available and there is also a growing awareness of the implications of protein-calorie malnutrition on national development. Many authorities now compare nutrition and education, respectively, to the hardware and software components of technology. Although in terms of percentage, the number of literates rose from 24.03 in 1961 to 29.34 in 1971, the number of illiterates increased in absolute number during this period. Most of our agriculture is managed by illiterate peasantry and unless there is a marriage between intellect and labour in rural India, there will be neither agrarian advance nor rural prosperity. Our agricultural future will depend, to a great extent, on how successful we are in involving youth and the illiterate both men and women in rural transformation. The urgency of population stabilisation hardly needs any emphasis, since all our efforts will have no effect in improving quality of life if population growth cannot be arrested and stabilised.

The se ond class compartment of spaceship earth is getting smaller and smaller, while the number of those who have to live there is getting larger and larger. Affluence is becoming a major claimant of world food and energy resources. Between 1967 and 1971, the developed market economies increased their agricultural exports on an average by 11 per cent per year, while the developing countries lost ground by 1 per cent. This is the net result of what is called the United Nations Development Decade. It is time the people living in the first class compartment realised that when the compartment of the poor bursts due to excessive pressure, the whole spaceship will crash. But the poor have to begin helping themselves.

During the last few years, we have started making real progress in improving our agricultural capability. While food production dropped by 17 million tonnes during the drought of 1965-66, the fall in production during the drought of 1972 is likely to be less than half this amount. This is certainly an index of real progress and encouragement towards greater effort.

To summarise the state of our agricultural balance sheet, we are endowed with considerable ecological diversity, a large volume of tapped and untapped sources of water, abundant sunlight, and large animal and human populations. Our liabilities, apart from those caused by population growth and aberrant weather, mostly arise from an improper use and management of these resources. Attempts to promote synergy, which is the only mechanism which can lead to rapid progress from small resources, have been few and halting. Our urgent needs hence are first, to develop and introduce in each ecological area an agricultural production technology which will lead to increased productivity based predominantly on the use of renewable resources and on the wise husbanding of non-renewable resources. We shall have to learn to produce more and more food from less and less land. Second we need to develop and introduce educational tools which will help to impart the latest technical skills to illiterate peasantry and which will enable educated youth to become catalysts of rural change. Finally, we need to develop and spread management and organisational techniques which will help those living in absolute poverty to overcome their handicaps and obtain their share of the fruits of agricultural advance.

THE EMERGING AGRICULTURAL TECHNOLOGY

It is clear that a synoptic view of our agricultural assets and liabilities stresses the fact that in view of the inelastic nature of land availability and the competing demands for its use, we have to adopt an agricultural technology which will help us to achieve our immediate goals of more food, more jobs and more income for the present population, without at the same time endangering the long-term production potential of the soil. It is probable that extensive ocean farming, hydroponics or soilless cultivation, test-tube cultivation, protein from petroleum and single cells and other similar techniques may contribute to our future food supply. In the immediate future, however, we shall have to rely primarily on mother earth to feed us and our animals. As far as we can judge now, soil will continue to be the most important medium for crop growth, since several of the other techniques will have to rely heavily on the use of non-renewable resources of energy.

We also do not know what the long term consequences will be of certain trends in ocean farming, such as induced upwelling. Upwelling is a physical, ocean-atmosphere process leading to the transfer of high concentrations of chemical nutrients from the sea bottom into the zone where there is active carbon assimilation, thereby producing food for fish. It has been estimated that about half of the world's fish production occurs in the restricted coastal upwelling areas. If man can artificially create upwelling, it is possible that there may be richer harvests of marine life for some time. No one, however, can predict what will happen in the long term. We already have the lesson of the Peruvian fisheries to remind us that if man in his greed tries to over-exploit a resource he will come to grief. In 1970 the catch of anchovies in Peru reached 12.3 million tonnes. It dropped dramatically to about 4 million tonnes in 1972 and is not yet showing any sign of recovery. Though the drop is partly due to a periodic ecological disturbance in the sea leading to the influx of warmer water, many authorities believe that over-fishing leading to the depletion of the basic renewal stock may also be a factor responsible for this big drop. A sad consequence of the drop in the availability of anchovies along the Peruvian coast is the dwindling in the population of the guano birds, from about 30 million a few years ago to about a million now. If the guano birds disappear, the finest natural fertiliser in the world formed by the deposits of these birds will also gradually get exhausted. Anchovies not only constitute the dominant food of the guanos, but also of poultry and pigs in North America. The drop in the availability of anchovies, therefore, escalated the demand for soy-bean as the main protein source in animal feed mixtures. The consequent sudden rise in soy-bean price led the Japanese to release rice for animal feed, rather than import soy-bean at very high prices. This illustrates the interdependence of biological and production factors and the consequences of one adverse event on other seemingly unrelated events.

The importance of the scientific management of the biosphere is thus obvious. Here we shall deal with some recent trends in the promotion and management of biological productivity, citing relevant situations in our country.

Attention to economic ecology

First among the emerging concepts of management of biological assets is attention to economic ecology. The prefix 'economic' before ecology is meant to underline the fact that what we need is as high an economic growth rate as possible through the use of the principles of ecology, rather than the kind of ecology discussed frequently in the affluent nations which is of the conservationist or zero growth rate kind, intended to preserve the high standards of living already achieved. Arable land in India can be placed under five groups—arid, semi-arid, humid, irrigated and hilly regions. It is obvious that there are numerous climatic variations in these groups. *Kharif* and *rabi* seasons have not the same significance in south India, as they have in the north. This is why agricultural technology becomes highly location and situation specific, necessitating a considerable amount of local research and testing work before a new technology can be recommended to the farmers. While ideas and concepts can be transplanted from one region to another, the actual material and techniques will have to be tailored to suit the local agro-ecological and socio-economic milieu.

The arid zone in our country occupies an area of 3.2 lakh km^2 of hot desert, mostly in Rajasthan, Gujarat, Haryana and Karnataka and 0.7 lakh km^2 of cold desert in Ladakh. In Ladakh, extreme aridity combined with low temperature limits the possibility of growing crops to about 5 months in a year. Hence, the strategy for agricultural growth in Ladakh has to depend largely on the cultivation of quick-growing cereals, oilseeds and fodder crops, and the rearing of goats to give pashmina wool. The hot desert regions, in contrast, have an abundance of sunshine, land and soils capable of responding to management, well-adapted grasses and trees, excellent breeds of sheep, goat and cattle and considerable reserves of ground water. Water, and not land, is the principal limiting factor and, therefore, all attempts have to be focussed on maximising income per litre of water. This will be possible only if the ecological balance is not further disturbed and a proper land use pattern is adopted.

Three examples may be cited to illustrate the trends which are aggravating the unfavourable consequences of aridity. First, the area used exclusively for grazing in western Rajasthan has dropped from 13.09 million hectares to 11.04 million hectares during 1951-61, while the population of grazing animals increased during the same period from 9.4 million to 14.4 million. The same trend of diminishing grazing area and rapidly expanding grazing population still persists. Second, while most of the land in the arid zone is fit only for forestry or range management, land is increasingly being brought under cropping. The areas cropped rose from 26 per cent in 1960 to 38 per cent in 1970, thus extending cultivation even to submarginal areas. Third, the area under forests is only 2 per cent, although the extent of land classified under barren uncultivable waste is 28 per cent and cultural waste is 18 per cent, all of which could be planted with tree species such as *Acacia tortilis*, *Prosopis juliflora* and *Eucalyptus* sp. Fruit trees, namely, *ber* and pomegranate can also be grown extensively.

Reclaiming the desert

Afforestation has to be the focal point for reclaiming the desert. Techniques for soil and water conservation and for sand dune stabilisation are fortunately available today. Large scale planting of shelter-belts could help to minimise wind erosion and decrease the dust over the desert. Scope for the establishment of pastures and grazing lands is great, and strip cropping involving the setting up of permanent grass strips to prevent wind damage will help to increase substantially the yield of crops, such as *bajra* and *moong*. If steps of this kind can be taken, it may be possible for the nomadic tribes, such as the Banjaras and the Gadiya Lohars, to start leading a more settled life.

Rajasthan has many fine breeds of sheep and research has shown that appropriate crossbreeding procedures can help to improve the yield and quality of wool and of mutton. Fortunately, techniques for artificial insemination have been developed and hence more widespread genetic improvement programmes are possible.

An important need in the desert areas is the preservation of organic matter for the soil. Unfortunately, because of the deficiency of fuel the available organic wastes are generally used for burning, and trees are cut in an unplanned manner. It is here that more extensive research and extension efforts on the utilisation of solar energy for purposes, such as heating, cooking, lighting and distilling water will be of great value. Often in the desert areas the water is saline and people have to walk several miles every day to fetch sweet water. Solar stills to produce water for drinking in such areas will be a great boon to the villagers.

Sophisticated techniques for raising crops in desert areas with very limited quantities of water are now becoming available. These involve cultivation of vegetables and high-value crops under air-inflated polyethylene houses using economic methods of water supply, such as drip or sprinkler irrigation. Since the Lathi aquifers of the Thar desert are rich, it may be possible to develop efficient water use system at least to raise community nurseries of different crops, so that transplanting can be done if there is a delayed onset of monsoon and for purposes, such as cultivation of vegetables, and for seed production.

Unfortunately, we have no arrangements now either to mitigate the rigour of a bad season or to derive maximum advantage from a good season. For example, this year provided a unique opportunity for planting a large number of trees in the desert and for seeding large areas with grasses. While the average annual rainfall of Barmer and Jaisalmer districts are 277.5 mm and 164.0 mm, respectively, 302 mm rain was received in just three days in Barmer and 377 mm in Jaisalmer between 10 August and 31 August. In spite of the shallow nature of the soils and the calcium carbonate pans which occur in the subsoil, thereby increasing run-off and reducing infiltration, abundant moisture was available to facilitate the establishment of trees, shrubs and grasses. The district administration tried its best to get the available seeds sown, but the magnitude of the programme was small in relation to the opportunities that were available.

Good weather code

What we need in such areas is a 'Good Weather Code', which will spell out the types of activities that should be undertaken in the event of rainfall being good. While we have scarcity manuals which tell us what to do when rains fail, we do not yet have a corresponding action code to indicate what we should do to capitalise on good weather. It is obvious that a written code by itself will be of no value if arrangement to implement its provisions, by way of extensive nurseries of trees, do not exist.

About 75 per cent of our cultivated areas is rain-fed, and since about 42 per cent of our food comes from such areas, there is variation in food production depending upon the amount and distribution of rainfall. Semi-arid areas where the mean annual potential evapotranspiration exceeds the mean annual rainfall, occur in many of our States. Such areas have been plagued for centuries by periodic droughts, floods, soil erosion, instability in production, drinking water scarcity, unemployment, underemployment and other forms of human suffering. In about 101 million hectares, crop fortunes are closely linked to the behaviour of the monsoon. These areas not only provide much of our millet and pulses but are also the major suppliers of industrial raw material, such as cotton and groundnut.

The earliest research effort on dryland agriculture was started by Tamhane in 1923 at Manjri. Subsequently, a rather comprehensive programme was evolved by Kanitkar to improve the productivity of rain-fed farming. This formed the basis for the Dry Farming Scheme started in 1933 by the Indian Council of Agricultural Research at Rohtak, Sholapur, Bijapur, Raichur and Hagari. The outcome of these projects was a series of dry farming practices commonly known as Bombay, Hyderabad and Madras Dry Farming Practices. The basic features of the dry farming practices developed in the past were bunding to conserve soil moisture, application of farmyard manure to supply plant nutrients, deep ploughing once in three years, shallow preparatory cultivation and interculture, low seed rate and wide spacing of crops. Official estimates placed the increase in crop yields from the adoption of this package of practices at about 15 per cent to 20 per cent over a base level of 200-400 kg per hectare. No wonder the package failed to catch the imagination and interests of the farming community. Nevertheless, these programmes did make a useful contribution in the areas of moisture conservation and erosion control.

Later in 1954 soil conservation research and demonstration centres were established in different parts of the country and they gathered valuable data on the capability of land, rainfall intensity and distribution run-off patterns, and response to fertiliser application. In addition to developing conservation practices appropriate to a region, these centres also provided an insight into the factors limiting production in dry farming areas. Lack of quick-maturing varieties was a major handicap in the early programmes. For instance, it was noted at the Bellary Research Centre that in late December the soil, which has a high clay content, cracks heavily because of loss of moisture. The flowering stage of the traditional varieties of cotton and *jowar* coincided with this period of rapid soil drying and hence their yields were poor. It was thus obvious that if cotton or *jowar* varieties which could be harvested by early December could be introduced into cultivation, much higher yields could be obtained. We had to wait until 1965 when thanks to hybrid *jowar* CSH.1, HB.1 *bajra* and PRS cotton varieties, which could all mature before the soil lost its moisture, good yields could be achieved even in years of subnormal rainfall.

Intensification of dryland research

It is experiences of this kind that led to the intensification of dryland farming research in 1970 through the initiation of an All-India Co-ordinated Research Project on Dryland Agriculture with the collaboration of the Government of Canada. Meanwhile, international interest in upgrading the productivity as well as the stability of production of the dry farming regions of Asia, Africa and Latin America grew and resulted in the establishment by the Consultative Group for International Agricultural Research of an International Crops Research Institute for the Semi-arid Tropics at Hyderabad in July 1972.

The new phase of dry farming research, has already resulted in considerable data on better moisture conservation and use, new cropping patterns, crop life-saving techniques and mid-season corrections in crop planning in the drought-prone areas. The pilot project areas attached to the dry farming research centres are helping to identify the socio-economic and operational constraints in the transfer of the technology from the research farm to the farmer's fields.

Since water is the major limiting factor, a priority area of research is the standardisation of techniques by which as much of the precipitation as possible can be conserved for crop use, either directly in the soil profile through infiltration or through run-off collection and storage. Deep ploughing, for example, promotes a vertical rather than a tangential flow of water in red soils with a dense subsoil. The cultivation of deep rooted crops, such as castor, red gram or *arhar* and cotton further helps in improving the soil texture and in adding organic matter through root deposition. Run-off storage structures are being developed both for individual small farms and for larger watersheds. Obviously, the most effective method will be the co-operative management of an entire watershed. If sufficient water can be collected in community-owned ponds, a life-saving irrigation can be given at the time of grain formation when the crop will benefit most from the supply of a little water.

In black soil areas with moderate rainfall, there is scope for double cropping or ratooning, provided suitable surface drainage can be introduced during the rainy season and appropriate tillage practices can be developed. Drainage and sound soil and water management will again need some degree of co-operative endeavour on the part of a watershed community. There is also great scope for introducing better inter-cropping practices in areas with annual rainfall ranging from 625 mm to 1000 mm.

Drought-escaping varieties

Progress has been made in identifying crop varieties which are relatively photo-insensitive and which have a shorter duration and the resulting ability to escape droughts. Early seedling vigour and good population performance are the other attributes of such strains. Suitable varieties in rice, *jowar*, *bajra*, minor millets, sunflower, safflower, castor, mustard, groundnut, pulses, such as *moong*, *urad*, *arhar*, and cow-pea and cotton are becoming available. As a result, different cropping patterns can be developed to suit different weather models. For example, some of the common weather aberrations are (i) early or delayed onset of monsoon; (ii) long breaks in the monsoon; and (iii) inadequate rainfall. Different crop schedules can be developed for each of these conditions.

If the monsoon is very early, short duration legumes could be taken followed by regular season crops. For normal sowing *jowar*, for late sowing *bajra*, and for very late sowing *setaria* are some of the possibilities. When there are long breaks in the monsoon, the *jowar* or *bajra* crops affected by drought could be ratooned. Crops with indeterminate growth habits such as castor or *arhar* regenerate fast if given a urea spray after the receipt of rains during a prolonged period of drought. The development of early maturing *arhar* varieties, such as Prabhat and Pusa Ageti has made it possible to take a pulse crop before wheat in north-western Uttar Pradesh. Since early varieties of *arhar* are now available, a crop of this pulses can be taken in north India between July and December. Again, with the help of dew or winter rains a crop of sunflower can be raised in the same field from February to April. Much better use of dew can be made in the north India during the *rabi* season. Plant physiologist, Asana has developed a model of a wheat plant which is capable of retaining dew. We need research of this kind in all rain-fed *rabi* crops. We should evolve a series of alternative cropping patterns for each soil and rainfall belt, to match different weather probabilities. It would also be necessary to build the appropriate seed and fertiliser buffers and organise community nurseries in order to put into practice alternative crop schedules, if the weather proves truant. The National Commission on Agriculture is planning to draw up a broad outline for the 'Drought Code' which could help the developmental administration to be ready for any weather pattern and initiate anticipatory action to mitigate the effects of drought, rather than be content with palliative action after the misfortune has set in.

Multiple and relay cropping

The potential of irrigated areas to produce much higher quantities of food, feed, fibre and fodder plants through multiple and relay cropping is now well-known. Owing to various difficulties and shortcomings in the water conveyance and delivery system, as well as because of the shortage of power, fertiliser and good seed, the full potential of the irrigated areas is yet to be realised. If these defects can be overcome and a minimum of two good crops raised, the production of about 8-10 tonnes of food and other grains per hectare per year, now being harvested in several of the experimental stations of agricultural universities, should not be beyond the reach of many small farmers. While taking up intensive farming practice, a continuous monitoring of the soil for major and micro-nutrients and for pathogens will be essential. Legumes should find a place in the rotation, and as a rule, crops sharing common pests and diseases should not succeed each other. It would be better to alternate deep and shallow rooted crops so as to tap nutrients from different soil layers.

New systems of cropping are rapidly coming into existence in many of our irrigated areas. Thus, in Punjab and Haryana, rice during *kharif* and wheat during *rabi* is gaining popularity. In West Bengal, wheat is becoming popular as a *rabi* crop in rice fields. Baisakhi *moong* and other strains developed in order to find place for a pulse crop during a season when the land is normally fallow are becoming popular as summer crops. In the rice fallows of south India, *jowar*, *bajra* and cotton can be raised during the off-seasons. In the case of several of these new cropping patterns, we need much more data on the most appropriate cultural practices, including fertiliser application and weed control.

Effective landuse

Our knowledge of the most effective land-use systems in the heavy rainfall areas is still fragmentary. Many of these areas, Assam, Meghalaya, Arunachal Pradesh, Nagaland, Mizoram, Tripura, Manipur and Kerala grow plantation crops and fruit trees in the medium and higher elevations. A viable alternative to shifting cultivation has to be found in the north-eastern Himalayan region. Similarly, in Kerala there is very little data on the optimum utilisation of garden lands occupied by crops, such as coconut, arecanut, mango and jackfruit. The current crop-mix in the garden lands of Kerala and Karnataka is the product of the technological possibilities as known until now to the farmers of these areas, but a fresh look is needed since the market conditions for some products, as for example arecanut, have considerably changed. By appropriate changes in the spacing of coconut and arecanut, some other crops of high value, namely, cocoa, cloves, and soy-beans can be grown in between the palms. New varieties of grasses and legumes are now available which can also be grown as intercrops in the arecanut or coconut plantations so that the farmer can maintain a few cross-bred cows for milk production. These and many other possibilities for capitalising on the ecological possibilities of the humid tropical regions are yet to receive intensive attention.

High-altitude research

High-altitude areas have also received relatively little scientific attention. Ecological conditions vary greatly even within short distances in these areas, depending upon aspect, latitude, altitude, slope, soil depth and distance from the plains. Large variations in temperature and rainfall occur, and the length of growing season is controlled by the time of occurrence of snow in winter and its disappearance in the spring. Erosion is a serious problem, and in several of these areas data are needed on minimum tillage, suitable implements to ensure timeliness of operations, fertiliser use and weed control. Both horticulture and nomadic sheep husbandry require considerable attention. For agriculture to start moving in these areas, marketing arrangements are prerequisites since in some of the Himalayan regions, owing to a variety of reasons, the producer may get as little as 10 per cent of the price paid by the consumer.

Besides rainfall, altitude and latitude the ecological conditions of soil and season need understanding in order to improve biological productivity. We have large areas affected by salinity and alkalinity where crops either do not grow, or give very poor yield. Soil salinity is also becoming a problem in black soils where irrigation facilities have recently been developed. An understanding of the nature of the problem and of the physical and chemical characteristics of the soil profile would be necessary to introduce the most appropriate corrective measures, such as gypsum application, drainage, crop and varietal choice, and fertiliser use. Fortunately, as a result of the work done at the Central Soil Salinity Research Institute, Karnal, and at other research centres and agricultural universities we now have techniques available for reclaiming such problem soils. Acid soils also require special care, and in particular, the most effective methods of phosphorus application will have to be worked out.

Strategies for ecological seasons

We are yet to work out detailed production strategies for each ecological season. We now know, for example, that in Assam the period between September to May is usually free of floods, since the major floods have either taken place in May-June or more commonly in August. There is tremendous potential in this area for exploiting ground water and for installing lift irrigation. An assured *rabi* crop can be taken if arrangements can be made to supply water. There are areas in Assam with over 250 mm winter rains, where even pending the establishment of an irrigation system, good crops of sunflower, soy-bean, barley, *moong* and even a short duration rice variety, such as *Bala* or *Pusa 2-21* can be taken. Similarly, the coastal areas of West Bengal, Orissa and Andhra Pradesh are exposed to recurrent floods and cyclones during August September. It is possible to tailor a cropping pattern which would escape or avoid the fury of the floods. For such flood-prone areas we need a 'Flood

Avoidance Code' which could provide the necessary guidelines to restructure the agricultural system in accordance with the probability of occurrence of floods.

The entire riverine or *diara* areas of Bihar and Uttar Pradesh will benefit greatly from arrangements of community tube wells. The Chhota Nagpur and Santhal Parganas area can grow fruits and vegetables and develop dairying so as to capture the emerging market in cities, such as Bokaro. We also know now that because of cloudy conditions and relatively greater incidence of pests and diseases during *kharif*, the yield of high-yielding varieties of rice is lower during this season than during *rabi*. Yet, while the total area under rice is over 37.0 million hectares, the area under *rabi* rice is only about 3 million hectares. The major problems in extending *rabi* rice cultivation are the cold temperatures of December to February and scarcity of water. Cold-tolerant strains are currently being selected and with more economical water management for which techniques are available, it should be possible to take a good *rabi* rice crop in the delta region of the east coast, where ground water is available a few metres below the ground. Thus, the scope for restructuring cropping patterns on ecological and marketing considerations is vast. For this we need to classify the existing cropping systems, which are largely the product of the home needs of the farmer and pest and disease syndromes, into classes, such as those with high-yield potential and low risk, high-yield potential and high risk, low-yield potential and low risk, and low-yield potential and high risk. Obviously, we should strive to eliminate the low-yield potential crops from the cropping system of each area and reduce the risk elements in the high-yield potential crops. Above all, effective purchase and marketing arrangements are vital, since the farmer is motivated not so much by yield per hectare but by net return per hectare.

Synergy in agriculture

Having discussed some of the broad features of crop planning on an ecological basis, we can now turn to the application of three other important concepts in agriculture. The first of these is the concept of synergy in agriculture. one of the most fascinating scientific developments of recent years. Synergy is not a new concept, since this mechanism which results in the product being something much more than the sum of the parts, has been the most potent tool involved in natural evolution. Symbiosis, or mutually beneficial relationships and co-ordinated functioning are essential ingredients of synergy. For developing high synergy cropping systems, an understanding of population behaviour and performance, rather than merely of the characteristics of individual plants or animals, is essential. Prudent observers of nature in the past had devised biological systems based on the release of synergistic interactions. To cite an example :

Chinese peasants over a thousand years ago had devised methods of producing high yields of fish with low inputs of money and technology. They did this on the basis of two principles. First, a body of water is a three-dimensional growing space. To treat it like a field by planting only one kind of crop is likely to result in wasting the majority of that space. Second, any fertile pond will produce a number of different fish food organisms. However, most fish are not omnivorous, but are rather selective in their diet. Thus, stocking single species in a pond wastes not only space but also food. Chinese fish culturists took advantage of these two characteristics of the pond environment through polyculture or stocking several types of fish. Recently, under an all-India co-ordinated project on composite fish culture, suitable species of fish have been identified which can give co-operatively about 3,000 kg of fish per hectare in about 6 months. The species involved are both Indian carps, namely, *catla*, *rohu* and *mrigal* and exotic carps, such as grass carp, silver carp and common carp. Such high synergy aquaculture systems can revolutionise fresh water fish production in our country.

Terrestrial and aquaculture systems can also be devised, where each element would contribute significantly to the functioning of the whole, resulting in a profitable farm ecosystem. The Chinese have again taken advantage of the possibility for raising pigs and ducks in conjunction with fish culture. In a 4.4 hectare Chinese farm in Malaysia, pigs, fish and aquatic plants were raised together. About 30 tonnes of pig meat were produced per year, with the primary feed being the aquatic water spinach *Ipomoea repens* which grew luxuriantly in the fish ponds fertilised by the pig manure. Besides the pigs, some 3000 kg of fish were cultured in the small ponds. The main food for the fish was algae, which grew well in the enriched ponds. Ducks could complement a system like this, their wastes being added to the ponds.

Changing plant architecture

The search for synergy has led both to the repatterning of plant architecture in many economic plants and to the development of crossbred farm animals which are efficient in the conversion of feed into the product for which they are raised by man. What the breeders now look for are the plant types which can maximise production per unit of area, time and water. Thus, plant types which will not shade each other or fall over each other and which will promote better light interception and carbon dioxide fixation are now sought after. In the earlier strains, many of the characteristics had been selected for performance under adverse circumstances and not for high yield under good management. Because of their plant and leaf characteristics, a larger number of productive tillers per square metre can be packed into the new varieties of wheat and rice, as compared to the old ones. Similarly, the distribution of the total dry matter produced by the plant between the part of commercial value and the remaining parts is much more favourable in the new strains. New plant types in *bajra* can respond to a population density of about 250,000 plants per hectare, in contrast to less than 100,000 plants in the case of the earlier strains. Similarly, in maize, dwarf varieties with smaller tassel, high nitrate-reductase activity and upper placement of the ear are under testing in several countries, and these can respond to a population density of about 150,000 plants per hectare. The concept of population explosion in fields has also permeated horticulture. Increasing emphasis is being placed in orchards on the selection of dwarfing root stocks. Some experts believe that the fruit orchards of the future may be lilliputian in nature, facilitating high management efficiency. Unfortunately, in our country root stock consciousness has not yet spread and citrus growers still raise orchards from seedlings, although budded plants on appropriate root stocks, such as trifoliate root stock in drought prone areas, can make a great difference in orchard productivity.

Apart from improving population performance and the yield potential of economic plants through a repatterning of plant architecture, growth rhythm and allocation of dry matter between the commercial and non-commercial portions of the plant, the other areas of concern have been in introducing a broad spectrum of resistance to pests and pathogens and in improving nutritional and cooking or processing quality. Unfortunately, breeding for resistance to pests and diseases is often a never-ending task. The resistance tends to break down, following the build-up in nature of new races of the pathogen capable of attacking a variety earlier released for its resistance. We are now witnessing this in the popular wheat varieties Kalyan Sona and Sonalika which at the time of their release in 1967 had a high degree of resistance to brown and yellow rusts. Kalyan Sona has become susceptible particularly to brown rust and there is no assurance that the resistance of Sonalika may hold out for long. Seeds of new strains have hence to be multiplied and distributed speedily. Dynamic varietal diversification and seed multiplication programmes are essential to sustain a good crop production programme.

Outwitting the pathogen

Will the struggle between the breeder and the pathogen be an endless one or will one outwit the other? This is an interesting question for which no clear-cut answer is yet in sight. The breeder is adopting a multi-pronged strategy. He is working on a type of resistance, technically referred to as horizontal or field resistance, which is likely to be of a more enduring type. He is also trying to develop escape mechanisms by trying to alter the growth phase of the plant in such a way that it does not synchronise with the peak multiplication and infectious phase of the pathogen. He is striving to develop strains called 'composite varieties' which can help to reduce the pressure on the pathogen in building up new and virulent races. He is also trying to understand the biochemistry and physiology of resistance, hoping in this way to find effective and cheap chemical methods of control. While all these approaches need to be followed with vigour, our immediate hopes lie in the genes for resistance found in the primitive cultivars and other wild and cultivated genetic material occurring particularly in the centres of diversity of plants. Thus, the rich collections of rice made by our scientists from the north-eastern Himalaya contain genes for resistance to a wide range of pests and pathogens infecting rice. Areas where the pests are endemic provide opportunities for screening for resistance. Under the all-India coordinated research programmes, such areas have been identified, and given an efficient seed multiplication and distribution machinery, we should be able to remain ahead of the pathogen in several crops.

Equally exciting are the opportunities now available to add a nutritional dimension to crop improvement programmes. According to several authorities, malnutrition in countries which have cereals as the staple food, is mostly the result of under-nutrition, arising in turn from inadequate purchasing power. Chronic illness and worm infection because of insanitary conditions, lack of community health care and ignorance about the feeding of infants resulting from poverty, all add to the problem. According to the report of the Task Force on Nutrition of the National Committee on Science and Technology (NCST), 90 per cent of our pre-school children have heights and weights much lower than those of children of corresponding ages in the U.S.A. Another important point made by the Task Force is that our nutritional problems are qualitatively very different from those of the richer nations and hence the remedies must be our own. For example, in richer nations where excessive intake of fat of the order of 75-100g daily has aggravated the problem of certain kinds of heart diseases, the emphasis has rightly been on reducing the fat content of the diet. The same situation holds good among the rich in our country. This section of the population, however, is very small and for a majority of our people, the inclusion of more fat in the diet is not only desirable but necessary. This is because fats and oils are not only concentrated sources of calories but act as important vehicles for some vitamins. The NCST Task Force has hence recommended that we should try to raise the per capita average consumption of fats from the current level of 10 g per day to at least 30-40 g per day. This would call for a 3-4 fold increase in oilseed production.

Apart from opening up the possibilities for sunflower and soybean production, we have not had so far any striking advance in oilseed research. Scope exists for improving the yield of groundnut, *til*, safflower and coconut, through better management and seeds. However, in the near future we may have to lean heavily on increasing the acreage under oilseed crops if we are to substantially increase the production of these crops. The position with regard to pulses is more or less similar. Increasing the area under oilseeds and pulses would be possible only through multiple cropping and by increasing the productivity of crops, such as rice and *jowar*, so that some land can be released from them.

More area for pulses, oilseeds

There is considerable scope for releasing areas from *jowar* and *bajra* for pulses or oilseeds in rain-fed areas by improving the productivity of these crops, thus replacing the old varieties by high-yielding ones. For example, calculations show that in Gujarat, which produced during 1969-70 one million tonnes of *bajra* from 1.73 million hectares, it is possible to produce 1.12 million tonnes from 1.60 million hectares merely by increasing the proportion of the area under high-yielding hybrids from the original 17 per cent to 30 per cent. Similar opportunities are now available in *jowar*, as a result of release of varieties such as 302, 604 and *Swarna*.

Genetic improvement of nutritive quality of basic staples is another venue of providing better nutrition, at no extra cost. Chemical fortification with limiting amino acids, which used to be the major approach advocated ten years ago, has given way now to attempts to improve genetically the amino acid balance and nutritive quality of crops of maize, *jowar*, barley, potato, wheat, and rice. This field of research was stimulated by the discovery a few years ago at the Purdue University in the U.S.A. of genes conferring a higher content of lysine, an essential amino acid, in the protein of certain strains of maize and more recently in *jowar*. This is of particular significance since the nutritional disorder pellagra has been found by the National Institute of Nutrition, Hyderabad, in areas where *jowar* is the staple food. Another important finding in this area is the identification in Sweden of a barley strain with high protein and lysine. It is interesting that both the *jowar* and barley lines originated in Ethiopia. This line of research may help to produce high-yielding-cum-high-nutritive quality strains. If this is coupled with the widespread preparation of home-made weaning foods in villages such as the Hyderabad mix, on the basis of locally available cereals, pulses and jaggery, a dent on the malnutrition problem can be made more easily.

Harmony and natural balance

The concept of harmony and natural balance involves the development of management concepts in areas, such as disease and pest control, and the balanced growth of different components of a production system. 'Prevention is better than cure' is the general motto in disease control, and we know that through appropriate immunisation, and sanitary and quarantine measure the health of farm animals can be maintained at a satisfactory level. Our scientists have been developing effective vaccines against the important diseases of cattle. Recently, a vaccine against lung worm of sheep has been developed using the principle of radiation attenuation. In general, however, the awareness of the need for quarantine and sanitation is not widespread.

Depending upon the cropping pattern, water availability and marketability of produce, profitable mixed farming systems can be developed. Where feed grain availability is low, ruminating animals could form a good mix with cereal and millet cultivation. Poultry rations usually contain as high as 60-70 per cent cereal grains. However, several agricultural and industrial by-products for example, rice bran, wheat bran, slaughter-house waste, fishery wastes, etc. could be used as poultry feed. Similarly, the serious drought in Maharashtra (1972) provided an opportunity to introduce new rations such as a mixture of bagasse, molasses and urea. Improved strains of fodder grasses and legumes are also becoming available and studies at the National Dairy Research Institute have shown that high-yielding crossbred cows can be maintained largely on high quality fodder.

More and more concepts, such as pest control, are giving way to procedures which help to raise good crops through better management with minimal assistance from chemical methods of control. Such integrated procedures of pest management involve an appropriate combination of methods, such as selection of resistant varieties, use of parasites and predators, both native and introduced, ecological control through modifications in cropping systems and agronomic practices, development of microbial pesticides, use of attractants and repellents including sex hormones, development of various methods of inducing sterility, and use of selective chemical insecticides. Such an integrated approach has become necessary to avoid dangers arising from the destruction of beneficial insects and natural enemies of pests, the persistence of some pesticides in the food chain, the origin of pesticide resistant insects and environmental contamination. Safer chemical pesticides are also being developed and in crops, such as *jowar*, the control of shoot-fly through either treating seeds with a suitable pesticide or an adjustment in date of sowing could make a big difference in yield.

Biological control of pests

Biological control which involves the control of pests through their natural enemies is receiving increasing attention. In the past, more emphasis had been placed on an inundation approach involving the mass breeding and release of indigenous natural enemies. Emphasis is now shifting to obtaining more effective parasites and predators from other areas where the same or related pests occur. In general, countries which have had the greatest successes in biological control are the ones which have imported the greatest number of natural enemies. A station of the Commonwealth Institute of Biological Control located at Bangalore helps to obtain natural enemies of pests of apple, cabbage, castor, coconut, cotton, potato, sugarcane, rice and aquatic weeds from other parts of the world. Predatory snails and hermit crabs have been found to be useful in controlling the giant African snail, which had become a menace in the Andaman islands and in parts of Kerala and Assam. Attempts are in progress in some countries in Africa to control water weeds, such as the water hyacinth and *Salvinia* through introduced parasites. If such parasites prove to be highly host-specific, we may also be able to initiate similar studies in our country. These aquatic weeds are causing serious problems in tanks and waterways particularly in eastern India and Kerala.

Economy through recycling

Economy and maximisation of farm incomes is a concept which is being used with great profit in diverse areas such as increasing the efficiency of nutrient supply, water use, energy release through recycling and effective use of all wastes and by-products, improved harvesting, storage, processing and utilisation. The major aim is to reduce waste in all possible ways, and decrease to the extent possible the dependence on non-renewable resources for increasing production. An integrated nutrient supply system involves the development in each block of an appropriate schedule of manuring with organic and inorganic manures. There is great scope for raising leguminous shrubs on bunds of irrigated fields or all along irrigation canals and rivers, to provide green leaf manure. It would be wise to introduce pulses and fodder legumes in all rotations. Success in conserving cow dung and other wastes for use as manure will depend upon the availability of fuel.

Devices, such as cow dung gas plants are yet to become popular. Meanwhile, rapid technological progress is taking place in which all wastes which contain cellulose can be converted into pipeline gas or liquid fuels. The conversion of grains through fermentation into usable ethyl alcohol, the growing of trees specifically for generating thermal power, the development of new high-yielding crops for industrial energy and recycling animal waste by anaerobic fermentation are some of the possibilities under economic assessment in several countries. Unlike the situation in rich nations, non-commercial sources of energy comprising dung, firewood and crop wastes constitute the major sources of energy supply in rural India and hence we can profit greatly from recent developments on the efficient use of wastes to supply power.

Fertiliser-use efficiency is very low at present and the common assumption of return from the applied nutrients is 10kg of grain per kg of nitrogen-phosphorus potassium NPK nutrients. Scope for improving fertiliser-use efficiency exists through procedures, such as adjusting fertiliser doses to soil test values, better water management, weed control, split application, placing the fertiliser a little below the soil surface, and use of nitrification inhibitors where leaching losses are likely to be high. Seed-cum-fertiliser drills help to achieve good seed germination and fertiliser distribution. When yields increase, deficiency of phosphorus and of micro-nutrients such as zinc become important, as was seen in the Punjab after the introduction of high-yielding varieties of wheat. A continuous monitoring of the status of soil fertility is therefore important.

There is apprehension that phosphorus reserves may get greatly depleted by the end of this century, therefore every attempt should be made to use wastes, such as basic slag from steel mills, other sources namely, rock phosphate and Laccadive sands, and also to promote the solubilisation of insoluble phosphates through microbial secretion of organic acids which dissolve phosphates. Rock phosphates and basic slag have been found to be suitable for application in acid soils. Fortunately, acid soils occur in the vicinity of steel factories and hence transportation costs can be minimised.

Cutting post-harvest losses

Techniques are also becoming available to minimise losses during harvest and post-harvest operations. A major problem in the safe storage of grains is the high moisture content often found, particularly in paddy. Studies carried out at the Paddy Processing Centre, Tiruvarur, on the effects of salt sprays both before and after harvests have shown that this technique could help to bring down rapidly the moisture content to about 12 per cent. We need much more work on the standardisation of effective methods of preventing pre- and post-harvest losses in grains, fruit and vegetables under different ecological conditions. Bad storage not only results in a quantitative loss of all food material, but more importantly, there could be considerable deterioration in nutritive quality. The problem is acute in crops, such as groundnut which develop aflatoxins following fungal infection.

The situation in processing and utilisation is dynamic. In some of the rich nations, where there is a move towards reducing the total per capita meat intake, so as to reduce the pressure on plant proteins which are needed to feed animals, food technologists are now developing textured vegetable proteins resembling meat products. Plant proteins which were not formerly of value in human nutrition are also now becoming usable processing and removing any toxic or anti-nutritional factor. For example, a milling technique called the 'liquid cyclone process' can help to remove gossypol from cotton seeds. Methods have been standardised in Sweden to remove the toxic glucosinolates present in rape and mustard seeds. Such detoxified rapeseed protein has still some anti-nutritional factors, which are currently being studied. A low cost 65 per cent protein concentrate can now be prepared from fresh coconuts. The process at the same time gives a high-grade oil. The Central Food Technological Research Laboratory at Mysore has standardised several useful milling and processing techniques, and particularly the improved methods of pulse milling deserve popularisation since they can save over 10 per cent of milling losses.

Changes in processing and utilisation can completely change the market value of a commodity. For example, until some years ago research on the improvement of *robusta* coffee had been given less importance in our country on the assumption that the world demand would be only for *arabica* coffee, which has a superior flavour. The advent of instant or soluble coffee has however changed the position since *robusta* has good solubility. Thus, while the annual average prices secured in 1961 in export auctions per 50 kg of similar grades of *arabica* and *robusta* were, respectively Rs 144.50 and Rs 70.50, these prices were Rs 223 and Rs 220.50 during 1970-71, thus practically wiping out the difference. Similarly, lac was regarded as a dying industry until recently. However, the price in (October 1973) of a tonne of lac in the U.K. market was £ 1450, while in October 1971 the price was only £ 340. Obviously, some important new use has been found for lac. Demand for tapioca has also greatly increased, and it is expected that by 1980 countries of the European Economic Community would be importing at least 4.4 million tonnes of tapioca. These few examples should suffice to indicate that in order both to maintain and develop further markets for agricultural produce, we have to keep ourselves very well informed about trends in their processing and utilisation. Quality control and improved packaging and forwarding techniques are equally important. All this calls for an agricultural technology and market intelligence unit which can keep our research workers constantly informed about the relative priorities they should assign to problems which have a bearing on the export trade.

Watching technological trends would also be important to stabilise the home market for labour-intensive cash crops such as cotton in the dry farming regions. Globally, it is becoming clear that cotton may face a serious threat from synthetic fibres unless cotton strains can be developed which can respond well to chemical finishing treatments capable of conferring on cotton 'easy care' properties, such as drip-drying and crease retention. The preliminary work done so far indicates that there is scope for screening varieties for these attributes.

An exciting era

We are thus in an exciting era in agricultural and food science. Thanks to the growing involvement of more and more physicists, chemists, climatologists, mathematicians and engineers in the study and solution of biological problems, we can hope for continued progress in unravelling new approaches to improve productivity. Remote sensing, satellite photography and satellite television have all great applications in soil and groundwater survey, crop censussing, disease forecasting, prediction of floods and cyclones, and in mass communication. The National Commission on Agriculture in an interim report on agricultural research and education has stressed the fact that in our legitimate concern for results of immediate applied value, we should not dry up sources of basic research. Research in production physiology, molecular biology, cellular biochemistry, design engineering, construction of production models on the basis of a systems approach, all deserve to be supported and intensified. If some of the current experiments designed to confer the ability to fix biological nitrogen on cereal crops (thus making them behave like legumes) meet with success during the next 10 years or so, this will be one of the greatest boons that scientists can confer on the poor cultivators. There is evidence that the current highest yields obtained in wheat and rice represent less than half of what is theoretically possible. Scientists have hence much to do.

While the onward march of science relevant to human

welfare must go on, it is our duty at every point of time to ensure that the people, for whose welfare the scientific work has been undertaken at public expense, benefit from the knowledge gathered and material developed.

SOCIAL AND EDUCATIONAL REQUIREMENTS OF NEW TECHNOLOGY

The emerging technology is based upon the understanding of the principles of ecology. A clear distinction must be drawn here between the different meanings which this term 'ecology', can have for people in different situations. In the developed world, the growing importance of the science of ecology is largely the result of the efforts of the conservation movement. Essentially, this is a movement which uses ecology to maintain for the already rich people of those countries the very high standards of living which they currently enjoy. It is a protective movement, which aims to prevent further depletion of already severely threatened or eroded resources, and a further degradation of the environment.

However, for the developing world, ecology has to be understood in a very different sense. Most people do not have even the bare necessities of life, and therefore, hardly any standard of living to conserve or to protect. Rapid economic growth is hence a prime necessity. Human wastes and civic effluents form a far greater source of pollution in the poor nations than scientific and industrial pollutants. In our situation, knowledge of ecology should be regarded as an instrument of balanced and rapid economic growth.

A publication entitled *The careless technology* (Taghi and Milton, 1972) points out with the help of 50 selected case studies, that a high proportion of the development efforts in the developing countries have been destructive, especially of precious natural resources and delicate but ill-understood natural balances. The authors demonstrate that time and again not enough forethought was given to the ecological consequences of developmental projects. However, the authors also admit that most of these projects were designed by experts from the developed countries, often with limited knowledge of the client countries, and based on the different and irrelevant experiences of their own countries. If such programmes were accepted by the poor nations, it was for other reasons which need not be gone into here. What is needed, however, is a close and detailed understanding of local ecosystems, and their application to local situations by those who are fully informed of the parameters of the problem. If development is not to be destructive, then the developing countries must take the responsibility for understanding their own ecological needs, resources and patterns and planning their development accordingly. Ecology has to be a positive force in the poor countries, one which supports the economic growth so urgently needed and not just a conserving force. This can be achieved when the people of each area participate, through block and district-level land-use and crop-planning forums, in the formulation of detailed land- and water-use plans for their areas. Land-use planning at the block-level, assisted by guidelines on market need and opportunities by a suitable authority at the state level, and on interstate crop adjustments and export opportunities by a central agency, would alone result in a dynamic agriculture where the profits of progress accrue to all sections of the community.

Village-level co-operation

For an efficient adoption of the technology at the field level, the need for the development by scientists of appropriate drought, good weather and flood avoidance codes for each agro-ecological area has been referred to. Such codes would be of immense benefit to the developmental administrators as well as to village *panchayats*, *zila parishads* and other agencies who have to get projects translated into field accomplishments. It is obvious that tasks, such as recycling of all wastes, and land-use planning based on an appropriate admixture of agriculture, animal husbandry, fishery and forestry, require considerable understanding and co-operation at the village level. The only approach to rapid economic development which can succeed is to optimise the advantages of our large population, vast numbers of whom are now neither participants nor beneficiaries of development activity.

For example, let us take the case of the control of *Pyrilla*, a serious pest of sugarcane. *Pyrilla* is not only affecting sugarcane but is now becoming a serious menace to other crops, such as wheat and *jowar*. The most economical and effective method of controlling this pest would be field sanitation involving the burning up of all trash after the harvest of sugarcane, and the collection of eggs of the pest from the lower surface of the leaf during April-May. These tasks can be easily accomplished by even village school boys and girls. If such early steps are taken, the small population of *Pyrilla* that may still remain is likely to be attacked by natural enemies during the rainy season and the problem may easily be controlled. If on the other hand, simple steps, such as crop sanitation, removal of eggs from the under-surface of the leaves at the appropriate time, and subsequent steps, such as attracting the nymphs and adults of this pest by light traps are not followed, then the pest assumes a serious dimension towards September—as it did in some areas of north India in the year 1973. Since the sugarcane plantation would be full grown at that time, it would be difficult to get into the field and spray the plants with chemicals. At this stage, aerial spraying or use of power sprayers is the only choice left. Though inevitable when the pest has assumed menacing proportions, it is obvious that making a habit of such a method in our country would be tantamount to bypassing our major strength, namely, our large population, and to increasing the already high cost of cultivation.

The emerging agricultural technology is of two major kinds with regard to the ease of adoption. In one kind, as for example, the new technology of wheat cultivation, the economic benefits derived by a farmer by adopting the technology are not influenced by what his neighbouring farmer does or does not do. In other words, in economic terms the technology is capable of successful individual adoption. In the other kind, the economic benefits conferred by the technology on the farmer will be proportional to the extent of co-operative action generated on the part of an entire village or watershed community. Rice and cotton cultivation and prevention of disease epidemics in cattle are good examples. Even in Punjab, with one of the finest farming communities in the world, the average yield of cotton is low, being only 368 kg per hectare. In contrast, in Egypt, where cotton cultivation is managed co-operatively without any infringement of individual ownership, the average yield is 780 kg per hectare. Pest control and water management in rice are best done co-operatively in a village. In fact, if this can be accomplished, even some of the fertiliser lost through leaching in drainage water can be recycled by collecting such water in a pond at the lowest point and redistributing it. The need to achieve a doubling in fertiliser response from the present low level of about 10 kg of grain per kg of NPK nutrients has already been stressed. It was pointed out earlier, that the emerging concept of pest avoidance is pest management and not just chemical control. All these aspects of the new technology would need understanding and co-operation among neighbouring small farmers. If this is not achieved, the risk element in crop production will be high. A low-cost and low-effort agriculture will be the poor cultivator's response to a high-risk farming situation, unless he has protection by means, such as crop insurance. This is an important reason for the relative stagnation of *kharif* crop production in our country, where in spite of moisture availability, the farmer hesitates to invest on inputs in areas which are prone to pests and diseases, water-logging and operational problems in land preparation.

Co-operative effort is not only needed in the delta area during the *kharif* season but even more importantly, in the dry farming regions. While an individual farmer can increase the storage of moisture in the soil profile of his own field through tillage, mulching and other measures, the possibilities for collecting all the run-off water and using it for a crop life-saving irrigation later, can be realised only if there is group action in accordance with the topo-sequence of the farms.

Changes in cultural practices

We also find that several basic changes in cultural practices may be needed to get the best out of the new crop varieties. For example, in dwarf wheats, sowing has to be shallow; first irrigation has to be at given the time of initiation of crown roots and population density should be higher. In rice, traditional practices such as low seed rate under direct seeding, wide spacing, deep planting and bunch planting under transplanted conditions, and drying the field to promote the establishment of seedlings are all intended to retard luxuriant vegetative growth in the earlier tall varieties, which have a proneness for both excessive vegetative growth and lodging or falling down.

In contrast, the new dwarf rice varieties need almost the opposite kind of treatment, if they are to reveal their full genetic potential for yield.

It is obvious that to accomplish all these tasks successfully we need to develop educational and organisational procedures which would on the one hand make the literate better equipped to discharge the functions of *gram sevak*, *gram sevika*, credit agent, teacher and other agents of change, and on the other make the illiterate highly skilled and efficient partners in adopting the latest scientific advances. Other obvious requirements, such as the timeliness of credit and input supply, and appropriate pricing and marketing arrangements need no reiteration. However, it may be pointed out that in addition to the procedures currently in operation for product pricing, we should also pay serious attention to evolving long-term pricing policies for factors of production, such as fertiliser, pumps, pesticides and others. Product pricing alone without attention to the pricing of means of production will tend to result in controversies and problems.

It is not only in agriculture and dairying that new techniques need to be popularised, but also in inland and marine fisheries. The possibilities of making full use of the three-dimensional space and the availability of different kinds of fish food in a pond, through stocking different kinds of fish which can derive their food from the bottom, and upper and middle levels has already been referred to. Similarly, there are opportunities for adopting new techniques in areas, such as the production of quality fish seed through induced breeding, the cultivation of air-breathing fish in the swampy areas, and the culture of frogs for export. In marine fisheries, also, culture techniques can be introduced to supplement the income from capture fisheries. Mussel culture, growing milk fish, mullets and certain species of prawns in coastal lagoons containing salt water, and pearl culture, can all improve the economy of the fishermen in our coastal areas.

To sustain high levels of biological productivity, we also need to generate a general awareness in the entire community of the crucial significance of conserving soil, water, flora and fauna. Like game and wild life sanctuaries, we need to develop crop gene sanctuaries in those parts of our country where valuable genes are found in the primitive cultivars and native flora. Such a step can help to prevent the erosion of valuable genes. In contrast to soil erosion, gene erosion is not visible to the naked eye and hence does not attract attention.

Changes in educational outlook

Having spoken about the extension needs of the new technology, it would be appropriate to turn to the social and educational infrastructure which is a prerequisite for the successful adoption of the technology.

What kind of education do we need which would be relevant to our society, dependent as it is on agriculture as its major activity ? And what practical steps can we take to change our educational system into such a one ?

The changes required are of two kinds : at one end we need to bring about a change in outlook, creating an awareness of biological surroundings and a consciousness of the possibilities of synergy. This can be done only when there is an inundation, so to speak, at every level of education of materials which will create such a consciousness. At the other end we need to give technical skills to illiterate and semi-literate adults, which will enable them to understand and efficiently use the new technological package. Between these two there are a wide range of activities which can be applied at every educational level.

During the early years of childhood, before the child begins to receive formal education, and in the primary school, the major emphasis should be on living in nature and with nature, learning about nature through direct observation, and using the materials provided in nature to develop scientific skills, aptitudes and habits of thought. How often are children in *balwadis* and primary schools forced to remain within the limiting walls of a barren and bare classroom, because of the false impression that education is something that must take place within a building ? How few children in *balwadis* are taken for walks and helped to learn about nature ? We need more educational games and kits which will make use of the play-way idea of teaching science in general, and agriculture in particular.

The traditional media of entertainment as well as the mass media of radio, cinema and television can also be harnessed to the cause. Even now, many of the new crop varieties are known in villages at some places as 'radio varieties', since information on the new strains reached the illiterate cultivators through the radio. It is a happy sign that newspapers are increasingly assigning more space to items relating to agriculture and rural development. While the English-language newspapers play an important role in conveying messages to the policy maker, the Indian-language press, besides the radio and cinema, forms the most significant medium of conveying information to villagers. Several of our leading newspapers now have whole time agricultural correspondents and experts specialising in agricultural subjects.

Role of banks and companies

Both banks and public and private sector companies can play a great role in combining their regular work with the art of communication. Banks can finance entire production programmes, as for example, the production of a lakh of tonnes of sunflower oil or the production of a certain quantity of soy-bean in a suitable area, and thereby assure the credit and other infrastructure for the entire production chain and not merely for components of the chain. Similarly, pesticides firms can sponsor programmes designed to ensure pest-proofing of important crops in the poorest villages in their area of operation. All such projects will provide excellent educational opportunities for the students of the area, besides serving as demonstrations of new techniques.

Work experience at the upper primary and secondary level too can be effective if carried out in a different manner. This idea of introducing work experience into schools seems rather artificial and unnecessary in our context. At an optimistic estimate, about 70 per cent of the children aged 6-11 are enrolled in primary schools. If we consider children up to the age of 14, and take account of wastage and stagnation in education, then the number of children between 6-14 who are not in school may be as large or larger than the number of children in school. Most of these children are already working, not indeed to gain work experience though they are gaining it no doubt, but out of sheer economic necessity. In these circumstances, bringing work experience into schools seems redundant. Would it not be more meaningful to carry educative experience out to the work, where the children already are anyway ? This means much more than open-air classrooms, or discussing arithmetic in terms of bags of manure or hectares sown or other agricultural operations, though of course, such activities are necessary and important. But it would mean much more and would imply a profound change in the school programme if such activities as allowing children to work in their own or others' farms for part or most of the day, planning for learning-oriented and not teaching-oriented education, and getting new kinds of teachers to deal with the new task are introduced.

Who is to teach work experience as conceived in this way ? The traditional school teacher, who is mostly drawn from the white-collar class and has little practical experience of agriculture may not always be the most suited to this task. In fact, it has already been observed in areas where the new technology has spread, that the technical knowledge of rural parents, who may be progressive farmers, is far ahead of the out-dated agriculture taught in the schools, even by qualified teachers. Why not allow such parents, or other local farmers, to teach part-time ? Often, even the children of farm families know more about the latest developments in agriculture than the non-agriculturist school teacher. Even at the post-graduate level of education, the Indian Agricultural Research Institute, New Delhi, which a few years ago initiated the practice of inviting farmers with practical wisdom as visiting professors for brief periods found the experience very rewarding to staff and students alike. Why not bring in more and more part-time teachers, people who have skills and knowledge in agriculture and related crafts, or at least send students out to them ? Some experiments along these lines are already being carried out.

Work projects for students

Another useful adaptation of the idea of work experience is to give academic recognition through credit to real economic work projects, self-chosen by students and carried out by them in their spare time, either alone or with the help of their families. A boy or girl who can run a simple project such as a poultry unit or a kitchen garden would have learnt much by way of independence, responsibility and initiative, as well by way of arithmetic, science and economics. It is needless to add that the conventional literacy skills of reading, writing and arithmetic will also be fully utilised in such projects. Of course, it means more time and effort on the part of teachers and administrators to identify and initiate such projects. Further, it requires the technical assistance of officials of agriculture departments and extension agencies. It is naturally much easier to provide artificial work in the classroom and call it work experience, than to help children to engage in real work and to assess it as it deserves. Children become responsible when they are obliged to carry responsibility. The majority of children in our country are already working and carrying responsibility. It is up to us to devise an education that will encourage and support them in their efforts by providing a place for such tasks. To quote Maslow (1972) the humanistic psychologist, speaking on the development of responsibility : It looks as if one way to breed grown-up people is to give them responsibility, to assume that they can take it and to let them sweat and struggle with it. Let them work it out themselves, rather than over-protecting them, indulging them or doing things for them. It is time that we use this as a basic principle in education.

Yet another useful form of work experience would be the school project. Apart from the practical and economic value of the school farm, garden or dairy, it would teach another vitally necessary attitude which has already been mentioned, this is, the necessity for co-operative endeavour. Even if each student had his own plot, or animal, or pond, he would learn, without being asked, to work in co-operation with his fellow students during certain operations, realise the necessity for certain activities to be undertaken by all at the same time, appreciate the economics of sharing and so forth. In this way, co-operative endeavour would become a necessity for the individual, for the success of each individual's project would be inevitably linked to the performance of thes ejoint operations at the right time and in the right way.

Involving university students

At the university stage fewer people are involved, but they need to be involved in a different way. In 1969-70, about 3 million students were enrolled in higher education, about 2.5 million men and 0.5 million women. Of this, only 1.6 per cent of the men and 0.4 per cent of the women were engaged in any kind of agricultural studies. Only 176 women were enrolled in agricultural universities. In a country with 80 per cent of the population engaged in agricultural pursuits and living in the rural areas it is sad that such a small fraction of men and women are engaged in studies which can contribute to rural development or agricultural productivity. It is especially regrettable that though women contribute equally to the labour force in agriculture, performing many of the key operations and most of the more tiresome ones, agriculture as a profession is not regarded as a suitable one for women at the higher stages of education. This reflects the gap between the educated classes, who are mostly drawn from the urban areas, and now-a-days also from the rural elites, and the rest of the population. Apart from providing more opportunities for higher education and technical studies in agriculture, we have also to think of other practical ways in which the great majority of university students can be helped to become involved in the work of rural development and to acquire some understanding and sympathy for the problems of the greater part of this country's population.

Making work-experience an integral part of university education would help to generate a greater sense of self-confidence and self-reliance on the part of the student. One approach to achieving this aim may lie in making an in-built provision in each of our development projects, for students' participation.

Student-work should not be regarded merely as social service or training, but must become a distinctive and advantageous part of the project. If this approach is accepted by the project authorities, students can become a source of great strength and dynamism to the project, when properly trained and deployed.

Therefore, every university student must be employed in an appropriate 'plan project' for a period of two months every year while he or she is at the university. A semester system of course curriculum organisation would help in the implementation of this idea, although this is not absolutely essential. The summer vacation can be restricted to one month, so that the formal teaching programmes do not suffer. The assignment of students to various projects will need proper planning and adequate consultation between the universities and project authorities. Needless to say, the assignment of students will be based on the principle of learning through work and would, therefore, involve a planned matching of the field of study with the field of work. Thus, students of History and Archaeology may work for the India Tourism Development Corporation, students of Zoology and Medicine in the family planning and preventive medicine programmes; those of Agriculture, Botany, Chemistry, Physics, Economics, Engineering and Home Economics in agricultural development and child nutrition programmes; and students of nearly all fields in pre-primary, primary and secondary education programmes.

All scientific institutions in the country run by central and state governments can provide opportunities for students to work in specific projects and can at the same time give a great fillip to the cottage industry movement by supplying detailed manufacturing drawings of new implements, machinery and processes. With these drawings, university students in engineering may be in a position to help village communities in starting small-scale industries, since rural credit is now becoming more easily available.

Technical literacy for farmers

The majority of our peasants are illiterate. Unfortunately, the proportion of illiteracy seems to be higher in areas, such as the arid and semi-arid regions where the scientific transformation of the rural economy requires a much greater understanding of the principles of economic ecology. Therefore, it is obvious that unless we seriously start programmes to impart the latest technical skills to illiterate peasantry by the method of learning by doing, we will not be able to accomplish our goals. The ICAR is proposing to set up a number of *krishi vigyan kendras* KVK to impart technical literacy to practising farmers, fishermen and others. These *kendras* would select in each area such means of economic growth which are most likely to give major benefits to the poorest sections of the community. In other words, those who are setting up a KVK will first have to make a survey of the agricultural potential of an area and then identify those aspects of growth which could help to improve the purchasing power of the poor. For example, in an exercise done in the union territories of Pondicherry and Karaikal, where a KVK has been approved for establishment, it was found that the following areas needed immediate attention, if the poor were to be benefited :

(a) Improving the income and reducing the underemployment of over 10,000 fishermen;
(b) improving the average per hectare rice yield to about 2,000 kg as soon as possible from the existing 1,400 kg; and
(c) introducing a scientific animal husbandry programme in order to produce more milk, both for marketing in Madras city and for making milk powder. A similar KVK in Punjab may deal with topics, such as tubewell technology, repair of implements and tractors, and scientific multiple cropping.

Having analysed the most effective methods of improving the income of the poorest sections of the community, and identified the major thrusts, the KVK has to provide training which will help the trainees to initiate change in their respective occupations. For example, in the case of Pondicherry fishermen the training will be in the area of coastal aquaculture, which will help them to undertake fish culture in coastal estuaries in addition to improving the techniques of fish capture. Similarly, the animal husbandry programme will impart skills in genetic upgrading, cultivation of nutritious grasses and legumes, the use of wastes enriched with urea as feed, health care through sanitation and immunisation, and better processing and marketing techniques.

Even if we are able to provide the educational infrastructure needed for agricultural reconstruction, we would still have to develop a social organisation which could help small farmers to overcome the limitations arising from the small size of farm holdings, lack of capacity to purchase the requisite inputs, and inability to get a fair price for the produce. To achieve this aim we shall have to devise strategies to generate social synergy.

Social synergy

What is social synergy? Ruth Benedict (1970) the anthropologist who first applied the concept of synergy in social sciences, says :

> Societies where non-aggression is conspicuous have social orders in which the individual by the same act and at the same time serves his own advantage and that of the group . . . . Non-aggression occurs in these societies, not because people are unselfish and put social obligations above personal desires, but because social arrangements make these two identical.
>
> Cultures with low social synergy are those in which the social structure provides for acts which are mutually opposed and counteractive, and cultures of high synergy where it provides for acts which are mutually reinforcing . . . In cultures with high social synergy, institutions ensure mutual advantage from their undertakings, while in societies with low social synergy the advantage of one individual becomes a victory over another, and the majority who are not victorious must shift as they can.

According to Maslow, 'The high synergy society is the one in which virtue pays . . . . High synergy societies all have techniques for working off humiliation, and the low synergy societies uniformly do not'.

To a biologist, there is sufficient evidence in Nature to prove that symbiosis, or the process of mutual assistance and support, is a necessary ingredient for synergy. However, it seems that the very concept of synergy has been very little used, or even understood, by social scientists in its application to man. Ruth Benedict was one of the few social scientists to apply this concept to societies, and it was developed later by Maslow, who, significantly enough is not considered an orthodox psychologist. A very significant definition of social synergy is the one just quoted. From this it appears that there is a close correlation between synergy and non-violence, a fact which should be of interest to us in the country of Mahatma Gandhi. It is evident that our society as at present organised is a low synergy society. What steps can we take to ensure that we move from this to a better state of affairs?

Individual and social goals

Individual goals have to be made to coincide with social goals. This can be done in many ways. Russia, China and Israel have all found their own ways to ensure this merging of individual and social goals. Most of these methods are related to the practices of child-rearing and education. In the Soviet Union, for instance, the system of rewards and punishments in schools is such that the individual is rewarded only when the peer group succeeds. At every stage, the success and happiness of the individual is related to the success of the group in such a way that each individual strives to maximise the success of the group. Some of the approaches described earlier, such as encouraging children and students to take up economic projects in a responsible way and linking them with academic success, would be good examples of social synergy at work.

This is not, however, the only means of achieving the goal. In a free economy, it is possible to conceive of a system whereby farmers could be motivated to produce what the nation considered necessary. This would involve a very complex set of arrangements, including pricing, availability of inputs, technical knowledge, land ownership and a variety of other things. However, it is clear that slogans and appeals to the social conscience cannot work, except for short periods during national crises. Slogans of 'grow more food' or 'self-reliance' are not adequate as inducement to persuade farmers even to grow anything, leave alone to do so in an ecologically balanced manner. It requires a far more widespread and dynamic movement of society to bring about such changes. In other words, it requires a release of synergy.

It may be asked who is the 'individual' whose interests have to be identified with the social interest ? Whom is the new technology to serve ? The first task is to identify the individual. It is obvious that it is the farmer of India, who must be served by the new technology in such a way as to release social synergy. He has three qualifications; he is essentially a small farmer, poor and illiterate.

A technology for the poor farmer

If slogans, such as the 'transformation of rural life' or 'the achievement of growth with social justice' are to be translated into reality, then the new technology must be such that it can be adopted by the small, poor and illiterate farmer. Do we have such a technology ? Yes, but as explained earlier, its adoption particularly during the south-west monsoon season requires a certain degree of co-operative effort and a changed outlook. These in turn imply far-reaching changes in education and social organisation as prerequisites.

At the village level it is necessary that there is co-operation between those who possess technical knowledge and those who are devoted to social service, and that both together identify the most important need of the village in getting its economy moving. If the need is correctly identified, and then properly attended to, it will act as a catalyst in releasing synergy. An important task of social workers is hence the identification of catalysts which can bring home, through tangible economic benefits, the value of co-operation to the small and marginal farmers.

So far, the discussion has been about an agriculture in which the ecological advantages of the different parts of our country can be maximised and the hazards minimised through appropriate land- and water-use planning in which (i) high synergy crop and animal production systems are introduced, (ii) recycling procedures used to promote a high growth rate in productivity on the basis of renewable resources of energy, farm and factory are closely linked; (iii) maximum economy and efficiency are effected in the use of all resources; (iv) export markets are nurtured through continuous attention to the changing quality needs of the clients; and (v) a fair and remunerative return is assured to the primary producer. This is an agriculture based on ecological awareness, in which synergy, harmony and economy are the basic principles, and of which recycling is a tool. These are in essence the principles on which Mahatma Gandhi developed most of his concepts of rural reconstruction, though he used a different language and a different set of examples which were valid at that time. We should not make the mistake of rejecting the principles because some of the examples used by Gandhi forty years ago may be out of date in the light of modern science. On the contrary, science and technology have in their search for a productive agriculture compatible with human growth and human welfare, uncovered the very same principles which Gandhi arrived at by a different route. If we can take the steps necessary to evolve the kind of agricultural system described so far, based on the most advanced principles of biological science, we can probably claim to have developed a gandhian agriculture, because this would be an agriculture where gandhian concepts become manifested in the form of an advanced rural economy, benefiting all sections of the community.

To achieve this, the tool has to be education, and the chosen method, co-operation. Social synergy has to be released by using appropriate educational and organisational methods as catalysts.

Transferring technology to the masses

The technology is now becoming available, but the mechanism for transferring it to the illiterate and small users in an effective manner does not exist. Ironically, there is a global communication network which makes the latest findings of science available almost immediately to research workers in any corner of the world; but what is urgently needed is such a communication network at the service of the poor farmer in our country. It is not only knowledge that is needed, but an approach which will be able to supply the right knowledge and tools to the right people at the right time and place. The worker on the spot, whether he is an agricultural officer, a teacher, a *gram sevak* or a social worker, must be able to identify the local problem or need which will act as a catalyst for promoting co-operative endeavour in that area—it may be lift irrigation in one place, dairying in another, pest control in a third, supply of farm machinery or fish fingerlings in a fourth and marketing in a fifth. In this network, the mass communication media, particularly the radio, television, cinema and the Indian-language press, have a very important role to play; so have the research and the extension worker, the education system and the drive for technical literacy.

Our prosperity depends on rapid economic growth, and this in turn depends on our performance in agriculture.

The future of our agriculture in its turn depends on the success with which we can help the small and illiterate farmers to take the many small steps which alone can lead to improved methods of farming. Science can only show the way; it is for us, the educated and the privileged class, to provide the will.

REFERENCES

Benedict, R., Synergy : Patterns of the good culture. *American Anthropologist*, vol. 17, (1970), p. 72.

Lowdermilk, W.C., The eleventh commandment in *Getting Agriculture Moving*, R.E. Borton, (ed.) *Agricultural Development Council*, New York (1966).

Maslow, A.H., *The Farther Reaches of Human Personality*, Pelican Gretna, La., (1972).

McNamara, R.S., *Address to the Board of Governors, World Bank Group*, (1973), pp. 16.

Meadows, D.H.; D.L., Randers; W.B. Behrens Meadows; J. *The Limits to Growth*, New York : Universe Books, (1972), pp. 205.

Paddock, William; Paul Paddock, *Famine 1972—America's Decisions : Who will Survive*, Boston : Little Brown & Co. (1967).

Taghi, Farvar, M ; J.P. Milton, *The Careless Technology*, New York : National History Press, (1972).

Verghese, B.G., *Beyond the Famine : An Approach to Regional Planning in Bihar*, 1967 (memeographed haper)

Verghese, B.G., A blessing code named famine, *Sunday World*, 18 March 1973.

IRRIGATION AND OUR AGRICULTURAL FUTURE 2

THE 1981 census has revealed that our population is still growing at an exponential rate of about 2.23 per cent. Population projections made by the Planning Commission, using two different alternatives (i.e., NRR=1 by 1996 or 2010) show that in 50 years from now we may have a population of about 1231 or 1375 million (Table 1).

TABLE 1 : **Estimated population of India : projections of the Perspective Planning Division of the Planning Commission**

Year	Assumption [a]	Population (Million)	Dependency Ratio [b]
1981	—	683.8	0.84
2001	A	940.3	0.58
2001	B	1,003.1	0.67
2031	A	1,231.7	0.57
2031	B	1,375.4	0.56

[a] Assumption A : NRR=1 in 1996

Assumption B : NRR=1 in 2010

[b] Dependency ratio : $\frac{(0\text{—}14+60+)}{15\text{—}59}$

If the programmes now planned for improving female literacy, economic emancipation of women and for widespread voluntary adoption of the small family norm succeed, it should be possible to contain the population size at 1231 million in

A.D. 2030-31. We will then need to produce 277 million tonnes of foodgrains to meet a per capita requirement of 225 kg per year.

Fortunately, we have a fairly large untapped production reservoir in most farming systems in our country. This is particularly true of the Indo-Gangetic plains and also of the black soil areas of central India. Because of the rapid growth in population and the consequent need of more land for domestic, industrial, communication and other purposes, land will be a shrinking resource for agriculture.

In other words, expansion in production will have to come largely through enhanced productivity and higher intensity of cropping. Our large requirement of foodgrains for domestic consumption also emphasises the importance of achieving a higher agricultural growth rate coupled with stability of production. This is where irrigation plays a pivotal role.

Once water is available, it is possible to introduce other components of technology, such as seeds of high-yielding varieties, improved soil health care and better post-harvest technology. Globally, irrigation has helped to elevate the yields of all major food crops (Table 2).

TABLE 2 : **Global impact of irrigation on rice yield (with optimum management)**

Class of land	Average yield t/ha
Good rainfall (120-270 growing days)	3.40
Naturally flooded	4.50
Full irrigation	7.00
Partial irrigation	5.75
Problem areas	2.80

In our country the introduction of high-yielding varieties of wheat and rice in areas covered with assured irrigation has helped in saving about 34 million hectares of land which would otherwise have been needed to produce the quantities of wheat and rice we now produce (Table 3).

TABLE 3 : **Impact of improved technology on land requirement in India**

Crop	Year	Per hectare yield (t)	Production ($t \times 10^6$)	Area saved by yield increase ($ha \times 10^6$)
Rice	1966-70	0.981	35.77	Nil
Rice	1979	1.328	53.77	14.33
Wheat	1961-66	0.830	10.95	Nil
Wheat	1979	1.574	35.51	20.22

The impact of irrigation on stabilising production is also evident from a comparison of the production of major grains, such as rice and wheat in Punjab where 80 per cent of the area is irrigated, with other states, such as Madhya Pradesh or Orissa where the area under irrigation is 13 and 28 per cent, respectively (Table 4).

TABLE 4 : **Area and production of rice**

State	Area ($ha \times 10^5$)			Production ($t \times 10^5$)		
	1978-79	1979-80	1980-81	1978-79	1979-80	1980-81
Madhya Pradesh	48.2	47.7	48.0	35.6	18.3	40.0
Orissa	43.7	41.2	42.0	44.0	29.2	43.3
Punjab	10.5	11.7	11.8	30.9	30.4	32.2
Uttar Pradesh	51.5	50.5	51.8	49.6	25.5	54.4

According to the Food and Agricultural Organisation's (FAO) statistics, the net area under irrigation throughout the world was 206.5 million hectares in 1979. Out of this area, 134.5 million hectares were in Asia. China and India have the largest irrigated area in the world with 49.2 and 39.1 million hectares, respectively, covered with irrigation facilities in 1979. Probably at present we have the largest programme in the world for creation of additional irrigation potential each year. For example, our target for 1980-81 was 2.5 million hectares and the anticipated achievement is 2.46 million hectares.

The national commitment to bring the maximum possible

area under irrigation by the end of this century finds expression in the Sixth Five-Year Plan (1980-85) approved by the National Development Council in February 1981. The following five-pronged strategy has been suggested for this purpose :

(a) conserving rain water in farm ponds, tanks, reservoirs and through watershed management;
(b) utilising the ground water potential in different parts of the country;
(c) harnessing surface water resources through major, medium and minor irrigation works;
(d) utilising the surplus water which goes to the sea through appropriate interbasin transfer river water; and
(e) intensifying research and development efforts in the field of solar desalination of sea water and other sources of brackish water.

In order to implement the five-point plan effectively, we should draw both inspiration and lessons from past experience. The various evolutionary steps in our irrigation history may be summarised briefly.

EARLY HISTORY

Water security, both for domestic and agricultural needs, has received attention since times immemorial. Diversion of flood flows through inundation canals, lift irrigation, storage of rain water in tanks and reservoirs and numerous other water conservation systems were introduced in different parts of the country, according to local possibilities. The Grand Anicut across tihe river Cauvery was built in the 2nd century. In south Inda tanks were invested with religious significance. No village was without a temple and no temple without a tank.

At the beginning of the 19th century, irrigation works thus included numerous wells all over the country, a large number of tanks in peninsular India and several inundation canals in north India. Some of these tanks and canals were constructed centuries back. Between 1836 and 1866, the Upper Ganga Canal, the Upper Bari Doab Canal and the Krishna and Godavari delta systems were constructed. These proved very remunerative. In those days, irrigation works were treated as commercial undertakings.

The First Famine Commission of 1880 set up following the great famine of 1876-78, however, emphasised the need for direct state initiative in the development of irrigation, particularly in drought-prone areas. The famines in 1897-98 and 1899-1900 led to the setting up of the first Irrigation Commission in 1901 to ascertain the utility of irrigation as a means of protection against famine, the extent of irrigation development and the scope for further irrigation works.

About this time, the gross area irrigated from public works in British India was about 7.5 million hectares of which 3 million hectares was from minor works like tanks, inundation canals, etc. for which no separate capital accounts were maintained. The area irrigated by protective works was only a little over 0.12 million hectares. Private works irrigated 5.7 million hectares, about 70 per cent by wells and the remaining from tanks, streams, channels, etc. The total gross irrigated area was 13.3 million hectares. There was a spurt in protective irrigation works in the first two decades of this century.

The total capital outlay on these protective works increased six-fold from Rs 2 crores in April 1903 to about Rs 12 crores in April 1921 while the overall outlay on irrigation works, protective and productive together, increased only about two-fold from Rs 40 crores in 1901 to Rs 79 crores in 1920-21. At the end of this period, the area irrigated was 10.4 million hectares by public works and 8.9 million hectares by private works in British India and 3.3 million hectares in the former princely states, a total of 22.6 million hectares.

The Bengal famine of 1943 underlined the urgency of increasing agricultural production to meet the needs of the growing population. The Grow More Food (GMF) campaign was launched in 1942. It relied mainly on the development of minor irrigation works and the restoration of derelict wells and tanks for speedy results. The Famine Enquiry Commission of 1944 emphasised the need to greatly expand private works. This was in line with the recommendation earlier made by the first Irrigation Commission (1901-03) and the Royal Commission on Agriculture (1928).

The construction of tubewells in the Indo-Gangetic valley

and Gujarat, taken up in the thirties, received a good fillip. Around 1945, the area irrigated from private sources in undivided India, excluding princely states, was 10 million hectares of which 4.4 million hectares was from wells. The progress made prior to Independence can be seen from the data given in Table 5.

TABLE 5 : **Progress of irrigation development in undivided India excluding princely states**

(*Net irrigated area in million hectares*)

Year	Public sector	Private sector	Total
1900	7.6	5.7	13.3
	(57)	(43)	(100)
1920-21	10.4	8.9	19.3
	(54)	(46)	(100)
1945	13.5	10.0	23.5
	(58)	(42)	(100)

Note : Figures in brackets indicate percentage to total.

In most parts of the country, 80 per cent of the annual rainfall is received during June to September from the south-west monsoon. As far as Gujarat, Rajasthan and Madhya Pradesh are concerned, the corresponding figure is as high as 90 per cent. It is the regularity of the south-west monsoon which is a major factor in determining the periodicity of droughts. The approximate probability of deficient rainfall (deficiency equal to or greater than 25 per cent of the normal) was worked out sometime ago for different meteorological sub-divisions. The conclusions are presented in Table 6.

During the past two decades, the prolonged break in monsoon during hot weather has drawn attention to the need for providing irrigation in wet areas also. Two such occurrences of long dry spells in August/September in the years 1979 and 1981 are fresh in our memory.

Overall, the pattern of rainfall has been observed to be uncertain in occurrence, marked by prolonged dry spells and

TABLE 6 : **Periodicity of drought in different meteorological subdivisions**

Meteorological subdivisions	Recurrence of the period of highly deficient rainfall
Assam	Very rare, once in 15 years
West Bengal, Madhya Pradesh, Konkan, coastal Andhra Pradesh, Maharashtra, Kerala, Bihar, Orissa	Once in 5 years
South interior Karnataka, eastern Uttar Pradesh, Vidarbha	Once in 4 years
Gujarat, eastern Rajasthan, western Uttar Pradesh, Tamil Nadu, Kashmir, Rayalaseema, Telengana	Once in 3 years
Western Rajasthan	Once in 2½ years

inter-spell variations in the time of commencement and withdrawal as well as the amount of total precipitation. Unlike in temperate countries where periods of maximum solar insolation and precipitation coincide, summer months are periods of minimum or no precipitation in our country. Irrigation structures are, therefore, essential in all parts of the country for all the three crop seasons, that is *kharif*, *rabi* and hot weather (summer).

Systematic studies are in progress now to assess the quantum of ground water. An approximation is given in Table 7.

TABLE 7 : **Estimates of ground water resources**

(*Million hectare metres*)

Contributing factor	At present	Ultimate on full development of irrigation
Rainfall	50	50
Seepage from canal systems including return flow from irrigation	11	25
Influent recharge from rivers	4	10
Total	65	85

It is obvious from these data that the possibility of increase in ground water storage would be from irrigation systems and use of monsoon waters in the rivers and streams.

Estimates of the country's water resources have been made from time to time. In the late forties, Dr. A.N. Khosla, then Chairman of the Central Waterways, Irrigation and Navigation Commission, estimated on the basis of an empirical formula evolved by him that the total annual surface and ground water resources are of the order of 167 million hectare metres. In a basin-wise assessment (1972), it was found that the surface water resources of various river basins aggregate to 180 million hectare metres.

The National Commission on Agriculture (NCA) in their report (1976) have assessed that the surface water derived from precipitation amounts to 115 million hectare metres. To this is added 20 million hectare metres brought in from catchments lying outside the country. The portion of the precipitation that goes into the soil is about 215 million hectare metres. A portion of it, roughly estimated at 165 million hectare metres is held as soil moisture and the remaining 50 million hectare metres percolates to the water table.

The surface moisture, though important for sustaining vegetation, cannot be used for irrigation purposes. The total water resources of the country, according to NCA, are thus 185 million hectare metres, comprising 135 million hectare metres and 50 million hectare metres from surface water and ground water, respectively. There is, however, an interchange at various stages between surface water and ground water, besides some recirculation. The ground water assessment by NCA is of the order of 67 million hectare metres, of which 45 million hectare metres regenerate during the non-monsoon period as surface water bringing the surface water total as 180 million hectare metres. On full development of water resources, the total ground water would increase to 85 million hectare metres and the surface water to 185 million hectare metres, including 45 million hectare metres regenerated from ground water.

WATER RESOURCES POTENTIAL

The National Commission on Agriculture assessed the surface water availability as presented in Table 8.

TABLE 8 : **Surface water availability as assessed by NCA**

(Million hectare metres)

	Average annual flow	Utilisable flow
Indus basin	7.7	4.6
Ganga basin	51.0	25.0
Brahmaputra basin (including Barak)	54.0	2.4
Mahanadi and other east flowing rivers up to Godavari	12.3	9.1
Godavari, Krishna and other east flowing southern rivers	22.5	19.0
West flowing rivers south of Tapi	21.8	3.0
Narmada and Tapi	6.2	4.9
West flowing rivers north of Narmada	2.5	2.0
Total	178.0 or 180.0	70.0

The exploitation of ground water is also restricted because of the depth of pumping, availability of power, recharge from irrigation systems and flood-flows in the rivers and streams. In arid areas, ground water is very valuable but it is saline in places and unusable in some locations.

However, with the new knowledge of stress physiology, soil science and modern irrigation techniques, it may be possible to grow some selected crops with moderately saline water and secure reasonable yields. Where good water is available in arid areas either locally or by transfer from another basin, it can be utilised for diluting saline ground water for irrigating a larger area.

Altogether, the utilisable surface flows aggregate to about 70 million hectare metres and ground water about 35 million hectare metres. This estimate is bound to increase in future with implementing schemes involving interbasin transfers and the recharge of ground water by monsoon water in some locations.

The suggestions made by Revelle and Lakshminarayana (1975) on underground storage of monsoon waters merit testing in pilot projects. However, not all this water would be available for irrigation as there would be demand for other purposes, such as municipal, industrial, including power plants and domestic uses. One estimate is that irrigation absorbs about 90 per cent of the utilisable water at present.

Taking the various factors into account and an economic use of water depth of 0.70 metre for irrigating crops, the present estimates indicate an ultimate irrigation potential of 113.5 million hectare metres of which contributions from surface water and ground water are 73.5 million hectare metres and 40 million hectare metres, respectively.

DEVELOPMENT OF IRRIGATION

Irrigation schemes were earlier categorised as given in Table 9 for administrative convenience.

TABLE 9 : **Criteria for classification of irrigation schemes**

Category	Criteria for Classification
Minor schemes	Cost up to Rs. 25 lakhs in plain areas and up to Rs 30 lakhs in hill areas
Medium schemes	Other than minor irrigation schemes with culturable command area (CCA) up to 10,000 hectares
Major schemes	With a CCA of more than 10,000 hectares

The above definitions were revised from year 1978-79 as given in Table 10, to facilitate better technical and administrative scrutiny of irrigation schemes.

After Independence, the country began an era of planned development starting with the first Five-Year Plan in 1951. This

TABLE 10 : **New criteria for classification of irrigation schemes**

Category	Criteria for Classification
Minor schemes	Those with CCA up to 2,000 hectares
Medium schemes	Those with CCA above 2000 up to 10,000 hectares
Major schemes	Those with CCA more than 10,000 hectares

resulted in a great spurt in irrigation development. As compared to the pre-plan irrigation benefits of 22.6 million hectare metres, the irrigation potential created by the end of 1979-80 is 56.60 million hectare metres.

An idea of the plan-wise progress in irrigation development and the investment made is given in Table 11.

TABLE 11 : **Investment and development of irrigation**

	Public Sector Outlay/ Expenditure (Rs crores)			Irrigation Potential Cumulative ha$\times 10^6$		
	Major and medium irrigation	Minor irrigation[b]	Total	Major and medium irrigation	Minor irrigation[b]	Total
Pre-Plan benefits				9.7	12.9	22.6
First Plan	380[a]	76	456	12.20	14.06	26.26
Second Plan	380	142	522	14.30	14.79	29.09
Third Plan	581	328	909	16.60	17.01	33.61
Annual Plan (1966-69)	434	326	760	18.10	19.00	37.10
Fourth Plan (1969-74)	237[c]	513	1,750	20.70	23.50	44.20
Fifth Plan (1974-78)	2,442[d]	631	3,073	24.82	27.30	52.12
Annual Plan (1978-79)	977	237	1,214	25.86	28.60	54.46
Annual Plan (1979-80)	1,079	260	1,339	20.60	30.00	56.60

[a] Includes Rs 80 crores incurred during the pre-plan period.
[b] Government outlays only.
[c] Excludes Plan outlay of Rs 50.54 crores on Cauvery basin projects.
[d] Excludes non-plan outlay of Rs 52.24 crores on Cauvery basin projects.

It is proposed to create an additional potential of 5.7 million hectares, and 8.0 million hectares respectively from major and medium irrigation and minor irrigation schemes during the Sixth Plan (1980-85). The approved outlays during the plan period are Rs. 8,448 crores and Rs. 1,810 crores for the two categories, respectively. It may be mentioned that the minor irrigation schemes, specially utilising ground water, are mostly funded from private sources and institutional finance. Thus there is a substantial step up of investment in the irrigation sector during the past decade.

MAJOR AND MEDIUM IRRIGATION SCHEMES

The important schemes initiated during the first two plan periods were the Bhakra-Nangal project, Rajasthan canal, Gandhisagar dam, Gandak, Kosi, Nagarjunasagar, Hirakud, Tungabhadra, Malaprabha and Ghatprabha projects. Later, the multi-purpose Beas project, Ramganga dam and canals, Tehri, Sri Ramsagar, Jayakwadi, Ukai, Kadana, Sardar Sarovar, Tawa, Teesta, etc. were taken up for utilising the monsoon waters. With the strengthening of survey and investigation organisations in the states, more projects to harness the monsoon waters are expected to be formulated during the sixth plan period.

The performance of major and medium schemes has been studied by the National Irrigation Commission (1972), the NCA (1976) and several committees. The irrigation potential created was not found to be fully utilised. The gap in the utilisation of the created potential by end of Fourth Plan (1973-74) was 2.1 million hectares, which has now increased to 4.0 million hectares by end of 1979-80. In some projects, water-logging and salinity damaged large areas. What was even more disturbing was the fact that the return in terms of increased agriculture production was far below the expectation. Some of the major deficiencies in the major and medium schemes were found to be the following :

1. There was need for modernisation of the pre-plan and early plan systems to provide water at the outlet delivery points to farmers at the right time and in the right quantity.

2. There was lack of adequate drainage, resulting in

water-logging conditions, because of excess water used in irrigating crops and also owing to soil factors.

3. The absence of distribution system within the outlet, and the non-introduction, of rotational distribution of water to the farmer was a serious shortcoming.

4. Inadequate attention had been paid to land consolidation, levelling and all other aspects which could promote better on-farm management of water.

5. There was a lack of anticipatory research on optimum water use, particularly in black soils with considerable moisture retention capacity.

6. Suitable infrastructure and extension service were lacking.

7. There was poor co-ordination between the concerned government organisations in the command areas.

MODERNISATION

Irrigation projects sanctioned for execution up to 1965 were designed to meet the pattern of irrigation of traditional crops. With the introduction of high-yielding varieties of seeds since 1965, several of the earlier projects have proved inadequate to meet the rather exacting demands for water in respect of high-yielding varieties of crops. Modernisation of the earlier canal systems listed in Table 12 has hence become essential.

The remodelling of the Western Yamuna canal and Ranbir canal has been completed. During the Fifth Plan, work on modernisation of Godavari barrage, Tribeni canal, Cauvery delta and Periyar canals had commenced. The weakness in the old structure, the capacity of the canals to cope with the latest cropping patterns, deficiencies in the control structure system, the causes of heavy losses in the irrigation channels, methods to augment canal supplies in tail reaches and other aspects in respect of modernisation are being analysed for some important projects.

Work on the modernisation of the irrigation system will be taken up actively in each State during the Sixth Plan. In respect of the problem encountered in some dams, a Dam Safety Unit has started functioning in the Central Water and

Power Commission and State Governments are also setting up similar units.

TABLE 12 : **Old irrigation systems**

Name of canal system	Year of construction	Area irrigated ha × 10^5
Godavari delta (Andhra Pradesh)	1890	5.58
Krishna delta (Andhra Pradesh)	1898	4.42
Sone canal (Bihar)	1879	3.47
Tribeni canal (Bihar)	1914	0.48
Western Yamuna canal (Haryana)	1892	4.81
Ranbir canal (Jammu & Kashmir)	1904	0.54
Tandula reservoir (Madhya Pradesh)	1921	0.67
Mahanadi canal (Madhya Pradesh)	1927	0.85
Nira left bank canal (Maharashtra)	1906	0.48
Godavari canal (Darna dam and Nander weir) (Maharashtra)	1916	0.32
Nira right bank canal (Maharashtra)	1938	0.35
Krishna Raj Sagar dam and canals (Karnataka)	1930	0.51
Mahanadi canals (Orissa)	1875 to 1895	1.12
Upper Bari Doab canal system (Punjab)	1879	3.35
Sirhind canal (Punjab)	1887	6.00
Ganga canal (Rajasthan)	1928	3.03
Cauvery delta system (Tamil Nadu)	1889	4.29
Periyar system (Tamil Nadu)	1897	0.62
Upper Ganga canal (Uttar Pradesh)	1854	6.99
Lower Ganga canal (Uttar Pradesh)	1878	5.28
Agra canal (Uttar Pradesh)	1873	1.38
Sarda canal (Uttar Pradesh)	1926	6.12
Eastern Yamuna canal (Uttar Pradesh)	1854	1.91
Midnapur canal (West Bengal)	1889	0.50
Damodar canal (West Bengal)	1935	0.73
Total		63.80

DRAINAGE

Irrigation and drainage go together. Crops need water in regulated doses at definite intervals. Inadequate water supply at certain critical stages in the growth of the plants may reduce yield considerably. On the other hand, excessive water can also cause great damage to crops. Drainage of superfluous water from irrigated land is, therefore, as necessary for the satisfactory growth of crops as the irrigation water itself.

It is not only accumulated surface water from heavy precipitation or flood waters that need to be drained to help crop growth but also the excessive water in the field owing to over-irrigation or seepage from adjacent channels, as well as percolation of irrigation water from the fields.

The growth of many agricultural crops is also sharply affected by the continued saturation of any substantial part of the root zone by ponded water on the surface or excess moisture availability in the soil. Often the excess soil moisture may be caused by a higher ground water table which again could be because of excessive irrigation, seepage, salinity and alkalinity. Poorly drained soils depress crop production in several ways. Often high water table conditions are associated with saline or alkaline soil conditions which affect crop yields. At times, some soils in natural condition have a high salt content which needs to be leached out by flooding and drainage.

The drainage problem is acute in the states of Punjab and Haryana. It also prevails in the command area of some of the irrigation projects in Uttar Pradesh, West Bengal, Gujarat, Madhya Pradesh and Maharashtra. The problem of drainage congestion is predominant in the alluvial plains of Punjab, Haryana, Uttar Pradesh, Bihar and the coastal plains of West Bengal and peninsular India.

Though precise data on the extent of water-logged area in the country are not available, the National Commission on Agriculture (1976) had estimated that a total area of 6 million hectares is waterlogged. Out of this area, 3.4 million hectares are subject to surface flooding mostly in the states of West Bengal, Orissa, Andhra Pradesh, Punjab, Uttar Pradesh, Gujarat, Tamil Nadu and Kerala. The remaining 2.6 million hectares have a high water table. Precise statistics of the extent of water-logged area in various states are yet to be compiled. This is a task which deserves to be taken up on a priority basis.

The extent of water-logging that takes place in the irrigation commands of various projects in the states should also be precisely ascertained. At present, such data are not readily available.

Of the post-Independence major irrigation projects where serious water-logging and consequent salinity problems have arisen, mention may be made of the Chambal project areas in Madhya Pradesh and Rajasthan, the Kosi and Gandak project areas in Bihar, Tungabhadra in Karnataka, Nagarjunasagar in Andhra Pradesh and the Kakrapar system in Gujarat.

A Central Water Utilisation Team visited several irrigation projects a few years ago. The team observed that inadequate drainage and consequent water-logging prevail in the Purna, Pravara, Neera projects in Maharashtra, at Dantiwada in Gujarat, Barna and Tawa in Madhya Pradesh, Lower Ganga canal in Uttar Pradesh, Malampuzha in Kerala, Periyar-Vaigai in Tamil Nadu, Tungabhadra in Andhra Pradesh and Karnataka, in the Sone system in Bihar, Ranbir and Pratapa canals in Jammu and Kashmir, at Jamuna in Assam, the Hirakud and Mahanadi delta in Orissa and the Krishna delta in Andhra Pradesh.

The drainage needs of salt-affected soils have their own specific particular problems. It is estimated that 7 million hectares of land are affected by salinity or alkalinity or both. A major portion of these salt affected lands lie in the otherwise fertile Indo-Gangetic plains of Punjab, Haryana and Uttar Pradesh. The other areas which have problems of salinity and alkalinity are the (i) semi-arid areas in the medium and deep black soils of Maharashtra, Karnataka, Madhya Pradesh, Andhra Pradesh and Gujarat, (ii) deltaic coastal areas particularly in West Bengal, Orissa and Gujarat, and (iii) the irrigated areas of Rajasthan and Gujarat.

One of the undesirable consequences of bringing irrigation waters to the arid and semi-arid areas is the soil salinity mostly because of rising ground-water table. This problem has been faced in all such irrigation projects in the country. The Central Soil Salinity Research Institute at Karnal has developed an effective package of reclamation and management on soils affected by alkalinity. Reclamation of saline soils, however, requires greater investment since either surface or sub-soil drainage will be needed. Since soil is the most precious resource of agriculture, steps should be taken not to compound this problem further and to reclaim the affected lands.

COMMAND AREA DEVELOPMENT

The Irrigation Commission in their report of March 1972 had analysed the reasons for (i) the gap between the irrigation potential created and the actual use of water, and (ii) the absence of the anticipated impact of irrigation on crop production and productivity. The commission observed that a series of co-ordinated measures were called for to optimize benefits from irrigated agriculture. It was emphasised that scientific crop planning suited to local soil and climatic conditions was an essential prerequisite.

The need for consolidation of holdings, levelling/shaping of lands, provision of field channels were considered essential to ensure equitable distribution of water to the farmers' fields. The commission also mentioned that the supply of the other inputs needed should be ensured, and research and extension efforts geared to support a forward looking agriculture. Attention was also invited to the need for the construction of rural roads, markets, storages and other infrastructural facilities in the command areas of irrigation projects. The commission stressed the need for a programme of integrated command area development involving co-operative efforts among the State Departments of Irrigation, Agriculture, Animal Husbandry, Co-operation, Community Development, Finance and Public Works, as well as various institutions, such as the Agriculture Refinance Corporation, land development banks, commercial banks, etc.

The commission was of the opinion that a special administrative agency for the co-ordinated and expeditious development of command areas under major and medium irrigation projects had become a necessity. The functions of the command area development agencies would be to assign tasks to various departments and institutional organisations, to enforce co-ordination among them and to see that the agreed programme was implemented.

In 1973, the State Governments were requested to set up command area development authorities for 50 irrigation projects which were identified in consultation with the state representatives. It was suggested that a senior officer should be appointed to head each authority and that whole-time officers of the rank of joint heads of departments in so far as irrigation, agriculture, soil conservation and co-operation were concerned, should be provided to assist the administrator of each command area.

In addition, it was suggested that an inter-departmental committee should be constituted under the chairmanship of the Chief Minister to keep under constant review the problems relating to the optimum utilisation of irrigation potential. The appointment of a whole-time secretary, to be designated as Secretary, Water Utilisation and Command Area Development, having the status of Additional Agricultural Production Commissioner was also suggested.

In December 1974, the Government of India approved a central sector scheme for Command Area Development (CAD) Programmes in selected irrigated commands to be taken up in the Fifth Five Year Plan. It was indicated that programmes would consist of the following components:

(a) modernisation and efficient operation of the irrigation system as well as development of main drainage system beyond the farmers' blocks of 40 hectares;
(b) construction of field channels;
(c) construction of field drains;
(d) land shaping and land levelling with consolidation of holdings;
(e) lining of field channels/water courses;
(f) exploitation of ground water, installation of tubewells, etc.;
(g) adoption and enforcement of a suitable cropping pattern;
(h) enforcement of an appropriate rostering system on irrigation;
(i) preparation of a plan for the supply of key inputs, such as credit, seeds, fertilizers, pesticides and implements;

(j) making arrangements for timely and adequate supply of various inputs; and
(k) strengthening of existing extension training and demonstration organisation.

The National Commission on Agriculture went into the various aspects of the Command Area Development Programme, and in their report of 1976 suggested several measures to optimise benefits from irrigated agriculture. The commission has laid great emphasis on the need for development of land in the command area in an integrated manner on the following lines :

(a) layout of plots and of common facilities such as water courses, field channels, drains and farm roads;
(b) consolidation of farmers' scattered plots into one or two operational holdings;
(c) construction of water courses and field channels;
(d) construction of field drains where necessary and linking them with connecting drains;
(e) provision of farm roads;
(f) land formation to suitable slopes; and
(g) introduction of the *warabandi* system for the rotational distribution of water.

With regard to the future irrigation projects, NCA suggested that the project report should be prepared in the following three parts : The first part should include all engineering works from the source of supply to outlets, including drains. The second part should deal with all engineering works in the command area comprising land levelling and shaping, construction of water courses, lined or unlined field channels, field drains and farm roads. Finally, the third part should relate to all other items pertaining to agriculture, animal husbandry, forestry communications and co-operation.

Progress of implementation

State Governments have so far set up 44 CAD Authorities for 71 projects out of a total of 76 irrigation projects with an ultimate irrigation potential of about 15 million hectares. These projects are spread over 16 states and one union territory in the country. During the last six years several activities have developed which include construction of field channels, land levelling/shaping, conjunctive use of surface and ground water, improvement of drainage channels and modernisation of the irrigation system.

An intensive extension procedure (training and visit system) has been brought into operation in a number or projects with good results. The World Bank and the Federal Republic of Germany are providing financial assistance to some of the CAD projects.

In physical terms, the achievements up to 1979-80 and during 1980-81 for some of the main items included in the CAD programme are summarised in Table 13.

TABLE 13 : **CAD achievements**

(*lakh hectares*)

Items	Cumulative progress up to March 1980	During 1980-81
Soil surveys	64.14	11.44
Topographical	32.75	8.93
Planning, design of OFD works	25.54	7.38
Construction of field channels	33.30	6.20
Lining of field channels	4.54	1.13
Construction of field drains	5.30	1.13
Land levelling/shaping	9.37	0.78

During the Sixth Plan period (1980-85), it is proposed to accelerate the programme considerably. An additional area of 40 lakh hectares is to be covered by field channels. Land levelling and shaping is also to be done in an area of 10 lakh hectares.

In financial terms, the total expenditure on CAD since its inception to the end of March 1980 has been Rs 252 crores. During the Sixth Plan an outlay of Rs 856 crores has been proposed : Rs 300 crores under the Central Sector and Rs 556 crores under the State Plan.

Problems and impact of CAD programme

The CAD programme has been recognised as an integral part of agricultural production efforts. The importance of a periodic review of the programme for its effectiveness in water management and optimum production from land and water resources is being realised. Action in this regard through project reviews, and socio-economic studies has been initiated as revealed in many seminars/workshops on CAD Programme.

The problems in black cotton soil areas in Tawa, Jayakwadi and Malaprabha pose a challenge in regard to appropriate land and water use planning. The drainage network planning and execution constitute another area of significance. A systems approach to production, processing and marketing is yet to be introduced in most Command Area Projects.

At the instance of the Ministry of Agriculture and Irrigation, the Programme Evaluation Organisation (PEO) of the Planning Commission conducted soil and water management pilot studies on seven irrigation projects: Gandak (Uttar Pradesh and Bihar), Mahanadi delta (Orissa), Nayyar (Kerala), Pochampad (Andhra Pradesh), Ukai-Kakrapar (Gujarat) and Navalgund (Karnataka) during 1978-80. The main objective of the study was to assess the impact of the soil and water management programme on the farmers, besides study on the strategy involved, organisational aspects and problems connected with the implementation of the programme.

The main conclusions and recommendations emerging from the studies as brought out in the Report of the PEO (January 1981) are briefly summarised.

Coordination. In two of the seven pilot projects namely, Nayyar and Mahanadi, no link could be established between the working of the Command Area Development Authority (CADA) and the pilot projects.

Project surveys. Before undertaking the implementation of the works, well planned surveys and investigations are necessary to determine the most suitable cropping pattern for the ayacut, and to formulate schemes for land levelling and shaping, water distribution and drainage beyond the outlets.

Maintenance of works. It was observed that the CADA had formed pipeline committees at each outlet level for the Pochampad Project for the maintenance and upkeep of physical works constructed under the pilot project. In the case of Navalgund, drops and diversion boxes constructed by the project were transferred to the beneficiaries for maintenance, while the channels were constructed by the farmers themselves. In the case of Western Gandak (Uttar Pradesh) it was reported that the State government had decided that the assets created by the pilot project would be maintained by CADA out of its own funds. No arrangement for the maintenance and upkeep of works had been thought of in the case of Gandak (Bihar), Mahanadi, Nayyar and Ukai-Kakrapar.

Irrigation in the case of Western Gandak (Uttar Pradesh), the area irrigated had increased by about 145 per cent during the post-project period as compared to pre-project stage. The farmers had switched over to canal irrigation as it was found by them to be cheaper and more convenient. Irrigation-intensive crops were also observed as the canal water was supplied in adequate quantity. In the case of East Gandak (Bihar), the percentage of area irrigated increased to 100 per cent compared to only 7 per cent before the commencement of the project. In the case of Ukai-Kakrapar, the percentage of irrigation had increased to 50 per cent in the *kharif* and 92 per cent in the *rabi* seasons, against 43 per cent in the *kharif* and no irrigation in *rabi* seasons during the pre-project period. In Navalgund, the irrigated area increased from 33 per cent to 83 per cent. There was some increase in the irrigation under the Nayyar project, while the increase in Pochampad could not be assessed for want of adequate data.

Cropping pattern. The impact of the availability of irrigation and changes in the cropping pattern had resulted in higher intensity of cropping. This change had been very significant in the case of Navalgund and East Gandak.

Yield. In some of the projects, there was a noticeable increase in yield per hectare for important crops. The percentage of increase in the level of returns per hectare for paddy, wheat and other crops was between 45 per cent to 81 per cent in the case of Gandak (Bihar). In the case of the Nayyar project, the level of returns remained almost the same for all other crops except paddy, which registered a marginal increase. During re-visits to the project areas, an all-round increase in yield was reported from Navalgund and West Gandak and an increase of about

36 per cent in the East Gandak area. In the case of Pochampad, the yield had gone up, after the availability of irrigation, during the last two years in the *rabi* season. No change had been reported from Ukai-Kakrapar, while a marginal decrease in yield was reported in the case of Mahanadi and Nayyar.

Employment. In the case of East Gandak (Bihar) there was a definite increase in the component of hired labour compared to family labour. The crop-wise employment per hectare in the case of wheat had shown a slight increase. In the case of Mahanadi, a 36 per cent increase in employment was observed in the pilot project areas. In the case of Nayyar, the intensity of employment from *kharif* increased from 108 man-days to 144 man-days but remained constant at 169 man-days during the *rabi* season. The stagnant employment position during the *rabi* season was reported to be because of the non-release of adequate irrigation water in the *rabi* season. In the case of Ukai-Kakrapar, increased employment was noticed because of switching over to high-yielding varieties of crops. In Navalgund there was general increase in employment in the *kharif* season.

Major gap-lack of a systems approach. The evaluation study highlights the significance of a systems approach to the problem of soil and water management in order to achieve efficiency in the conveyance of water to the field, scientific application of water to crops and adoption of cropping patterns which would confer the maximum benefits to the farmers. Genuine interdisciplinary and interdepartmental team work is essential if the irrigation command is to be managed on sound principles of ecology, economics, energy requirements and employment generation.

MINOR IRRIGATION PROGRAMME

Minor irrigation includes all ground water development and surface water development through irrigation projects (both flow and lift) having CCA up to 2,000 hectares. Drainage and embankment projects costing less than Rs 2 lakhs each are also included. In some areas, micro-storage works to improve moisture regime in the vicinity and percolation tanks to replenish ground water are also constructed under this programme.

Minor surface water flow irrigation projects, comprising

storage and diversion works occupy a conspicuous place in the complex of irrigated agriculture in the country, particularly in the undulating area south of the Vindhyas, and in the hilly regions. These provide the only means of irrigation in several drought-prone tracts and are labour intensive, offering extensive opportunity for rural employment. These are also of considerable help in recharging the meagre resources of ground water in the hard rock areas.

Surface water lift irrigation schemes are useful where available surface water cannot be used for irrigation through construction of flow irrigation schemes owing to topographical limitations. The initial investment on these schemes is comparatively low, and they can be completed very quickly. These schemes also enable the use of the available surface flow at places where the maximum benefit from irrigation can be derived.

Ground water development forms the bulk of the minor irrigation programme. It is essentially a farmers' own programme implemented primarily through individual and co-operative effort with finance obtained largely from institutional sources. The programme thus imposes very little burden on the public exchequer.

The programme of ground water development has several other advantages and has become a vital factor in promoting modern agriculture. Ground water is widely distributed and provides an instant and assured source of irrigation in the hands of the cultivators. It provides critical help in improving the status of irrigation supply and in controlling water-logging and salinisation in the canal commands.

Financing of the programme

The outlay for the Minor Irrigation Programme is being derived mainly from two sources (i) public sector funds as part of the State Plan outlays, and (ii) institutional sources, such as land development banks, co-operative banks and commercial banks with refinance facilities from the Agricultural Refinance and Development Corporation (ARDC). The World Bank has also made available a substantial amount for minor irrigation, particularly for ground water development. The World Bank credit is being channelled through the ARDC. Apart from normal plan resources, public sector funds in the form of central grants are also being made available for minor irrigation under the special Central Sector Programmes such as Small Farmers Development Agency, Drought Prone Areas Programme, Integrated Rural Development and Tribal Sub-Plan.

Surface water flow irrigation projects are mostly financed from public sector funds as part of the State Plan outlays are made available in the form of central grants under the special Central Sector Programmes. Surface Water Lift Irrigation Projects are financed partly from institutional sources. The utilisation of public sector funds in the field of ground water development is confined to such items as purchase of drilling equipment, cost of staff, ground water surveys, contribution to share capital and advances to the Tubewell Corporations, and subsidies that are made available to the small farmers or the Tubewell Corporations, since water rates realised are lower than the economic rates.

In Uttar Pradesh, Assam, Jammu and Kashmir, Himachal Pradesh, public tubewells are being constructed exclusively from public sector funds. The loan funds for private wells, tubewells, pumpsets, etc. are mobilised exclusively from institutional sources.

In addition to what has been mentioned earlier, there are also sizable investments made by the cultivators from their own resources in the field of minor irrigation.

Financial progress

The investments made in the various plan periods since the inception of the First Plan are given in Table 14.

Area irrigated through minor irrigation works

Data on the area brought under irrigation through minor irrigation are given in Tables 15, 16 and 17.

The institutional investment during 1980-81 and 1981-82 are likely to be of the order of Rs 300 crores and Rs 335 crores respectively.

Ground water sanctuaries

During the severe drought year of 1979, a programme for the establishment of ground water sanctuaries was developed by the Ministry of Agriculture, Government of India. The concept of

TABLE 14 : **Investments made in minor irrigation programmes**

(Rs. in crores)

Plan Period	Plan outlays	Institu-tional	Total
First Plan	76	Neg.	76
Second Plan	142	19	161
Third Plan	328	115	443
Annual Plans (1966-69)	326	237	563
Fourth Plan (1969-74)	513	661	1,174
Fifth Plan (1974-78)	631	780	1,411
During 1978-79	237	240	477
During 1979-80	260	250	510
Total	2,513	2,302	4,815
During 1980-81	256	300	556
Target for 1981-82	301	335	636

a ground water sanctuary involves the setting aside of a suitable area or locality from which ground water will be extracted only during very dry years, when other sources of water get exhausted. Methods of enriching the aquifer, namely, planting of suitable trees which can enhance profile storage will have to be developed. Artificial recharge methods will have to be developed in hard rock areas. The establishment of a grid of ground water sanctuaries in areas prone to severe water shortage during dry years will be an important component of our water security system.

TABLE 15 : **Minor irrigation benefits—1950-51 to 1984-85**

(million hectares)

Period	Ground water	Surface water	Total
Pre-Plan (1950-51)	6.50	6.40	12.90
End of First Plan (1955-56)	7.63	6.43	14.06
End of Second Plan (1960-61)	8.30	6.45	14.75
End of Third Plan (1965-66)	10.52	6.48	17.00
End of Three Annual Plans (1968-69)	12.50	6.50	19.00
End of Fourth Plan (1973-74)	16.50	7.00	23.50
End of Fifth Plan (1977-78)	19.80	7.50	27.30
End of 1979-80	22.00	8.00	30.00
End of Sixth Plan (1984-85): Target	29.00	9.00	38.00
Ultimate potential on full development	40.00	15.00	55.00

TABLE 16: Physical achievements in ground water programme

('000 numbers)

Period	Dug wells	Private shallow tubewells	Electrical pump sets	Diesel pump sets	Public deep tubewell
Pre-Plan	3,960	3	21	66	2.4
End of 1960-61	4,540	20	200	230	8.9
End of 1968-69	6,110	360	1,090	720	4.7
End of 1973-74	6,700	1,040	2,430	1,750	22.0
End of 1977-78	7,425	1,700	3,300	2,500	30.0
End of 1979-80	7,780	2,110	3,950	2,650	36.0
End of 1984-85 (target)	8,980	3,310	6,500	3,550	51.0
Ultimate feasible	12,000	4,000	12,000	5,000	70.0

TABLE 17: Institutional investment in minor irrigation

Period	Rs. crores
During 1951-56	N.A.
During 1956-61	18
During 1961-66	100
During 1966-69	205
During 1969-74	600
During 1974-78	700
During 1978-80	440
During 1980-85 (Target)	1,500

Energy management

Rural electrification coupled with the assured supply of power is the backbone of the minor irrigation programme, particularly that of ground water development in so far as it provides the most economical and efficient means of lift water. Diesel pumping and the use of animal operated water lifting appliances are the alternatives but they are comparatively more expensive in operation. Short supply and the hike in the price of imported diesel have become constraints in the minor irrigation programmes in recent years. The situation makes it imperative that the rural electrification programme is given an added momentum. The Sixth Plan has hence accorded the highest priority to the energy sector.

The Rural Electrification Corporation (REC) set up by the Government of India in 1969-70 in pursuance of the recommendations made by the All-India Rural Credit Review Committee, has played a significant role in accelerating the rural electrification programme and putting it on a sound technical footing.

Over the years, the REC has evolved a number of loan categories with varied terms and conditions suited to the socio-economic, geographical diversity of the country and in accordance with government directives. The States have been classified into above average (AA), average (A) and below average (BA) categories. The average in this case is the national average of village electrification. Within each State, areas have been classified into ordinary advanced (OA), ordinary backward (OB) and specially underdeveloped categories. The terms and conditions of loan for backward and specially underdeveloped areas are much softer than those for advanced areas.

Recently, the REC has introduced a Special Project Agriculture (SPA) at a cost of Rs 360 crores for the energisation of six lakh pumpsets during the Sixth Plan. This programme will be financed by the commercial banks, ARDC and the REC on an equal basis. Two types of schemes are being financed under this programme, SPA (1) involving an 8-year loan up to Rs 30 lakhs for each project and SPA (2) envisaging a 14-year loan up to Rs 50 lakhs for each project. In both cases, there will be a moratorium of two years on repayment of loan. The programme is expected to accelerate the energisation of pumpsets through the involvement of commercial banks.

Ground water organisation

Ground water is the main component of the minor irrigation programme. The first large scale venture in scientific planning and development of ground water was undertaken in India in 1934 when a project for the construction of about 1,500 tubewells in the Indo-Gangetic basin in Uttar Pradesh (in the Meerut region) was initiated. This project was formulated after pooling all the knowledge about the hydrogeological conditions and hydrological parameters that was available with different organisations concerned at that time. Some special experiments were carried out to determine the size and the design of the proposed tubewells.

The success of this project led in the course of time to the initiation of two activities in the field of ground water at the national level. The Geological Survey of India (GSI), set up a special division for hydrogeological investigations on a systematic basis. The GSI covered a total area of 7,25,747 km^2 under these surveys which comprised mainly testing and sampling of the quality of ground water, measuring ground water levels and fluctuations in some wells and also collection of some hydrometeorological data.

The other activity taken up was the drilling of exploratory holes, including electrical logging of the holes in alluvial and sedimentary areas considered geologically favourable for economic production of ground water on a large scale through deep tubewells. A special organisation called the Exploratory Tubewells Organisation (ETO) was set up under the Union Department of Agriculture for this purpose in 1954. The exploration was phased in accordance with the priorities indicated by the States. Till the end of March, 1971, ETO had completed exploration in a total area of 2,34,570 km^2 covering parts of nearly all the States. In all, 911 exploratory holes (787 exploratory and 124 observation/slim holes), had been drilled, of which 382 turned out to be successful and the rest were abandoned. Out of the areas explored, about 70,000 km^2 were proved to be ground water-worthy for further development. A potential for construction of about 15,300 medium capacity tubewells yielding more than 12 LMP at a draw down of about 6 metres had been established in the proven areas.

Although ETO had been started primarily for a systematic and scientific exploration of the ground water resources, the organisation was also pressed into action for the construction of emergency tubewells under drought relief operations in famine hit areas of Rajasthan and Bihar, in the three years preceding 1968. In all, ETO drilled a total of 1,434 production wells of which 1,183 proved successful and the others abandoned.

Central ground water board

The Central Ground Water Board created in 1972 by the

merger of the Ground Water Wing of the Geological Survey of India with erstwhile ETO under the Ministry of Agriculture has become a unified agency at the national level which deals with all matters connected with ground water. The board is headed by a chairman and has two major wings : one for hydro-geological investigation and the other for exploratory drilling. These wings are headed by the chief hydrogeologist and the chief engineer (drilling), respectively.

The main activities of the board include macro-level hydro-geological investigations, deep exploratory drilling coupled with geophysical logging and pump tests to study the subsurface hydrogeological features and monitoring water table behaviour of about 3,000 wells.

Different types of hydrogeological formations are met with within the country, including alluvial formations, semi-consolidated formations and hard rock formations having basalt as well as crystalline rocks. The location, depth, design and spacing of wells are determined by these formations.

The chief objectives of the above mentioned activities of the Central Ground Water Board (CGWB) are to study the nature and lithology of geological formations below the ground surface, their water bearing and water transmitting properties, depth of water table etc. in different regions. Hydrogeological investigations cover reconnaissance studies of pits, lithological logs of wells, water table measurements and testing the chemical quality of water.

Based on these investigations, exploratory drilling is done in selected spots to carry out studies on sub-surface geology with a view to locating ground water zones. Pump sets are installed on selected exploratory bores to determine the aquifer properties relating to storage and transmission of water. The reports and data compiled by the CGWB are being used by the state ground water organisations to formulate projects when seeking institutional credit.

Out of a total area of about 28 lakh km^2 requiring hydro-geological investigations, an area of about 14.4 lakh km^2 has been covered up to the end of the Fifth Plan. About 1.7 lakh km^2 have been covered during the years 1978-79 and 1979-80. During the Sixth Plan (1980-85), an additional area of 6.6 lakh km^2 is proposed to be covered.

State ground water organisations

In most States, organisations have come up for micro-level ground water surveys and investigations. Their main work is to prepare the technical feasibility report at block level for ground water potential and availability and types of structure feasible. These reports are required for the sanction of minor irrigation schemes by ARDC. Similarly, REC also sanctions schemes for energisation of pumpsets only when a ground water availability certificate has been given by the state ground water organisations.

BUILDING A NATIONAL WATER SECURITY SYSTEM

Water security is basic to food security. Fortunately, we are favourably placed with regard to the feasibility of building an enduring and effective national water security system. Such a system should meet the water needs of (i) human and animal population, (ii) agriculture, and (iii) industry and infrastructure. The quality of water needed for these purposes will vary. A priority task is the provision of safe drinking water to the people living in 2,30,000 villages, who at present do not have even one source of pure drinking water.

The provision of clean drinking water in villages is essential for the health and vitality of farming families. Human migration often becomes necessary in drought prone and desert areas because of the lack of water and fodder for farm animals. The national water security system should hence pay specific attention to the water requirements of our vast animal population.

The major components of a water national security system will be :

(a) harvesting, storage (both above and underground) and efficient use of rain water;
(b) harnessing surface and ground water sources and using them in an integrated manner;
(c) effective use of dew in rabi crops;
(d) establishment of ground water sanctuaries at hot spot locations facing acute water scarcity in scanty rainfall years; and
(e) stepping up research and development efforts in the solar desalination of brackish and sea water.

To optimise the benefits from our investment in irrigation, we should bring about a close co-ordination between drinking water supply programmes and irrigation projects.

Another area in relation to water security which needs attention is energy supply and management. In States such as Punjab, energy management holds the key to successful drought management. Production of crops can be kept at a near-normal level even when there is a severe drought, provided adequate energy for pumping ground water is available (Table 4). Besides electricity and diesel, biogas operated pumps need to be popularised. The ultimate answer to this problem will be the use of solar energy through photovolatic systems. Wind energy can also be used in desert, coastal and hill areas. An integrated energy supply system will have to be developed for each block.

TASKS AHEAD

Water management

Scientific water management is possible only if the physical engineering features of an irrigation project and agricultural development are closely linked. In most of our irrigation projects, there exists a wide gap between the development and utilisation of irrigation potential. This is unfortunate in view of the huge investments made in such projects. The results of an analysis carried out in the Sarda Sahayak command area by the Water Technology Centre of the Indian Agricultural Research Institute are shown in Fig 1.

The large gap is indicative of the fact that the development of the command area did not keep pace with the construction of the irrigation system. Our irrigation departments have generally tended to concentrate on developing irrigation potential. Commensurate attention to the development of the command area and to on-farm management of water is still not forthcoming in an adequate measure. An analysis of water management in 30 irrigation projects supported by the World Bank has shown that in only 9 projects was adequate attention paid to water management.

The reasons for poor water management vary from project to project, but in general, they were related to weak institutional performance, poor selection of water control equipment,

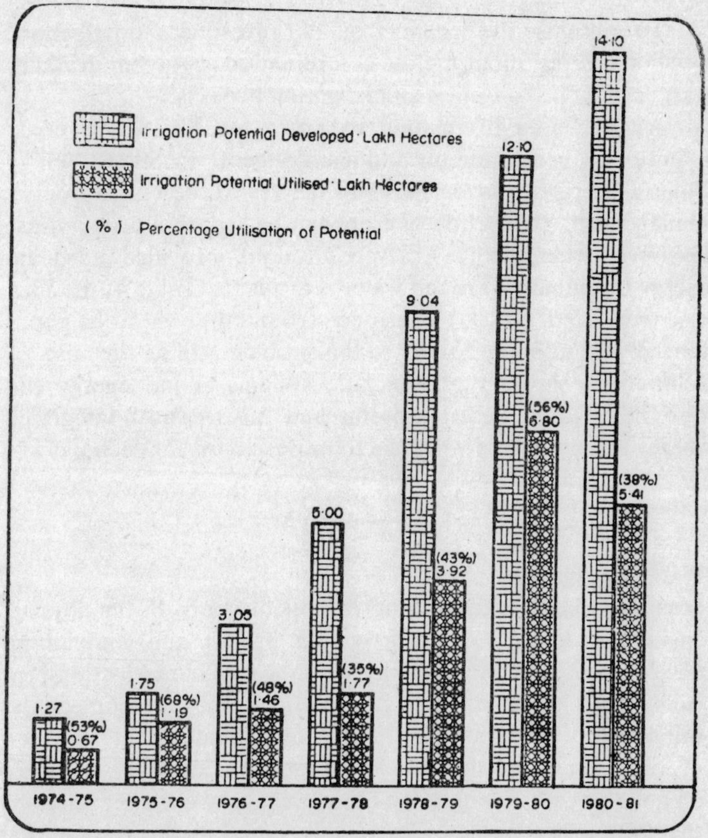

FIG. 1 : *Sarda Sahayak Canal Project—Utilisation of irrigation potential*

inadequate farmers' participation and financial constraints. This emphasises the need for training and establishing a cadre of water technologists and managers, who could introduce a systems approach in irrigation. It will be desirable to establish a national staff college for apex level training on command area management. Such a national level staff college should be linked to appropriate national and state institutions and to appropriate universities.

Public policies

Irrigation is a state subject under the Constitution and policies relating to water rates are evolved by the State Governments. According to the latest estimate, the loss from irrigation works amounted to Rs 427 crores during 1979-80. At the current rate of loss, the total losses during the Sixth Plan period will amount to nearly Rs 2,200 crores. Unless water is regarded as a valuable commodity, its wasteful use will persist.

The question of the introduction of charges in flow irrigation systems on a volumetric basis should be given serious consideration wherever this has not been done. Supply of water from tubewells is being made on a volumetric basis in some states. Ideally, farmers' own co-operatives should manage the water delivery system so that there is both equitable and economical use of water.

Another area which needs attention is legislative enactments in relation to irrigation. The Central Government had circulated a model irrigation bill and also a model bill to regulate the exploitation of ground water. States which have not yet done so will have to review the existing legislation in the light of the suggestions contained in the model bills. A suitable machinery will also have to be developed to take speedy and just decisions on interstate water disputes.

Land and water use planning

The Sixth Plan has suggested the setting up of central and state land use boards in order to assist farmers in taking to farming systems which are economically and scientifically sound. Such land use boards can take advantage of modern techniques, such as remote sensing, while developing land use plans. The best fertiliser to the farmer is assured and remunerative marketing. Therefore, marketing and other post-harvest aspects of farming should receive adequate attention.

Farmers' participation

Irrigation arrangements are made for the benefit of farmers. The users of water should hence have a total sense of participation in the conservation and management of water resources. The existing administrative arrangements for water delivery are not tailored to generate this sense of involvement. Management

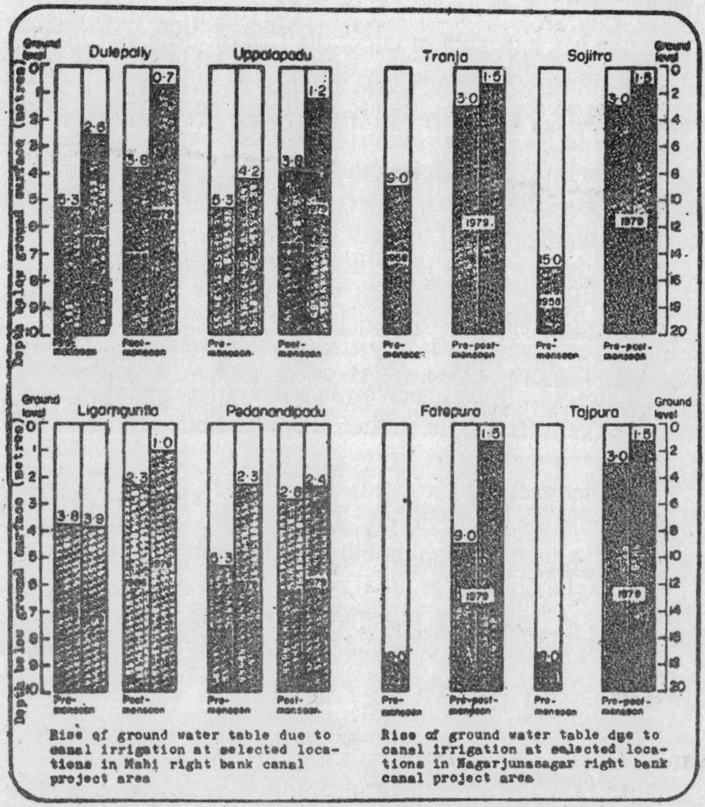

FIG. 2 : *Rise of ground water table*

of water should be a joint sector activity involving both government and farmers. The existing structures of command area authorities need suitable modification to achieve this aim.

Interdepartmental co-ordination

For efficient water use, it is obvious that the irrigation, agriculture and electricity departments will have to function as members of a symphony orchestra. The existing linkages among these departments are rather weak and sometimes non-existent. Agricultural universities and research institutes have also not been fully involved in water management. In fact, much before an irrigation project is due for completion, the agricultural university should undertake anticipatory research on optimum water use pattern taking into consideration the soil and climatic factors. Unfortunately, because of the absence of such anticipatory research, we are not able to derive full benefit now from any water resource for several years after the creation of the resource.

Irrigating arid land

The Rajasthan canal is one of the largest man-made canals of the world in desert areas. It is designed to utilise 8 million acre feet of surplus Ravi-Beas water for irrigating the arid zone of western Rajasthan. The project was started in 1958 and Stage I which will help to irrigate 5.34 lakh hectares will be completed in 1983. Land use planning and cropping strategy in the entire Rajasthan canal area requires careful review.

Monitoring

There is need for an integrated monitoring mechanism which will provide us with continuous information on the positive and negative impact of irrigation projects. The positive impact should be measured in terms of additional production per unit of time and water, additional employment and income generated. There is no purpose in just giving figures on area under irrigation without an accompanying statement on the impact of water on productivity, intensity of cropping, diversification of labour use and agrarian prosperity.

The analysis of the negative impact of irrigation should cover fields such as water-logging, salinisation and erosion. The public health aspects should also receive equal attention, since there is growing evidence that irrigation projects could also lead to the spread of water-borne diseases and sometimes cause nutritional disorders. Climatic impact studies of irrigation projects also deserve attention.

REFERENCES

The National Commission on Agriculture (1976).

Government of India, *Report of the Irrigation Commission*, Vol. III, (1972).

Roger Revelle and V. Lakshminarayanan, The Ganges water machine, *Science*, 188, (1975), pp. 611-16.

RAINFALL AND DRYLAND AGRICULTURE 3

RAINFALL AND FOODGRAINS PRODUCTION

THE EFFECT of rainfall on crop production in our country will be evident from the peaks and troughs in the production of foodgrains experienced from 1960-61 to 1978-79 (Table 1).

TABLE 1 : **Peak and trough points of foodgrains production during 1960-61 to 1978-79**

(*in million tonnes*)

Year	Foodgrains Production/ Adjusted Actual Production	Peak Point	Trough Point
1960-61	82.3		82.3
1961-62	82.4	82.4	
1962-63	80.3		80.3
1963-64	80.7		
1964-65	89.4	89.4	
1965-66	72.3		72.3
1966-67	74.2		
1967-68	95.1	95.1	
1968-69	94.0		94.0
1969-70	99.5		
1970-71	108.4	108.4	
1971-72	105.2		
1972-73	97.0		97.0
1973-74	104.7	104.7	
1974-75	99.8		99.8
1975-76	121.0	121.0	
1976-77	111.2		111.2
1977-78	126.4		
1978-79	131.4	131.4	

It is noteworthy that :

1. The level of foodgrains production at each successive peak point is higher than that at the preceding peak. This is true also of the troughs.

2. Production during troughs of 1970s has been consistently larger than the peak levels of production achieved during the 1960s.

The above observations point to the obvious inherent strength that Indian agriculture has been acquiring over time, thanks to a larger area under irrigation.

3. Notwithstanding the above, we observe an unnerving feature in the form of every peak being followed by a trough in the following years. While peaks which have been occurring with almost a regular interval of two years are a source of legitimate pride, the troughs serve as warning signals against complacency, and urge the need for constant preparedness to meet the ensuing challenges. Eternal vigilance against factors causing instability in production is a pre-condition for a dynamic agricultural system.

4. Risks in agricultural production arising from (i) weather aberrations, (ii) pest epidemics, and (iii) inadequate public policy support, are high, particularly in the crops growing during the south-west monsoon period.

In the first decade of the 21st century we may have to grow foodgrains to meet the needs of about one billion people. In addition, the food requirements of a large animal population will have to be met. The needs of the human and animal population for water, work, food, fodder and fuel can, obviously, be met only by improving our capability to conserve and use every drop of water. The national water conservation and utilisation strategy has, therefore, been accorded high priority in the sixth plan framework recently endorsed by the National Development Council. The strategy consists of 4 major components :

(a) Harvesting, conserving and utilising rain water effectively in dryland areas on a watershed basis;
(b) harnessing our surface and ground water resources through major, medium and minor irrigation projects;

(c) bringing about appropriate interbasin transfer of water by linking some of the major river systems; and
(d) intensifying research and development efforts in the field of solar desalination of sea water.

Rainfall, water from the melting of snow and dew during winter are all important sources of moisture for crops in the northern part of the country. The rainfall is, however, uneven in space and time and occurs largely during 3-4 months of the year. Consequently, drought and floods may occur in the same area during some years. In spite of all efforts on the irrigation front, nearly 30 per cent of the cultivated area is drought prone. In another 40 per cent of the area, crop growth depends entirely on rainfall. It is in such areas that improved dryland farming technology becomes so vital for maximising production per unit of water.

URGENCY OF RATIONAL WATER DEVELOPMENT AND MANAGEMENT

Taking a global view, Tolba (1980) has pleaded for greater attention to the conservation and scientific management of water in the light of the following facts :

1. According to the World Health Organization, 1,200 million people, or 30 per cent of the present world population, lack safe drinking water, and 1,400 million people have no sanitary waste disposal facilities. Lack of proper excreta disposal has an immediate impact on water quality, especially in areas where safe water is in short supply. It contaminates the water sources, and thus contributes to the spread of diseases. Currently, some 5 million people die every year from such water-borne diseases as cholera, typhoid, diarrhoea, dysentery, schistosomiasis, malaria and intestinal worm infections.

2. The daily minimum water demand for a human being varies between 1.5 litres and 20 litres, depending on climate and physical activity. The daily per capita in-house water use varies from 3 litres to 700 litres. A ten-year study in Singapore indicates that as domestic water use goes up, disease rates tended to go down. It concluded that 90 litres of high-quality water seemed to be the 'social minimum' for the prevention of

water-borne diseases. Beyond 90 litres, the improvements were of an aesthetic nature rather than in health.

3. Agriculture is the greatest user of water, accounting for 80 per cent of all consumption. It takes approximately 1000 tons of water to grow one ton of grain, and 2000 tons to grow 1 ton of rice. In addition, animal husbandry and fisheries require significant quantity of water.

4. In 1975 according to the Food and Agricultural Organization (FAO), the total areas irrigated in the world amounted to 223 million hectares, of which 92 million hectares was in the developing countries. Some 15 per cent of the world's cropland is irrigated, yielding from 30 per cent to 40 per cent of all agricultural production. The amount of water used by irrigated crops is nearly 1,300,000 million cubic metres, but because of losses in storage, conveyance and use, total amount used increases to almost 3,000,000 million cubic metres.

By 1990 FAO estimates, that the total area irrigated in the world would increase to 273 million hectares, of which 119 million hectares would be in developing countries. Expanding and maintaining irrigated areas up to 1990 is going to be a challenging task, and its magnitude can be judged by the following requirements for the developing market economy countries only :

22.5 million hectares of new irrigation;
45 million hectares of irrigation improvement;
78.2 million hectares of drainage improvement, including 52.4 million hectares on irrigated land;
438.000 million m^3 of additional water; and
$ 97, 800 million of investment at 1975 prices.

5. Increased agricultural activities in marginal areas have often over-exploited water availability. In many areas, more groundwater is being withdrawn than can be replenished naturally, thus contributing to major management problems.

6. Industry is a heavy user of water. For example, in the United States, industrial water demands account for nearly 40 per cent of the total water requirements, and five major industrial groups—food and kindred products, pulp and paper,

chemicals, petroleum, coal products and primary metals—account for slightly more than 85 per cent of total industrial requirements. However, nearly 60 per cent to 80 per cent of water required for industrial processing is for cooling and need not be of a high quality.

According to the Lima Convention, 25 per cent of the global industrial production should be in developing countries by the year 2000. This means that we must have more water available for industrial processes, and at the same time ensure that the effluents do not pollute the water sources and thus degrade the quality of available supply.

7. Irrational use of water is contributing to the loss of productive soil owing to waterlogging, salinisation, alkalinisation and erosion. On a global scale, at least 200,000 to 300,000 hectares of irrigated land is lost every year due to salinisation and waterlogging. In some parts of the world the water level is increasing at the rate of one cm every day. Current estimates indicate that the 20-25 million hectares of land that is saline at present, was fertile and productive at one time.

8. Water conservation practices have not received adequate attention so far, both in the developed and developing countries. The efficiency of use of irrigation water is still low in most countries, and losses of up to 70 per cent to 80 per cent are not exactly uncommon. Over-watering is often endemic, and it is virtually certain that most current estimates of water needs for irrigation are grossly overstated to account for this loss. Similarly, in the industrial sector, many products can be manufactured with significantly less water than currently being used. For example, water requirements to manufacture one ton of paperboard vary from 62,000 litres to 376,000 litres, the higher figure being over six times the lower one. In some urban centres of developing countries, as much as 50 per cent of all the water stored and conveyed is being lost because of leakages.

SOME ASPECTS OF CURRENT RESEARCH IN INDIA

The work currently in progress in our country in the area of forecasting monsoon rainfall, ground water storage and recharge studies and agronomic aspects of rain water management are summarised here.

Forecasting monsoon rainfall

The work in progress at the India Meteorological Department, is summarised as follows :

There are three principle aspects of predicting monsoon rainfall :

(a) the dates of onset and withdrawal of monsoon over different parts of the country;
(b) The total quantum of monsoon rainfall during the hundred-day period from the beginning of June to mid-September; and
(c) spells of heavy and lean rainfall which lead to floods and droughts during the monsoon season.

Currently, the meteorological department uses a mix of statistical prediction methods and methods based on physics of the atmosphere to solve these three prediction problems.

Date of onset

The date of onset is predicted by statistical association between the predict and (the date of onset) with certain antecedent features, which are the predictors. The relationship is expressed by a regression equation. The four main predictors, which are used for this purpose, are :

(a) the wind direction over New Delhi in the upper troposhere (300 mb);
(b) the upper tropospheric wind direction in the southern hemisphere, represented by the 200 mb wind direction at Darwin in January;
(c) the upper tropospheric features reflected by the difference of 200 mb February winds between Trivandrum and Madras; and
(d) the southward component of the upper tropospheric winds over eastern India (200 mb Calcutta wind).

After considerable screening of a wide variety of predictors, it has been observed that these four predictors exhibit the closest degree of association with the date of onset of the monsoon rains over the extreme southern tip of peninsular India.

There are differences of opinion over what constitutes an onset of the monsoon rains. It has to be noted that there could be no unique definition of an onset, which will satisfy all users. In the meteorological department, the onset is generally defined by a sudden increase in precipitation which persists over several days, and a gradual change in the air-mass characteristics.

Prediction of seasonal and monthly rainfalls

The earliest attempt to forecast the total quantum of monsoon rainfall was by Sir Gilbert Walker in the early 1920s. The method was based on statistical correlations between the total quantum of monsoon rainfall and antecedent features over different parts of the world. Unfortunately, when we plot the total monsoon rainfall against time, we obtain a time series which is not stationary, that is, the statistical properties of the time series keep changing over the years. Thus, some of the factors which Sir Gilbert observed to be highly correlated with monsoon rainfall in 1924, are now observed to exhibit only very weak correlations. In some instances, the direction of the association has also changed. An earlier positive correlation has been replaced by a negative one.

Long-range seasonal forecasts are prepared for only two regions of the country, where the interannual variability of rainfall is the largest. These two regions are (i) north-west India, and (ii) the Indian Peninsula. The principal predictors that are currently used are :

(a) South American pressure in April and May;
(b) the position of a zone of high pressure in the mid-troposphere in April along 75°E; and
(c) monthly mean temperatures at few selected Indian stations in March and April.

For reasons stated earlier, the success achieved by this technique has been limited. Recently, a new statistical technique has been introduced to predict the seasonal rainfall. This uses a mathematical model based on Auto Regressive Integrated

Moving Averages (ARIMA). The model assumes that the statistical properties of the behaviour of meteorological elements, such as rainfall, is partly determined by its past history (autoregressive component), and partly by changes which are purely random. The sequence of random changes, which best describes the behaviour of the time series is obtained by designing a series of weighting factors.

The results obtained by the ARIMA model have been encouraging for the last two monsoons. For 1979, the method predicted a deficiency of rainfall over north-west India and the peninsula by about 15 per cent. The actual deficiency was larger. But, interestingly enough, the prediction was in the right direction. Similarly, for 1980 the prediction was normal over peninsula and above normal over north-west India. The prediction was generally correct.

From 1980, the ARIMA method has been extended to obtain a monthly forecast for 30 meteorological subdivisions over India in 1980. It was observed during June, July and August this year, that the forecast was correct in about 15 subdivisions, and partially correct in 10 subdivisions. It was not successful in the remaining 4-5 sub-divisions out of 30. This statistical technique is being improved.

Short period fluctuations in monsoon rainfall

Short period fluctuations in monsoon rainfall occur between the beginning of June and the middle of September. The duration of this fluctuation is of the order of 5-7 days.

There are four principal meteorological systems which lead to short period fluctuations :

(a) periodical shifts in the position of the monsoon trough;
(b) the formation and movement of depressions in northern Bay of Bengal;
(c) mid-tropospheric low pressure systems; and
(d) off-shore vortices along the west coast of India.

The monsoon trough

The monsoon trough is an elongated low-pressure system, whose axis is aligned roughly in an east-west direction along the Indo-Gangetic plains. When this axis moves north to the southern periphery of the Himalaya, there is an abrupt cessation of rainfall over the west coast and the central parts of the country, but there is an equally abrupt rise in rainfall over north-east India and the Himalayan foothills. Such a situation is known as a 'break' in monsoon rainfall. Under 'break' conditions, the catchment of many of the Himalayan rivers, such as the Kosi receives abundant rainfall leading to floods over north-east India, but the rest of India is largely dry. The normal duration of a 'break' is 4-5 days, but there have been instances when the 'break' extended to over 15 days, as in 1979.

Monsoon depressions

These are low pressure systems which form over the north Bay of Bengal. They move in a north-westerly direction across central India before recurving towards the north. Heavy rainfall is usually observed in the south-western sector of these depressions. Some depressions form *in situ* over the north Bay of Bengal, while some could be traced as the westward passage of the remnants of cyclonic disturbances originating in the Pacific.

Mid-tropospheric low pressure systems

They are low pressure systems which extend in the lower troposphere between 2 km and 6 km. They are usually not observed at the earth's surface. Their preferred location is over Gujarat, Saurashtra, Kutch and north Maharashtra. Very heavy rainfall is observed in these States with the formation of a mid-tropospheric low pressure system. The normal life span of a mid-tropospheric low is about 5 days.

Off-shore vortices

These vortices are observed over north Kerala, coastal Karnataka and the south Konkan coastal zones. The dimensions of these vortices are small compared to that of a depression or a tropical cyclone. But, notwithstanding their small aerial extent, they are capable of generating very heavy rain over the west coast of India.

Interannual variability of monsoon rain

Considerable research is now in progress in trying to understand why the monsoon is good in certain years and poor in others. No firm results have yet emerged regarding the cycles or periodicities in monsoon rainfall. Studies of periodicity, have shown a mild rising trend at a few stations north of 14°N from the beginning of this century, but no such trend has been observed over any other part of the country. It is difficult to assign any predictive value to these trends.

The monsoon experiment and future developments

An International Monsoon Experiment, known as MONEX, was launched between May and September, 1979. The U.S.A., U.S.S.R., France, Australia, and many other countries, in addition to India, took part in this experiment. The data that were collected are now being analysed.

As India enters the space age, the observing platforms from space are likely to reveal many unknown features of the monsoon in the years to come. The Indian National Geostationary Satellite (INSAT), which will be launched in 1982, will have an important meteorological payload. The meteorological department is planning to set up a network of 110 data collection platforms over the inaccessible regions of the Himalayan foothills and other parts of the country. The meteorological data from these platforms will be obtained via INSAT. They will be collected and processed at a new centre being built for this purpose in New Delhi. Subsequently, the satellite signals will be converted into meteorological variables, which will be used for disseminating warnings against natural disasters, such as heavy rainfall, floods, and the passage of tropical cyclones.

The meteorological department is also developing mathematical models which seek to simulate the behaviour of the monsoon. The outcome from these models is obtained on an electronic computer. By these means it should be possible to determine what will be the likely response of the monsoon if changes were made in external conditions that govern the monsoon. For example, if the sea was much warmer than usual in certain years, or if large areas of the country were deprived of their natural vegetation by cutting down forests, or if in a certain year there was heavy snowfall over the Himalaya, the computer should be able to tell us what would be the likely repercussion of such changes on monsoon rainfall.

Rainwater in relation to aquifer recharge and utilisation

The development of ground water resources require a precise evaluation of the total recharge occurring to the ground water body from rainfall. For a quick appraisal of the resources an empirical relation needs to be established to estimate the ground water recharge component from rainfall. The work in progress under the aegis of the Central Ground Water Board is on the following lines.

Rainfall infiltration is primarily dependent on the duration and intensity of rainfall, soil characteristics having a bearing on infiltration rate; topographic slopes; land use; agronomic practices; weather conditions preceding, during and succeeding rainfall period; and depth to water table. These conditions impose a limit on the threshold value of rainfall required to effect ground water recharge.

These recharge components are being estimated by the Central Ground Water Board (CGWB) in varied hydrogeological and climatological situations, such as hard rock areas and alluvial areas, and in different climatic conditions, namely arid, semi-arid and humid zones of the country. A few illustrative studies from different parts of the country are listed and described here.

Ghaggar project area (CGWB)

Studies were carried out under the above project in Ambala, Kurukshetra, Karnal, Jind, Hissar and Sirsa districts of Haryana; Ropar, Patiala, Sangrur, Bhatinda, Faridkot and Ferozepur districts of Punjab; the Union Territory of Chandigarh; and the Ganga Nagar district of Rajasthan. The studies showed that in the arid zone, against the seasonal rainfall of 441.7 mm during 1976, the recharge component was only 34 mm, that is, about 7.8 per cent, but in 1977 although the rainfall was 43 per cent above mean seasonal rainfall, there was no recharge. In semi-arid zones, long-term mean seasonal rainfall does not contribute to ground water recharge. Only years giving more than 10 per cent above mean seasonal rainfall contribute to ground water recharge. In the humid zone, the recharge contributes to 16 per cent and 15 per cent of the seasonal rainfall for 1976 and 1977 respectively.

United Nations Development Programme Phase II, Rajasthan and Gujarat

Under UNDP Phase II, parts of Bikaner, Nagaur, Sikar, Jhunjhunu and Churu districts were covered by water balance studies. Long term average monthly values of potential evaporation in Bikaner were found to be correctly representative for the western arid part of the Rajasthan project area and that of potential evaporation in Jodhpur for the eastern semi-arid part. Jhunjhunu and Didwana in the Sikar basin area were representative of the semi-arid part of the project area. The long-term mean recharge values computed for the station were 30.3 mm at Jhunjhunu and 35.1 mm at Didwana. The average of 33 mm corresponds to about 8 per cent of the average annual rainfall. The recharge studies in Gujarat were carried out in the district of Ahmedabad, Patan, Idar, Deesa and Chanasma.

Indo-British Betwa ground water project area

During 1976-79, water balance studies were carried out in the Betwa catchment area covering parts of Madhya Pradesh and Uttar Pradesh. The results obtained are given in Table 2.

TABLE 2 : **Average values based on analysis of data over a period of 50 years (1926-75)**

Item	mm
Annual rainfall	1138
Soil moisture recharge	175
Net rainfall	593
Run-off	339 (29.8% of rainfall)
Ground water recharge	75 (6.6% of rainfall)
Base flow	30-250

Studies in Vedavati River Basin Project

The Vedavati River Basin Project was concerned mainly to establish the water balance in a typical drought-prone hard rock environment. Evaluation of rainfall contribution to ground water body in the Chinnahagiri subbasin was carried out under this project. The Chinnahagiri catchment is the western part of the Vedavati basin, which is devoid of influence from extra basinal waters and extraneous causes for water level fluctuations.

The results obtained from the studies are as follows:

1.	Total rainfall of the days on which ground water recharge occurred	278 mm
2.	Run-off which occurred on the days during which effective ground water recharge took place	5.4 mm
3.	Rainfall which is distributed as ground water recharge and evapotranspiration	276 mm
4.	Estimated surface storage in the catchment	48 mm
5.	Run-off that occurred on the days when there was no recharge to ground water body	0.85 mm
6.	Evaporation taken as 77% of rainfall	255 mm
7.	If all the depression storage and soil moisture, etc. is evaporated, balance of ET to be met from remaining rainfall	158 mm
8.	Therefore, rainfall reaching ground=(3—4—7) water table	70 mm
9.	Percentage in terms of rainfall	21%

Studies by the Department of Mines and Geology, Karnataka
The results of studies in two basins carried out by the ground water cell of the Department of Mines and Geology, Karnataka, are given here.

Karanjia basin, Bidar district. The Karanjia river is a seventh order tributary of river Manjira which joins the Godavari. It has a drainage catchment of 2896 km^2. The watershed of Karanjia is underlain by the Cretaceous basalts and Tertiary laterites which occur as capping on basalt at and above 600 msl. During a calendar year, 9.68 per cent of the total precipitation is estimated to be added as recharge to ground water storage. Volumetrically, 242.11 mm^3 of water is added to ground water storage during a normal year.

The Karanjia river watershed typifies a drainage catchment of semi-arid climate in Karnataka State, with an annual rainfall between 700 mm and 1000 mm.

Estimated recharge to soil moisture storage in the Karanjia watershed is 70.8 mm^3 per annum comprising 8.43 per cent of the annual normal precipitation. The empirical estimation of recharge to soil moisture storage are based on the following assumptions :

1. The initial moisture at the beginning of monsoon is around zero.
2. The soil is charged to available water storage capacity by the end of the rainfall season.
3. Intermediate variations in the soil moisture storage during the monsoon comprised a part of evapotranspiration.

Satnala basin, Bijapur district. The Satnala is a seventh order tributary of Bhima river with a catchment area of 1624 km^2. It lies between longitude 16°47′ : 17°13′ and latitude 75°37′ : 76°10′.

Rainfall is the main source of recharge to ground water. The recharge (R) was estimated for the years of analysis (1970, 1973, 1974 and 1975), by casting the water balance equation in the modified form, by substituting measured values in equation given :

$$R=P-(ET+QO+ET)$$

Where P=Precipitation
ET=Evapotranspiration
QO=Discharge (exclusive of ground water outflow)
R=Recharge which includes recharge to soil moisture storage and ground water storage

During the year of a normal rainfall, 9.68 per cent of precipitation is estimated to be added as a recharge to ground water storage.

Studies in parts of Nagaur district by the Central Arid Zone Research Institute, Jodhpur

The Central Arid Zone Research Institute (CAZRI), Jodhpur

carried out studies in 2 areas of 344 and 258 sq km, respectively, in the Nagaur district to determine ground water recharge. Study area no. 1 lies in sand dunes and study area no. 2 is bounded by high ridges of eroded Vindhyan limestone and sandstone. Rain gauges were installed with a density of 1 for 15 sq km in area no. 1, and 1 for 26 sq km in area no. 2. Pre-monsoon and post-monsoon observations of the various hydrologic parameters, namely, static water level, yield, total soluble salt content, etc. were recorded in the representative wells. Study area no. 1 is underlain by Vindhyan shale, limestone and sandstone and tertiary sandstones, while study area no. 2 is underlain by the Vindhyan limestone and sandstones. The data collected during 1977 and 1978 are given in Table 3 :

TABLE 3 : **Recharge estimation by CAZRI in parts of Nagaur district**

Study area	Formation	Year	Total rainfall MCM	Recharge to aquifer MCM	Percentage rainfall as recharge
No. 1	Vindhyan shale, limestone and	1977	1011.91	103.73	10.25
	sandstone and Tertiary sandstone	1978	426.40	211.44	49.58
No. 2	Vindhyan limestone	1977	721.97	35.21	4.88
	and sandstone	1978	389.86	14.67	3.76

The experimental determination of the recharge from rainfall and other sources was made by Goel and co-workers (1971-73) by using radioactive tracers. The tracer in this case was Tritium and the technique used was developed in 1968 by Munich and his associates. It is based on tracing the movement downwards in the soil on its way towards the water table of a layer of moisture tagged with tritated water. The downward movement of the tagged layer is caused by the recharge of water from above. The injection of tritium is made below the root zone and away from the trees. The results obtained are given in Table 4.

TABLE 4 : **Results of tritium injection studies**

Item	Western U.P.	Punjab	Haryana
No. of sites	45	21	14
Date of injection	June 1971	June 1972	June 1973
Date of sampling	Oct. 1971	Nov. 1972	Dec. 1973
Average total recharge (in cm)	21.5	8.2	8
Average total rainfall (in cm)	99	46	47
Average irrigation (in cm)	10	21	7
Total recharge (%)	22	18	17
Recharge owing to rainfall only (%)	20	12	15

Recently, Datta and co-workers* of the Physical Research Laboratory, Ahmedabad, have carried out these experiments in the Sabarmati basin, Gujarat, and have come to the conclusion that downward movement of soil moisture varies from 5 cm to 280 cm per year and that the average recharge to unconfined aquifers for the two-year period, 1976-78 is about 8 per cent of the total water input and 15 per cent in the case of confined aquifers. However, the results varied from 1.4 per cent to 33 per cent.

The recharge data are being utilised for the estimation of the ground water potential of each region. Such data are of prime importance in proper and planned exploitation and management of ground water resources. Hence, research in this area needs to be greatly intensified.

Ground water sanctuaries

A proposal was mooted in 1979 that suitable locations may be identified in chronically drought prone areas where steps to enrich the aquifer through combined engineering and afforestation techniques could be initiated. Such 'ground water sanctuaries' should be utilised for the supply of water for human and

* Personal communication.

animal needs in years characterised by the failure of the south-west monsoon. The Government of India has sanctioned a pilot project for the establishment of such sanctuaries.

Moisture conservation and use: Studies conducted under the All-India Co-ordinated Dryland Farming Project of the Indian Council of Agricultural Research (ICAR)

Improving storage in the soil profile

The entry of rain water into the soil is through the surface, which should be kept in a condition to receive more and more of the rain water. Among other things, the ability of the soil to soak as much water as possible is dependent on :

(a) off-season tillage;
(b) organic mulches for the *rabi* or late *kharif* crops;
(c) vertical mulch for the low rainfall *regurs*;
(d) advancing the sowing time of *rabi* crops planted below the Vindhyan region;
(e) deep tillage in textural profiles;
(f) tillage for cutting the hard plough pans in the alluviums of north India; and
(g) farming on grade.

Off-season tillage. Shallow surface cultivation immediately after the harvest of the crop, and later in the off-season, helps in keeping the soil open and also helps in the control of weeds.

In the sub-humid red soil regions, as well as in the semi-arid red soil regions, off-season tillage has been found to be very useful. In subnormal years, the advantages are more significant (Table 5).

Organic mulches. Organic mulches are found to improve water intake, and therefore, would be useful for the late *kharif* or *rabi* sitations. However, in our country their use is limited by the fact that the crop residues essentially form a part of the fodder for bovines.

Vertical mulch. The *regurs* of the Deccan region have low infiltration, because of the heavy texture of the soils. Sometimes, this is compounded by sodiumisation and low rainfall.

In such situations, vertical mulch helps. This is essentially,

TABLE 5 : Effect of off-season tillage on yield of sorghum (CSH-6) in the semi-arid red soils of Hyderabad

(*in quintal per hectare*)

System	Average Yield 1978 (Normal year)	1979 (Subnormal year)
Plough and plant system (direct sowing)	9.3	4.9
Off-season tillage	13.4	12.4

providing 45 cm deep and 22.5 cm wide furrows across the slope at 4 m to 8 m intervals and packing them with stalks of sorghum or cotton, so that the packing extends beyond the soil surface by about 15 cm. This helps to improve water intake leading to higher yields. The benefits are greater in low rainfall years (Table 6).

TABLE 6 : Effect of vertical mulch on the yield of sorghum (M35-1) in the Bellary region

(*in quintals per hectare*)

Treatment	Yield 1972-73 (subnormal)	Yield 1975-76 (normal)
Control	0.2	10.8
Vertical mulch at 4 m interval	4.0	11.2
Vertical mulch at 8 m interval	2.8	12.5

Advancing sowing time. Below the Vindhyan region, where temperature transition from *kharif* to *rabi* is not abrupt, crops should be sown much ahead of the conventional dates. Even though the highest rainfall is received by the first fortnight of September, farmers in the Deccan *rabi* region sow almost after the cessation of the rains.

Region	*Sowing time*
Bijapur	Last week of September
Solapur	First week of October
Bellary	Second week of October

However, by providing surface drainage, crops can be sown at least 4 weeks ahead when part of the crop growth would be completed with the rains. The yields obtained in an experiment at Solapur are given in Table 7.

TABLE 7 : **Effect of advanced sowing of crops on yield of crops (Solapur 1971)**

(*in quintals per hectare*)

Sowing time	Yield			
	Sorghum	Safflower	Gram	Wheat
September 8	8.8	12.4	8.4	4.7
September 20	5.4	9.9	7.4	4.6
October 7*	4.2	7.2	4.4	2.1
October 20	1.5	4.0	4.1	2.1

* normal date of sowing

Tillage. Surface tillage in the off-season is seen to be advantageous. Tillage to break the plough pans in the Gangetic alluvial plains permits the roots of crops, particularly the adventitious roots, to move deeper and tap subsoil fertility as well as water. Similarly, in textural profiles, as in the red soils of Anantapur, deep ploughing helps in better root development of crops and higher final yields. Thus, such edaphic factors which do not affect the movement of water but affect root development need be ameliorated for optimised use of the stored water in the soil profile.

Farming on grade. The conventional practice in the past of soil and moisture conservation has been contour bunding. Today it is realised that contour bunds might create waterlogging and crop losses in *regurs* areas. In light soils, such a practice excludes the possibility of water harvesting at the lower elements of the slope.

Nowadays, in light soils and shallow to medium *regurs*, graded bunds are suggested for areas with slopes more than

1.5 per cent. In deep *regurs*, only keyline cultivation on grade is recommended.

Between the graded bunds, sowing of crops should be parallel to the bunds, similarly, with the keylines. Then, with eventual intercultural operations, the crop rows can be ridged leaving furrows in between crop rows. This system does not involve the use of any additional tools or equipment and the farmers can adopt it with their own existing implements, such as country plough or blade harrows. Such a land configuration leads to improved water intake and increased yields to the tune of 15 per cent. Some synergistic effects might be observed when it is coupled with improved crop husbandry.

Another simple method of increasing water intake is by providing dead-furrows at regular intervals of 2-4 m. These furrows arrest run-off and provide more time to water to move into the soil profile. This method is useful in low rainfall areas.

The bed-furrow system is yet another method of land configuration, but it needs special tools which are not within the easy reach of small and marginal farmers. Similarly, border graded strips which are found to be useful in the subhumid red soils of the Bangalore region, need investment.

Run-off recycling to donor areas. Run-off is inevitable in the tropics. It varies from 10 per cent in the low rainfall *regurs* of Bellary to 40 per cent in the high rainfall *regurs* of the Malwa plateau. The conventional water harvesting systems had been the tanks. They are still in existence in many parts of south India. In Madhya Pradesh according to revenue records, tanks were common, but today they are few and far between. This is largely because the tanks belonged to the community and, consequently, were not well managed. Further, the water from the tanks is used in the lower reaches to grow the more inefficient water users, such as rice. The donor area is, therefore, not benefited.

It had been the endeavour of the All-India Co-ordinated Research Project for Dryland Agriculture to create small ponds (250/m^3 ha) and provide water to the donor area for critical irrigation to the *kharif* crops; or to recharge the soil profile with irrigation to grow *rabi* crops in deep or heavy soils.

The benefit from such critical irrigation has been high, that is, as much as 20 kg grain per hectare per mm. However, there are still certain problems that need solution before such systems are adopted in the drylands of India. They include:

(a) High seepage in the light soils (eg. red soils, alluvial soils).
(b) Lack of cheap sealant; and
(c) Lack of efficient methods for lifting water and for its use.

The research information collected so far is piecemeal. A major effort is required in this direction from hydrologists, soil physicists, agricultural engineers and agronomists.

Crop weather watch groups and contingency plans

Several States have set up state-level crop weather watch groups. Such groups study the behaviour of the monsoon and plan the future course of action in crop management under rain-fed situations. They would also suggest any mid-season corrections required for standing crops.

As far as the rains in Andhra Pradesh were concerned for the year 1980, the south-west monsoon had set in a week in advance and good rains were received throughout the state, and about 60 per cent area of the state received above normal rainfall. But this was immediately followed by a dry spell from 18 June to 25 June, particularly in parts of Rayalaseema and coastal Andhra Pradesh. However, this was followed by a wet spell up to 4 July. There was again a dry spell during the first 20 days of July followed by a wet spell of 10 days in the remaining period of the month. There were only isolated showers in north coastal Andhra Pradesh up to 20 July. The next wet spell was from 31 July to 6 August with a dry spell for a week followed again by a wet spell. Ultimately, from 1 September there was a dry spell in many parts of the state.

Taking an overall view, it has to be stated that run-off causing events were less (i.e. the intensity of the rains was not severe enough to cause any run-off). Consequently, many tanks and even wells which largely depended on the rainfall for their recharge, were less filled and the conventional rice plantings were delayed more so in those fields which depended on the tanks.

The crop weather watch group suggested that mobile nutrients, such as nitrogen required special management and needed to be applied in splits in smaller doses for dryland crops. Similarly, wherever there was a dry spell weeding should receive the utmost attention in those crops.

In the low rainfall areas of Anantapur and the adjacent areas in Cuddapah and Chittoor, considerable area under sorghum could not be covered for want of rains, even though groundnut was sown to a large extent (78%). The plant stands were very poor for want of moisture and the crop was also suffering. In order to cover the unsown lands, alternate crop strategy was suggested which included setaria + redgram (2:1), setaria + castor (2:1) and groundnut + redgram (5:1). Another suggestion was to shift from spreading varieties to bunch varieties. The cut-off date was given as the end August for groundnut. During the early part of August pearl millet was suggested as an alternate cereal crop. Finally, to cover the fodder requirements, horse-gram with phosphate application (20 kg P_2O_5/ha) was suggested as this was found to enhance the yields of grain by almost 100 per cent and the yield of fodder by 200 per cent.

Yet another important aspect that was covered by the watch group was pest surveillance. There were no major pests on sorghum, but there was an apprehension that green-gram sown as a sole crop in Telangana might be affected by virus. However, the incidence was not high. In areas where the incidence was noted, it was observed that local varieties were less affected and whenever fertiliser was applied, the incidence was less. In fact sucking pests which are the vectors for this disease were also observed to be fewer. There was adequate preparedness for tackling the pod borer in red gram. The leaf webber on groundnut was a problem in certain parts, but early diagnosis of the malady before webbing and a simple dusting with BHC were recommended to control this pest. Semilooper on castor was another pest that received attention and against which proper plant protection measures were suggested. At the end of August there was likely to be infestation by the natural hymonopterous parasite (*Microplitis maculipennis*); wherever it was observed, the pesticide spray schedules were suggested to be withdrawn.

While the crop weather watch group can suggest crop planning or mid-season correction, depending on the forecast made available, it is necessary that the climatological information based on rainfall over the last few years (50-60 years) be utilised even for advance planning, particularly to suggest alternate crop strategies.

Experiences during 1979

During the drought of 1979 which affected the country in varying degrees, the ICAR project was able to show that the adoption of improved crop practices with moderate levels of fertilisers and use of high-yielding varieties insulated almost all the crops against moisture stress. In fact, both on the research farms and on the farmers' fields there were areas where crops were outstanding during the drought. Short duration crops and varieties performed far better compared to longer duration crops and varieties. For example, in the Malwa plateau soybean yielded 18.7 quintals per hectare as against *Kali tur* whose yield was only 5.5 quintals per hectare. Similarly, in Dantiwada, while sorghum failed, pearl millet yielded 5.9 quintals per hectare. In Varanasi rice failed whereas pearl millet and black gram yielded 11.6 and 10.5 quintals per hectare respectively, Among varieties of rice, DR-92, a 93-day duration yielded 15.3 quintals per hectare at Bhubaneswar as against TNAU-64-64 with a duration of 106 days which yielded 1.8 quintals per hectare. At Jhansi CSH-5 sorghum with a 122-day duration yielded 5.3 quintals per hectare as against 12.1 quintals per hectare of MSH-36 with an 83-day duration. Finally, all the fertilised crops were seen to tap moisture from lower depths and hence could withstand drought better than unfertilised crops.

There is great scope in our country for more efficient use of rain water through watershed management in rain-fed areas and command area development in irrigated areas. Under conditions of small and often fragmented holdings, watershed management would involve co-operative endeavour on the part of the watershed community. Thus, the social engineering aspects of watershed management are as important as the purely technological strategy. It is only by combining technology with social action that rain water can provide the maximum benefit to dryland farmers, both through surface water storages and through aquifer recharge. The operational research project undertaken by the Central Soil Conservation Research and Training Institute of the ICAR at Sukhomajri indicates the immense potential that is available for elevating and stabilising crop production in rainfed areas in the hills. The conservation of water in small ponds and tanks had in the past been a way of life with our village communities. In South India this practice had been institutionalised by introducing the principle that every village should have a temple and that every temple should have a tank. Unfortunately, many of these water conservation practices have tended to get discarded in preference to large and expensive water storage projects. If we can spread the message of scientific water harvesting and recycling all over rainfed areas, the economy of such areas could be rapidly improved.

REFERENCES

Tolba, Mostafa K., Water management for arid lands in developing countries, Pergamon Press, New York (1980).

Goel, *et al.*, Annual Reports of the Central Arid Zone Research Institute, Jodhpur (1971-73).

Swaminathan, M.S., Disasters facing the eighties, *Science Today*, July, 1980.

AGRICULTURAL EVOLUTION, PRODUCTIVE EMPLOYMENT AND RURAL PROSPERITY

4

THE PROBLEM of a technological upgrading of agriculture is a complex one involving a dynamic interaction of scientific and socio-economic factors with the environment. There is so much variability not only in socio-economic conditions and attitudes but also in the biological and physical environment, that agricultural and biological research offers a great challenge to intellect and ingenuity. We are now on the threshold of a new era in our agriculture, an era which, if we are wise and if scientists, educationists, administrators, political leaders and farmers all work together, could lead to greater stability of production, qualitative adequacy of food, rural prosperity, productive employment, national self-reliance and above all harmonious co-existence of plants, animals and man in a mutually symbiotic and permanently productive bio-system.

Landmarks in agricultural evolution

Taking world agriculture as a whole, the selection of plants suitable for domestication from the extensive wild flora and their subsequent improvement through conscious or unconscious breeding, the conversion of geological deposits into soils and planned efforts to conserve and provide water to crops, constituted the major components of progress until the 17th century. The next significant advance came with the introduction of cereal-legume rotations and addition of nutrients in the form of fertilisers in the 18th and 19th centuries. The beginning of this century marked the rediscovery of Mendel's laws of inheritance and the use of the principles of genetics in the tailoring of plants adapted to the changing physico-chemical, biological, technological, economic and social components of the environment. This development in turn triggered rapid progress in industrial activity related to agriculture, particularly those relating to fertilisers, pesticides and other agricultural chemicals, machinery and post-harvest technology. A few of the significant landmarks of this recent evolutionary phase are indicated in Table 1. Countries which have taken advantage of these scientific developments are faced today with the problem of surpluses of farm and animal produce, while those who neglected them are fighting for food self-sufficiency.

TABLE 1 : **Some significant milestones in agricultural advance in the 20th century**

Milestone	Approximate year of finding or widespread use
Hybrid maize	1933
Chlorinated hydrocarbons for insect control	1945
Minimum tillage	1945
Foliar feeding	1945
Direct application of anhydrous ammonia	1947
Hybrid sorghum	1957
Chemical weed control	1958
Systemic biocides	1959
Dwarf wheat	1961
Dwarf rice	1965
Opaque-2 maize	1965
Hiproly barley	1968
Hybrid barley	1969
Hybrid cotton	1970

In several countries of the world, during the first half of this century more and more food and milk were being produced, respectively, from less and less land and cow population. In contrast, during this period productivity remained stagnant in many of our important food crops, although a rise in total production occurred owing to an increase in the area, both under cultivation and under irrigation.

In India, organised scientific effort in agriculture began with the establishment of the Indian Agricultural Research Institute (IARI) in 1905. Research, however, did not make any appreciable impact on production except in crops, such as sugarcane, largely because of the absence of the developmental substrate essential for research results to strike roots. Research, particularly in the fields of plant breeding and plant protection, did, however, help to minimise the fluctuations in production, (except those caused by the weather) in crops such as wheat and rice. Developments in the post-independence era, for example, the initiation of the community development programme, national extension network, irrigation projects, the setting up of fertiliser factories, and finally, the intensive agriculture district programme, provided the stimulus for a radical reorientation of agricultural research policies and goals. The high-yielding varieties programme and the national demonstration programme initiated in 1965 generated a feedback relationship between agricultural scientists on the one hand and extension agencies and farmers on the other, which is vital for a dynamic research programme.

Reorientation of research goals

Half of a scientist's difficulties are over once the problem needing solution is clearly formulated. The widespread awareness now in evidence of the role of science in promoting agrarian prosperity has in turn led to a re-examination and reorientation of research programmes. For example, the following are some of the major research goals in crop breeding set for themselves by the scientists of the IARI :

(a) Enhancement of the content of oral contraceptive principles, such as diosgenin present in some plants, so as to help in the population control programme;
(b) combining yield with the genetic upgrading of the quality and quantity of nutrients present in cereals, pulses, tuber crops and other food, as well as in fodder and feed crops, so as to contribute towards the elimination of protein calorie malnutrition;
(c) development of varieties suitable for increasing the income and employment potential of farms of small size through a series of multiple and mixed cropping systems, based on choices and alternatives from an economic standpoint and on sound principles of ecology from the scientific standpoint;

(d) achieving stability of production as well as improvement in yield in areas characterised by low and uncertain rainfall and adverse environmental problems, such as flood or alkalinity or salinity;

(e) development of strains in the major agricultural and horticultural plants which would help to achieve the yield potential theoretically possible under a given environment;

(f) breeding varieties of crops which can stimulate the development of industries in areas characterised by poverty and population pressure, such as the monoculture rice belts;

(g) upgrading the quality and yield of industrial crops, such as fibre, sugar and oilseed crops;

(h) development and use of genetic techniques for accelerating the pace of breeding for better yield and quality in perennial crops such as fruit and forest trees, plantation crops, namely, coffee, rubber and pepper, and palms such as coconut and arecanut;

(i) tailoring varieties in appropriate plants to the specifications of the food industry and of the export market; and

(j) collection and conservation of gene pools.

Development of high-yielding varieties

Exploitation of F_1 hybrid vigour as in maize, sorghum and pearl millet, the introduction of a plant type possessing a dwarf and non-lodging habit and relative photo-insensitivity as in wheat and rice, and population improvement procedures as in maize and sorghum have been the major genetic mechanisms employed so far in developing crop varieties which respond well to good soil fertility and management. In many of the currently available high-yielding varieties, the total dry matter production is similar to that of the earlier tall varieties, but the harvest index (i.e., the ratio of grain to total dry matter) is far better, resulting in higher yield. A further improvement in total dry matter production together with a high harvest index can be achieved. For achieving this, conceptual models of different crop plants, termed 'ideotype' by Donald (1968), based on a synthesis of knowledge from morphology, physiology, biochemistry, climatology, ecology and pathology would have to be constructed and used in plant breeding programmes.

Some of the selection criteria that will form the basis for the development of new varieties in the future are given in Table 2. In our country, endowed with abundant sunlight, a major criterion of new varieties should be improved photosynthetic capability which can be achieved through selection of plants having better light-receiving systems, and leaf surface characteristics most conductive to CO_2 compensation points.

TABLE 2: **Characteristics of crop ideotypes**

Hybrid vigour or additive gene action
Early maturity
High photosynthetic ability
Low photorespiration
Photo-insensitivity
High response to nutrients
Multiple resistance to insects and diseases
Better protein quantity and quality
Synchronised development of inflorescences
Crop canopies that can retain and fix a maximum of CO_2

How high can be the yield of high-yielding varieties?

During a 12 hour day length, about 500 calories per cm^2 of radiation are received on earth. Of this, only 222 calories per cm^2 are in the visible part of the light spectrum and thus useful for photosynthesis. If all this energy is converted into dry matter by plants, 77 g per m^2 per day can be obtained, which is equivalent to 770 kg per hectare per day (Loomis, Williams and Duncan, 1967). Theoretically, therefore, there is a possibility of producing 2810 tonnes per hectare of dry matter during a year, provided that the photosynthetic rate is not limited by other factors, such as carbon dioxide, water and nutrition. If a harvest index of 0.5 can be reached, we can get, theoretically, an economic yield of about 140.5 tonnes per hectare per year. In practice, however, about 25 tonnes of grains per hectare per year is the maximum reported so far. The potential yield per day, the highest yield obtained in any national demonstration or trial and the average yield of some of the major cereals,

TABLE 3 : **Average and highest productivity reported in India in trials and demonstrations**

Crops	Average	q/ha Highest	cal/kg	Vegetation period	cal/ha$\times 10^6$ +	cal/ha/day$\times 10_9$
			Cereals and Millets			
Rice	16.0	100.00	3520	120	35.20	2.93
Maize	11.3	110.00	3630	90	39.93	4.43
Wheat	11.7	71.63	3440	120	24.64	2.05
Sorghum	5.2	98.00	3550	130	34.79	2.67
Bajra	3.8	67.10	3270	130	21.94	1.68

Crop	Average	q/ha Highest	cal/kg	Vegetation period	cal/ha$\times 10^6$	Edible	cal/ha/day$\times 10^5$
			Tuber and Root Crops				
Potato	80.0	411.00	840	120	34.52	95%	2.62
Tapioca	130.0	480.00	1530	300	73.44	85%	2.44
Sweet-potato	58.0	372.00	1140	135	42.40	85%	3.14
Yam	58.0	190.00	1130	135	21.47	85%	1.59

Source : Data collected by Dr S.K. Sinha, IARI.

millets, pulses, oilseeds and tuber crops are indicated in Table 3. It would be obvious from this data, that while we work towards realising the theoretical potential, we have a long way to go before our average yield attains a respectable relationship with the highest yield already reached in the country. The potential for the future is immense, since the maximum yield of the economic product obtained so far in any multiple cropping system is only about 20 tonnes per hectare per year. The scope for research on enhancing the production potential is particularly great in pulses, oilseeds and tuber crops.

Agronomy for high yields

The agronomic practices adopted will determine whether or not the yield potential of a variety will be realised. Some of the new trends in agronomy are listed in Table 4. The photo-insensitive nature of the new varieties makes it possible to

TABLE 4 : **Recent trends in agronomic research**

High plant density
Weed free environments
Minimum tillage
Controlled release of fertiliser and bacterial fertilisers
Foliar feeding
Use of low cost anhydrous ammonia as a nitrogen fertiliser
Soil moisture control through irrigation and alteration of structure and permeability
CO_2 fertilisation
Co-ordinated pest and disease control
Aerial application of fertiliser, pesticides and agricultural chemicals

think and plan *de novo* on such problems as sowing dates and seasons. For example, the new hybrids of maize give a much higher yield during the *rabi* season than during *kharif*, wherever the temperatures during *rabi* are not too low for maize (Table 5).

An important aspect of the agronomic practices should be the 'breeding' of soils suited for sustained high productivity. This would involve simultaneous attention to the physical, biological,

TABLE 5 : **Mean performance of certain maize varieties during *rabi* and *kharif* seasons of 1965 and 1968 at Hyderabad**

Variety	*Kharif* Mean Grain Yield	*Rabi* kg/ha	Percentage of *Kharif*	
Local	5359	5181	96.7	
Deccan	5624	7848	139.5	
Ganga-3	5745	7169	124.7	
Ganga-2	5642	5937	105.2	Based on one year data
Ganga-101	4632	5872	126.8	Based on two years data
Amber	4881	8577	175.7	
Jawahar	5219	8280	158.7	

Source : Data from all-India co-ordinated trials.

chemical and topographical facets of soil fertility. Intensive agriculture based on modern plant breeding without coincident steps in soil breeding would result, ultimately, in agricultural disaster rather than agicultural progress. Unfortunately, there has been little realisation of this position so far.

Pest and disease control

It is practically impossible to breed a variety possessing resistance to all strains of all pests and diseases as well as high yield and quality. This is, because of the wide variability occurring within the pest and pathogen populations, and also because of the various forms of negative relationships existing in the plant with regard to mechanisms of resistance. For example, rusts of wheat survive best in the host plant when the cells contain high sugar. In contrast, pathogens, such as *Alternaria* and *Helminthosporium* grow better when the level of sugar in the cell is low. Hence, what is needed in every crop plant is the development of a co-ordinated strategy of control, involving an appropriate admixture of genetic, chemical and agronomic approaches. Diseases and pests, which can be avoided by simple agronomic procedures, such as a change in the date of sowing, are best eradicated in this manner. A striking example for this is the raising of a seed potato crop in the Punjab during the aphid-free season. With the rapid development of the seed industry, seed-borne diseases can be controlled through seed treatment. Genetic control will be the method of choice where usable sources of resistance are readily available and where a disease or pest is very widespread in its occurrence. The approaches likely to give the best results in sorghum are indicated in Table 6. Such exercises will have to be done for each crop.

TABLE 6 : **Co-ordinated disease and pest control in *Sorghum vulgare***

Disease/pest	Causal Agent	Strategy of Control		
		Genetic	Chemical	Agronomic
Sugar disease	*Sphacelia sorghi*	−	+	+
Downy mildew	*Sclerospora sorghi*	+	−	+
Grain smut	*Sphacelotheca sorghi*	−	+	−
Loose smut	*Sphaecelotheca cruenta*	−	+	−
Leaf rust	*Puccinia purpuria*	+	+	−
Leaf blight	*Helminthosporium turcicum*	+	−	−
Shoot fly	*Atherigona varia soccata*	−	+	+
Stemborer	*Chilozonellus*	+	+	−
Midge	*Contarinia sorghicola*	−	+	+

Development of an ecology-cum-economics based multiple cropping 'cafeteria' system

Multiple or relay cropping would help to increase the income and employment potential of holdings of small size. However, intensive exploitation of land and unscientific crop rotation could lead to very undesirable long-term consequences. There should, therefore, be some ground rules in the introduction of multiple cropping patterns. Among these are :

1. No two crops sharing in common the same pests and diseases should be grown in succession.

2. One crop should be deep rooted and another with more shallow roots so that different layers of the soil can be tapped for nutrients. Varieties of crops also differ in rooting pattern and if a deep-rooted crop such as cotton is grown during *kharif*, a wheat variety such as Sonalika or Sharbati Sonora may

suffer less from micro-nutrient deficiency than Kalyan Sona which also taps nutrients from the lower layers of the soil.

3. For the restoration of soil fertility, at least one leguminous crop should find place in the rotation. If the stalks of maize are not needed for feeding cattle, their incorporation in the soil would help to improve soil structure. On the above lines, we could evolve for each agroclimatic area a multiple cropping 'cafeteria' with a wide choice of alternative crops from which the farmer can choose an appropriate combination suited to his need and input-mobilising potential and the demands of the market. The yields obtained in some multiple cropping systems under trials conducted in model agronomic centres are shown in Fig. 1.

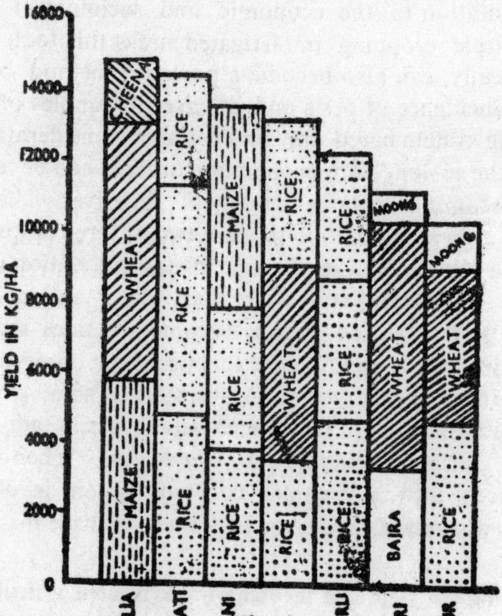

FIG. 1 : *Highest total production of cereal-pulse crops in 3 crops single year rotations.*

Multiple cropping is a very potent instrument for improving the economic position of a farmer with a small holding and for banishing underemployment and unemployment. Studies*

* Personal communication.

in the Agricultural Economics Department of the Punjab Agricultural University have clearly shown that the employment potential of agriculture can be greatly enhanced by double cropping in lands with irrigation facilities. Studies have also revealed that in the Ludhiana district, there has been an appreciable increase in real income among all classes of farmers, big, medium and small, as well as among landless labour. This is not true in many other IADP districts where the farming technology has not become as advanced as in Punjab. Inasmuch as 69 per cent of our work-force will depend upon agriculture for employment, the social significance of a technological upgrading of the employment potential of our cropping systems is obvious.

In addition to the economic and sociological advantages of multiple cropping in irrigated areas this tool, if deployed scientifically, can also become a powerful method of minimising the incidence of pests and diseases. Examples of a multiple cropping system based only on economic considerations and on one of the ecology-cum-economics concepts can be cited. With water becoming available in many of the river valley projects, there is a great temptation to grow two or three crops of rice one after the other. Even in summer, paddy cultivation is becoming popular, but already it is clear that where summer paddy is grown pests, such as jassids become a serious menace in the succeeding *kharif* paddy crop; this has been observed in parts of Bihar in recent years. Conversely, in some parts of Bihar where a monoculture of tobacco was formerly adopted, there was a serious incidence of *orabanche*. When tobacco is introduced into a multiple corpping system involving crops such as wheat and maize, the *orabanche* menace may recede.

Enhancing the yield and income of unirrigated agriculture

Recent research has shown, that apart from the limitations imposed by low and uncertain moisture levels, the missing links in elevating and stabilising yields of rain-fed agriculture have been the non-availability of crop varieties of suitable duration and growth rhythm, poor plant population, absence of attention to rectifying the defects in soil structure, improper tillage, lack of application of nutrients and plant protection procedures and poor storage and marketing. In addition, problems, such as fragmentation of holdings and lack of organised supply of inputs made the few steps taken in the past in the field of soil and moisture conservation even less effective than they might have otherwise been.

Much progress can be achieved in rain-fed farming if a new technology is introduced, comprised of the following components :

(a) Land consolidation and soil conservation;
(b) improvement in tillage leading to better soil structure and root penetration;
(c) addition of organic matter in the form of plant residues with a view to improving the physical and biological characteristics of the soil;
(d) adoption of water harvesting procedures resulting in storing as much of the precipitation as possible for the use of crops;
(e) addition of plant nutrients through deep placement of fertilisers and foliar feeding, if necessary by aircraft;
(f) improving the biological fixation of nitrogen through the use of efficient strains of rhizobia, particularly those which are tolerant to salt and use of pelleted bacterial cultures for buffering the bacteria against acidity and alkalinity;
(g) the introduction of photo-insensitive and quick-maturing crops with a series of double and mixed crop rotations from which the farmer can be advised to adopt the one which is most suited to the likely weather pattern during a season and to giving him the maximum income;
(h) increasing the density of plant population through paired rows and other techniques;
(i) popularisation of crops such as soy-bean, high-protein maize, macaroni wheat, short-duration varieties of castor and cotton and perennial crops, for example, cashewnut, oil palm and dates, which can form the base for small scale food industries and export earnings;
(j) popularisation of high-yielding fodder grasses and high protein *bajra*; and
(k) genetic upgrading of the non-descript cattle population by an extensive programme of artificial insemination

using superior breeds, particularly European breeds, acclimatised in the tropical parts of Australia.

While the above would constitute the major ingredients of an immediate action plan, a systematic survey and development of ground water resources should be continued so as to further increase the income potential of agriculture in the dry areas (Indian Agricultural Research Institute 1970).

Banishing malnutrition

The major contributions of agricultural research in banishing malnutrition are the following :

Genetic upgrading of protein quality in staple grains

It is now possible to upgrade the quality of proteins in cereals, millets and other food crops very considerably by genetic techniques. Composite varieties of maize possessing protein rich in lysine have been recently released under the names Shakti, Rattan and Protina. The last mentioned composite was developed at the Uttar Pradesh Agricultural University, Pantnagar. Varieties of rice and wheat as well as a new cereal, triticale, are being screened for protein properties. A great merit of this approach is that a dent on the malnutrition problem can be easily made without any special educational effort or added expense.

Increasing the production of pulse crops

New short-duration and high-yielding varieties of the major pulse crops such as *Cajanus cajan*, *Phaseolus aureus* and *Phaseolus mungo* have been developed, so that pulse crops can find a place in crop rotations in irrigated areas. Much of the area under pulses is rain-fed and for these areas both better varieties and suitable methods of applying rhizobial cultures are being developed.

Increasing vegetable and fruit production

These crops have received very little scientific attention so far. In recent years, several new varieties and hybrids have been developed and released in vegetable crops. If these are grown with an integrated schedule of pest control, the production can go up substantially. Research on fruit tree improvement through the development of good rootstock, new varieties and better management practices is now receiving serious attention. The new mango varieties developed at the IARI offer great promise. A demonstration orchard with plants raised on dwarfing root stocks and dwarf hybrid varieties is being developed at the IARI to show how the new plant type can facilitate good orchard management.

Increasing animal production

It is well-known that India is the largest reservoir of under-utilised cows in the world. The problem of improving animal productivity has three aspects, health care, increasing the production of fodder and feed, and the genetic upgrading of the milk-yielding potential of our breeds, more particularly of non-descript cows and buffaloes. With regard to the fodder problem, the main emphasis is on the development of high-yielding-cum-high quality fodder crops, so that the supply of concentrates to animals becomes unnecessary. Maize and millets could also be increasingly used as animal feeds.

A useful approach to the rapid genetic upgrading of the milk yielding potential of cows may be the use of 'tropicalised' versions of European breeds in our artificial insemination programmes. The value of this approach has become apparent from the results of the cross-breeding experiments carried out at the IARI between Sahiwals and Friesians from Australia. India could sponsor, with profit, a collecting team of animal geneticists to the tropical parts of Australia, Latin America and Africa, to collect European breeds introduced two to three centuries ago and which have undergone selection for adaptation to tropical climate.

Need for exploiting synergistic interactions

If agricultural research is to be effective in canalising the powerful tools of modern science for the eradication of hunger and poverty, the most important need is to achieve synergistic interactions among scientists working in different disciplines on the one hand and among scientists, extension workers and political and administrative leaders on the other. Synergy or the mechanism which makes the whole something very much more than the sum of the parts, has been the most potent principle involved in evolutionary advance and is the only mechanism which can help a poor nation to realise its economic aspirations. To cite one example of the use of this principle in evolution, our important cereal bread wheat, has three parents, *Triticum monococcum*, *Aegilops squarrosa* and *Aegilops speltoides* which are individually poor plants but collectively make the king of cereals. Harnessing and maximising such synergistic effects should be the primary goals of our agricultural research and development policies.

TOWARDS SELF-RELIANCE IN AGRICULTURE

Having considered some of the important scientific developments in agriculture, it would be appropriate to deal with a few urgent national needs. Recent events have underlined the importance of producing the food, feed and industrial raw material we need within the country itself as speedily as possible. Such an approach will also help to revive our rural economy. There are immense possibilities for immediate action both in eliminating imports of agricultural material and in harnessing the available resources of nutrient supply. This may be illustrated with two examples, the first relating to the stepping up of oilseed production and the second, to improving the availability of phosphatic fertilisers.

Increasing oilseed production

Currently in India (1974), there are 16.5 million hectares under major oilseeds producing about 9 million tonnes of oilseeds. Our requirements of vegetable oil for food and industrial purposes at the current levels of consumption will be 12 million tonnes of oilseeds, by the end of the fourth plan in 1974. This would require a growth rate of over 5 per cent. Taking groundnut, sunflower and soy-bean as examples we can examine what the possibilities are.

Groundnut

The bulk of the area under oilseeds and the total production in the country is accounted for by groundnut (8 million hectares producing 6 million tonnes). Consequently, the groundnut crop should be given top priority for purposes of both research and development since any impact of these on production will be more on this crop than on any other.

It is appropriate to fix a target for the unit area of production. Since groundnut figures also in many multiple cropping patterns, another dimension to be added to this target is that of time. We might fix the target then, not in terms of production of nuts in shell as is generally done, but that of oil extracted. It would appear that a target of one tonne of oil per hectare in 120 days should be an ideal towards which we should immediately work. This target takes into consideration, the yield of nuts in shell, the shelling percentage, the oil content and maturity. In other words, we must aim at a per day oil production of 8.5 kg per hectare. From the point of varietal input towards this direction, we have a few bunch varieties (Ah 1192, J-11 and KG. 61-240) whose per day oil production exceeds 9.0 kg per hectare.

The States of Gujarat, Andhra Pradesh, Tamil Nadu, Maharashtra and Karnataka account for over 80 per cent of the area under groundnut. A districtwise survey of these states reveals that a third of the total number of districts accounts for nearly 2/3 of the total production. This would mean that there exist in the country, pockets of groundnut cultivation whose contribution to the total production is out of proportion to their contribution to the total area. The strategy for increased groundnut production has, therefore, to be two-fold, one for areas of advanced agronomy and another for the rest.

In the areas of advanced agronomy, the aim should be one of maximising yields from the varietal and plant protection aspects. For the rest of the areas which are generally subjected to water and nutritional stress (and which also are generally mixed cropped), the strategy should be one of stabilising the yields at a fairly economical level so that the cultivator does not suffer from ruinous losses, as he does at present.

Currently the national average yield of groundnut is 7.7 quintals of nuts in shell. Only in a few States, such as Tamil Nadu and Punjab has the average yield gone above one tonne per hectare. It is an interesting and revealing point that in the 1940s the national average for groundnut production was above one tonne per hectare and that this has steadily fallen down by two quintals over a 30-year period. This is also a period when groundnut area and production have doubled. Thus, the main reason for the decline in the yield per unit area, is the extension of groundnut cultivation to marginal, unprofitable areas because of the compulsions of marketing and trade forces, and price structure. While delimiting the groundnut cultivation only to productive regions is a long term crop planning objective, current efforts should be to identify the causes of low yields in the different areas, to study the conditions of groundnut cultivation, and to seek ameliorative measures. Some of the major causes for low yields are :

Poor plant population. One of the most important causes for low yields in groundnut, all over the country, is the patchy stand of the crop at the time of harvesting by the cultivator. Very frequently, the conditions are so bad that the farmer is hardly able to harvest 40 per cent of the sown area. Thus, no matter how good the variety, with reference to the yield of the surviving plants the production is at a low level. This patchy stand is due mainly to seed-borne and soil-borne diseases, and soil-borne pests, for example, the whitegrub. Fortunately, the necessary plant protection measures have been identified by the various research groups. The main difficulty in their large-scale application is the cost and availability of the fungicides and pesticides.

Weeds. In a typical *kharif* crop, the toll taken by the weeds competing for nutrition with the crop of groundnut is high. Unlike in other crops, interculturing operations cannot be carried throughout the crop season since it would disturb the pegs that have entered the ground and are forming into pods. Thus, this crop is well suited for the chemical control of weeds. The weedicide, the dose and time of application have been identified and the only consideration is the availability and cost of the weedicide.

Leaf spot and collar rot diseases. The leaf spot disease caused by two species of *Cercospora* takes a heavy toll particularly of the erect varieties of groundnut. The damage caused by this disease can be of varying intensities depending on the stage of the crop at which initial infection commences. Although spreading varieties suffer lesser damage than erect varieties, it has not been possible to incorporate the tikka tolerance of spreading varieties into erect ones. Effective chemical control measures have been formulated. 855 kg per hectare of pod yield (or 54 per cent) is accounted for by the tikka disease.

The collar rot disease is caused by *Aspergillus niger* and can account for 40 per cent reduction in yield in some regions. Genetic sources of resistance to this disease have been identified. Seed dressing with fungicides has also been formulated and control of this disease is hence easy.

Whitegrub. Among the pests of groundnut the most devastating is the whitegrub (*Holotricha sp.*). The loss of the crop attacked by this pest is total. Soil application of insecticides, such as phorate is effective against this pest as well as against aphids, but its general application is limited by the high cost of treatment. On account of the attractive prices offered to the groundnut crop, it is the practice in some areas to crop it with groundnut continuously, both in the *kharif* and in the summer season with irrigation. This practice of monoculture of groundnut has resulted in the heavy build up of the whitegrub, thereby increasing its damaging role. Cropping patterns should be so adjusted as to avoid this loss.

Rainfall distribution. It is not generally recognised that groundnut is not a crop of high water requirement. Yields of over a tonne of nuts per hectare can be, and have been, harvested under rainfall as low as 250 to 350 mm during the crop season. What is of greater significance is the distribution or scatter of the rainfall. Even in regions of heavy or assured rainfall, there are droughty spells at the initial and later stages of growth which seriously limit yields. This is also the reason why the yields of the summer irrigated crop are invariably higher. It has been observed that there is a negative correlation between yield and rainfall during November, particularly in the southern regions. While erect varieties are generally harvested by November, spreading and semispreading varieties would suffer by this rainfall. The manipulations for adjustment are mainly agronomical and varietal. Early maturity is important not only in erect but also in spreading varieties. Implements for interculture for purposes of moisture conservation assume a significance in this connection.

In the case of bunch varieties of groundnut, the kernels lack dormancy and hence, if conditions, particularly of soil moisture are favourable, the seeds germinate resulting in a loss of the product which could be quite heavy. Further harvesting operations are rendered more difficult and expensive, if flooding of the field before harvesting is to be avoided from considerations of lack of dormancy of the seed. Prolonged dormancy again is not required if the seeds are to be used for sowing in the *rabi* or summer irrigated crops. An ideal condition would be dormancy of 20-30 days. Bunch cultures with 21 days dormancy have been identified. Dormancy itself has been classified into two groups, depending on the site of the dormancy principle, namely, the seed coat or the embryo. In the case of the former, even prolonged dormancy would not present any difficulty since a slight mechanical removal of the seed coat would be adequate for purposes of germination.

While discussing the targets of groundnut production, the yield of one tonne of oil per hectare in 120 days was mentioned as a suitable target so far as yields per unit area is concerned. With the present levels of oil recovery (25 per cent) and shelling (75 per cent) this would imply hectare yield of four tonnes of nuts in shell. Can this be obtained? The questions to be considered in this connection are :

1. What are the areas and seasons under which yields of such high order can be realised?

2. What are the inputs necessary in terms of varieties, fertiliser and plant protection chemicals, storage facilities, milling or crushing, etc.?

With reference to the first question, the seasons that would facilitate four tonne hectare yields are, obviously, the summer irrigated and the *kharif* seasons with assured, well-distributed rainfall. In the former category there are at present (1974) about 400,000 hectares with almost an equivalent area potential under the new major and minor irrigation projects. This entire area, mainly in Andhra Pradesh, Tamil Nadu, Karnataka, Orissa and Maharashtra can be expected to produce four tonnes per hectare provided the other inputs are available. Regarding the *kharif* season, the areas of assured well-distributed rainfall, good retentive soil are the Dharwar area of Karnataka, Pollachi area of Tamil Nadu, Khargone area of Madhya Pradesh,

Saurashtra area of Gujarat, Saharanpur area of Uttar Pradesh and Ambala, and the Ludhiana (irrigated) area of Haryana and Punjab. Additional new areas are also likely to come under this category with the implementation of new major and minor irrigation projects.

With reference to the second question, so far as the varietal input is concerned, the genotypes that have yielded more than four tonnes of nuts in shell per hectare have been identified. The problem will be only of rapid seed multiplication. In regard to other inputs, particular attention must be paid to giving the seed the dressing required with fungicide. Rhizobial culture should be applied to the soil and where necessary, borax as well. The application of calcium at the pegging stage and molybdenum and zinc will be beneficial in some areas. The application of weedicides could help to maintain a suitable plant population. In other words, at present the areas and the package of practices which can give rise to a groundnut yield of four tonnes per hectare are known.

From the foregoing it is apparent that the main reason for the low levels of groundnut production in the country is the inadequacy of extension efforts. Some of the measures to be taken in this direction are as follows:

1. Large scale seed production programme is necessary. The multiplication ratio in groundnut is very low, being in the neighbourhood of 15 or 16. As a consequence, the spread of improved varieties has not been as rapid as in other oilseed or grain crops. The current position of the area under improved varieties in the different states of India is indicated in Table 7.

It will be seen from Table 7 that the spread of improved strains ranges from nearly 90 per cent in Gujarat to 7.7 per cent in Rajasthan, the national average being 58.54 per cent. It should be pointed out that the improved varieties listed are all old varieties, and perhaps with the exceptions of J-11, all the others will have to be replaced by newer varieties already under pre-release multiplication, such as M-13, C-145, C-148, KG-61-240, Pol-1, TMV-10, TG-1, TG-3, NG-268, TMV-7, S-206, T-64 etc. Even if we target for a coverage of 0.1 million hectares with these improved varieties, this would mean a seed production programme for 10,000

TABLE 7

State	Improved varieties	Total area under groundnut (ha.)	Area under improved varieties (ha.)	Percentage of area under improved varieties
Gujarat	J-11, Punjab-1 AK-12-24	1,798,000	1,608,166	89.44
Andhra Pradesh	TMV-2, 3, Spanish Improved	1,187,300	913,985	76.98
Maharashtra	AK-12-24, J-11, Karad-4-11, Kopergaon-1	1,000,400	223,052	22.30
Tamil Nadu	TMV-1, 2, 3, 4	882,600	413,890	46.89
Uttar Pradesh	T-28, T-32, T-64	357,400	246,000	68.83
Rajasthan	AK-12-24, Pb-1	239,500	22,678	7.73
Mysore	TMV-2, Spanish Improved, HG-8	801,500	193,585	24.15
Orissa	AK-12-24	696,000	38,600	5.54
Madhya Pradesh	AK-12-24	420,100	311,290	74.10
Haryana	Pb-1, C-501	15,400	7,379	47.91
Punjab	C, 501, Pb-1	240,300	157,840	65.68
Total		7,066,100	4,136,465	58.54

tonnes annually, which in its own turn would mean the cropping of 10,000 hectares only for this purpose. Therefore, what is needed is a dynamic seed production programme.

2. There should be large scale seed treatment programme. At present, cultivators retain from their previous produce, nuts for the subsequent sowings, and seed dressings with rhizobium and fungicides are only done sporadically. Since dressings help to eliminate patchy stands, there should be a drive to have the seeds shelled and suitably treated.

3. The extension of the package programme over large areas of assured rainfall or irrigation is essential. Considerable

areas of high productivity potential are still to be covered by the package programme. A large scale implementation of this would ensure sizable contribution to production.

4. There is need to stabilise yields in scarce rainfall areas. In large tracts under uncertain rainfall conditions, stabilising the yield is of the utmost importance. In this programme, varieties identified as those of greater adaptability to wide fluctuations in the environment should be grown specially. Again, moisture conservation and other dry farming practices should be adopted.

5. Extensive rhizobia inoculation of areas newly brought under groundnut (e.g. new irrigation projects) should be carried out.

6. Raising groundnut with one presowing irrigation before the onset of the monsoon, for the groundnut-wheat rotation, should be attempted in Punjab, Haryana and western Uttar Pradesh.

7. The introduction of new patterns of mixed cropping, such as castor and groundnut (in Gujarat), tapioca and groundnut, interplanting groundnut in coconut plantations etc. is necessary.

8. There should be allocation of specified areas, varieties and package of practices for the export trade (annual requirement about 70,000 tonnes in 1974).

9. Aerial spraying of the groundnut crop in areas of endemic infection of red hairy caterpillar with suitable insecticides (e.g. Parathion 0.05 per cent) should be carried out.

Sunflower

Sunflower oil is one of the finest edible oils. The refined oil can be used as such without hydrogenation, but hydrogenation presents no difficulty. This is one crop in which the season of planting, photoperiod, and within limits, altitude are not limiting factors. Thus, two to three crops in a year can be raised at many locations depending on the rainfall pattern and irrigation facility. The oil can be extracted by the usual pressing. In the U.S.S.R., the factory oil recovery is reported to be nearly 44 per cent. The present yield of oil in the U.S.S.R. is around 825 kilograms per hectare. There is very good scope for adopting this oilseed crop in India in a big way.

Four commercially grown Russian varieties were obtained from the U.S.S.R. in 1969. These varieties were grown at 12 centres in the *rabi* season 1969-70 and at 25 centres in the *kharif* season in 1970. The trials were continued in 1971.

All the varieties have shown photo-insensitivity and have done well in all representative locations in the country in both the seasons and under irrigated and non-irrigated conditions. At several locations, seed yields are comparable to the yields obtained in the U.S.S.R. and other countries. Under unirrigated conditions, an average of 1413 kg per hectare was obtained at Digraj (Maharashtra) with only 75 mm rainfall during crop growth, and 1352 kg per hectare at Jalgaon with 283 mm rainfall. It was observed that yields as high as 3207 kg per hectare were obtained from an irrigated *kharif* crop at Coimbatore. In the northern States, *rabi* and spring-summer crops have done well. In the States of Maharashtra, Mysore and Tamil Nadu, better results have been obtained in the *kharif* sowing. One variety, Armavirskij 3497, has given a better performance on an all-India basis. The oil content is generally lower than that reported in the U.S.S.R. (4-5 per cent less). This may be because of the shorter duration of the crop in India (short photoperiod from the point of view of oil formation).

The most important item of work in sunflower production is the maintenance of the standard of the selected commercial varieties. Continuous selection within a variety following a fixed number of steps, is the keynote of the Russian technique in maintaining the standard and effecting further improvement in a variety. Unless this is done in India, the material of promising Russian varieties we already have, or which we may import in future can be expected to deteriorate rather quickly. To accomplish this, there is need to have simultaneous arrangements for large scale multiplication and production of seed from the material coming out of the final stage of the selection process.

The world germplasm could be evaluated for use as direct introduction or for utilisation in breeding work. Collections are already available from the U.S.S.R., U.S.A., Hungary,

Ethiopia, Rumania and Argentina. Breeding for disease resistance has to be taken up urgently since diseases caused by *Macrophomina* and *Rhizoctonia* have already been found to cause damage. Production of hybrid seed using male sterility and the development of composites, will be other important lines of work. Already, such material has been obtained for utilisation in breeding.

Only exploratory work has been done on the agronomic aspects which forms the basis of the presently recommended package of practices. The standardisation of packages of practices for different agro-climatic conditions based on experimental data obtained from different agronomic experiments is an urgent requirement.

Data have to be collected to establish how far sunflower can replace, advantageously, the traditional *rabi* or *kharif* oilseed and other crops in different parts of the country. In view of the low prices for foodgrains, such as sorghum, *bajra* and maize, farmers are in search of an alternative and more remunerative crop to replace the millets. The sunflower plant, owing to its characteristic growth habit (single stem and medium height in commercial oil-yielding varieties) may well adjust with several *kharif* and *rabi* crops as an intercrop.

Soy-bean

An all-India co-ordinated research project on soy-bean was initiated in 1967 by the Indian Council of Agricultural Research. Although there is awareness of the important role of the soy-bean, with its 40 per cent protein and 20 per cent oil content, inadequate attention has so far been given to strengthen soy-bean research and production.

The request to the U.S.A. for import of 135,000 tonnes of soy-bean oil for the year 1970-71 provides some indication of our immediate requirements. The baby food, Balahar contains 15 per cent soy, 15 per cent groundnut and 70 per cent wheat. Production target of Balahar was about 60,000 tonnes for the year 1974 and was likely to increase in subsequent years. Antibiotic factories are also buying soy-bean in large quantities. In addition, there are several enterprising concerns which have started making infant foods or other products, which require soy-bean. Consequently, the Union Ministry of

TABLE 8 : **Soy-bean varieties suitable for different parts of India**

Varieties	Areas for which suitable	Crop season	Yield range (kg/ha)
Bragg	Punjab, Haryana, Rajasthan, Delhi, Uttar Pradesh, (including Kumaon hills), Bihar, West Bengal, Madhya Pradesh, (northern central), Maharashtra (Vidharba), Gujarat (northern)	*Kharif*	2000-3500
Punjab-I	”	”	”
Lee	”	”	1800-2500
	Himachal Pradesh (Kulu Valley, Simla and Solan hills)	Summer crop	2000-2500
Clark-63	Punjab, Haryana, Rajasthan, Delhi, Uttar Pradesh, (including Kumaon hills), Bihar, West Bengal, Madhya Pradesh, (northern central), Maharashtra (Vidharba), Gujarat (northern)	For early maturity in *kharif*	1500-1800
	”	For spring-summer crop	1500-2000
	Srinagar Valley	Summer crop	1500-2000

J-231	Maharashtra, Gujarat (southern)	*Kharif*	1500-2000
Hill	Maharashtra (Vidharba), Karnataka	For early maturity in cotton-soy-bean combination in Vidharba, both crops in Karnataka	1000-1400 (Solid crop)
Davis	Karnataka	Both summer and winter crops	1100-1500
S-3	Tamil Nadu, Karnataka, Andhra Pradesh	Summer (irrigated) Winter (rainfed)	1200-1500
Improved Pelican	,,	,,	1100-1500

Agriculture has prepared plans for a rapid expansion in acreage. The target for soy-bean acreage for 1973-74 was about 600,000 hectares.

Although soy-bean is not a new crop to India, the improved high-yielding varieties of soy-bean which were imported from the U.S.A. are new to the environment of this country. During this short period of four years much progress has been made in the field of soy-bean research. Varieties suitable for cultivation in the different parts of the country have been identified (Table 8) and through organised production, marketing and utilisation programmes, soy-bean can make substantial contributions to both our immediate oil and protein needs. The immediate task is to produce the 135,000 tonnes originally asked for from the United States.

Augmenting the availability of phosphatic fertilisers through the mobilisation of indigenous sources and wastes

The target of P_2O_5 production for the year 1971-72 is 0.33 million tonnes and for the year 1975-76, 0.56 million tonnes. This estimate has been made assuming the import of rock phosphate to the tune of about 0.75 million tonnes of ground and unground natural phosphates and the utilisation of indigenous rock phosphates of only high quality. The actual P_2O_5 consumption target for 1970-71 was 0.462 million tonnes while the estimated one for 1975-76 was 2.1 million tonnes. The natural sources of indigenous phosphate available in the country are indicated in Table 9. Recent agronomic experiments have revealed the crucial role of phosphorus in getting the expected return from the application of nitrogen to high-yielding varieties. Hence, every effort should be made to augment the availability of phosphorus to our crops. Three major sources which can be exploited with profit in acid soils are :

(a) Basic slag, a by-product of the steel industry at present wasted;
(b) rock phosphate deposits; and
(c) phosphorus rich sands of the Arabian Sea islands.

Distribution of acid soils

There are at least 6.5 million hectares of strongly acid soils of below 5.5 pH. These soils are deficient in both calcium and phosphorus and require lime and phosphatic fertiliser besides nitrogen, and in many cases trace elements also for satisfactory crop production. These are the soils in which finely ground rock phosphate and basic slag, both of which are of low grade for the manufacture of phosphatic fertilisers, can be directly used. Fortunately, many of these acid soils are located very near steel plants with the results that transport costs will not be high.

Use of basic slag

Basic slag, a by-product from our steel mills is an important waste material for crop production in the country. The total annual production of basic slag from 7 steel mills is over 1.13 million tonnes and it will be more than 1.5 million tonnes when the Bokaro plant comes into full production. Out of the seven mills, four produce on an average 125,000-200,000 tonnes and two 340,000-500,000 tonnes. Indian basic slag is poor in respect of phosphorus composition (around 2% P_2O_5 on an average, except the slag from one steel mill which contains 7 per cent) but its lime and contents of secondary and trace elements are high. The total P_2O_5 available from basic slag annually is about 53,000 tonnes. Apart from P_2O_5 it will also supply active lime equivalent of 1.4 million tonnes of $CaCO_3$. It has been conclusively proved in a series of laboratory, pot culture and field experiments on a number of different acid soil areas in the country, that basic slag in spite of its low P_2O_5 content is an efficient supplier of phosphorus and other nutrients to crops and also an efficient amendment for acid soils.

For the efficient use of these sources of phosphate in acid soils it is necessary not only to grind them finely, but also to broadcast and mix with soil thoroughly in order that both of them may interact and release the phosphorus for utilisation by plants. In the economics of usage of these sources, the cost of grinding and transporting them occupy a prominent position. On equal phosphorus basis also the amount of P_2O_5 required to give the same benefit as from an easily available source of phosphatic fertiliser is about twice the latter and this also enters into the question of economics. As against this, the cost of the manufacture of the finished product is the main item that is avoided by the direct use of rock phosphate and basic slags.

Rock phosphate deposits

The range of P_2O_5 content in the rock phosphate deposits which are not suitable for industrial utilisation is from 10 per cent to 30 per cent and on an average may be taken to have the same order of P_2O_5 content as superphosphate fertiliser which contains 16 per cent P_2O_5 (Table 9). As such, on an average, the cost of

TABLE 9: **Indigenous sources of P_2O_5**

Place	State	Average percentage of P_2O_5 in the mineral	Estimated extent of deposit or production
Rock Phosphate Deposits			
Kasipatnam	Andhra Pradesh	40-42*	
Udaipur	Rajasthan	30-37*	100 million tonnes
Kashmir	Jammu and Kashmir	26-28	Not fully exploited
Tiruchirapalli	Tamil Nadu	21-26	0.13 million tonnes
Singbhum	Bihar	18-25	1 million tonnes
Mussoorie	Uttar Pradesh	15-20	8 to 10 million tonnes
Sirmur and Mahasu	Himachal Pradesh	11-18	In small belts but widespread
Laccadive	Island	12-16	A few million tonnes
Jaisalmer	Rajasthan	10-12	4.8 million tonnes
Basic Slag Deposits			
Tatanagar	Bihar	7.2	
Bokaro	Bihar		
Durgapur and Burnpur	West Bengal		
Rourkela	Orissa	2.1	1.13-1.50 million tonnes
Bhilai	Madhya Pradesh		
Bhadravati	Karnataka		
Salem	Tamil Nadu		
Ramagundam	Andhra Pradesh		

*Suitable for industrial use.

transport of this source of rock phosphate per unit of material would be nearly the same as that of superphosphate from its factory. However, nearly double the amount of P_2O_5 in this form will have to be applied to get the same benefit as from superphosphate. The rock phosphate deposit analysing from 20 per cent to 30 per cent P_2O_5 will be much cheaper from the point of view of transport cost than that from weight for weight superphosphate and also for about equal effect on the plant. This is certainly so in the case of rock phosphate deposits from Udaipur and Kasipatnam which contain more than 30 per cent P_2O_5. In all other cases the transport cost of rock phosphate will compare favourably with equal effect on plant growth, only for a range of distribution which is half the distance that the superphosphate is to cover. This factor can be taken into account in defining the area around which the deposit is to be distributed for direct application on the neighbouring acid soils. In other cases, the extra cost in transport has to be balanced from saving in the manufacturing cost of superphosphate.

Rock phosphate has to be ground before it can be chemically treated for the manufacture of easily available phosphatic fertiliser. Therefore, the grinding cost of rock phosphate will be common to both. This can be ground by ball mills which are indigenously available in the country and more may be installed at the site of these deposits, if necessary, for direct transport to the surrounding areas.

Grinding arrangements and economic considerations

Basic slag is a harder material and also has much lower P_2O_5 content. The primary crushing of basic slag is to be done by jaw crushers which are used in many factories and workshops. Many of these have a grinding capacity of about 5 tonnes of lumpy slag per day to a size less than 5 mm. The ball mills take charge of the crushed basic slag in the next stage. These are of the same type as are those used for grinding ores, minerals etc. The grinding capacity of the ball mills is usually 100-120 kg in 24 hours for grinding to a fineness of more than 80 per cent passing through 100 mesh.

The cost of grinding basic slag so that 80 per cent of the material passes through 100 mesh has been estimated by the

National Physical Laboratory as Rs 66 per tonne when done on a small scale. The cost is expected to come down to Rs 39 per tonne if ground on large scale of about 50 tonnes per day. In order that basic slag of about 2 per cent is to be ground to give the same P_2O_5 as superphosphate which contains 16 per cent P_2O_5 the grinding charges of basic slag will be four times more than the quantity of rock phosphate needed for the manufacture of superphosphate to supply equal P_2O_5. The transport charges of basic slag would also be eight times that of superphosphate for the same content of the nutrient. To neutralise the latter effect, the distance over which basic slag can be transported from the site to the factory may be restricted to about 1/8 of that for superphosphate in the case of all other basic slags and about 1/2 in the case of the Tata basic slag. The cost of grinding basic slag of about two per cent P_2O_5 content comes to about Rs 3.20 per kg of P_2O_5 for the small scale grinding, and Rs 1.60 per kg for large scale grinding as compared to non-pool price of Rs 1.76 kg of P_2O_5 in terms of superphosphate and of Re 0.48 per kg and 0.59 per kg of P_2O_5 in terms of imported rock phosphate from the United Arab Republic and Morocco respectively. The cost of the Tata basic slag thus would come to Re 0.91 for the small scale grinding and Re 0.46 for the large scale grinding.

Agronomic considerations

Datta and Motsara (1968) have suggested that the basic slag should be applied which has been ground to contain 80 per cent material to pass through 100 mesh. Mandal and Jha (1970) have shown that 20-30 mesh size particle of basic slag is sufficient. On the latter basis, the cost of grinding is expected to be reduced to about 75 per cent of the earlier requirement of 80 per cent material to pass through 100 mesh.

Datta and Motsara have shown from their data, that the favourable effects of basic slag application in acid soils is because of its effect on the microbial population of soil and in improving water-stable aggregates, in mineralisation of organic matter and improvement of soil fertility. In field experiments with wheat it was found that basic slag was superior to superphosphate and was at par with, if not slightly better than, a combined application of superphosphate and lime at the same doses. The results of the *rabi* 1966 trial, at Palampur in Himachal Pradesh are given in Table 10. All the basic slags and super+lime were superior to superphosphate in producing wheat and gram at Palampur. Basic slag (Bhilai) gave higher yield followed by super+lime. All treatments were superior to the control.

TABLE 10 : **Wheat (Var. C-253) yield in quintals/ha (Palampur) rabi, 1966 grain yield**

Treatment	Level			Mean for
	I	II	III	treatment
Control				8.40
1. B.S. (Bhilai)	24.46	32.61	35.54	30.87
2. B.S. (Durgapur)	22.25	30.33	34.46	29.15
3. B.S. (Tata)	25.50	27.96	29.95	27.57
4. Superphosphate	21.68	24.68	25.73	24.03
5. Super+Lime	24.88	29.47	35.62	29.99
Mean for levels	23.75	29.08	32.12	–

Source : Dutta and Motsara (1970)

Thus rock phosphate and basic slag can be distributed advantageously to acid soils round about the source of their origin. This will be feasible for almost all the sources except those occurring in Udaipur which can still be reserved for fertiliser grade phosphorus while the one at Jaisalmer may be turned to other sources of phosphatic fertilisers, such as dicalcium phosphate which requires only hydrochloric acid for its manufacture and which is easily available in the country. Recent work done in the Division of Soil Science and Agricultural Chemistry at the IARI has shown that coating seeds of wheat and maize with dicalcium phosphate increases the efficiency of utilisation of phosphorus nearly twice that of an equal amount of P_2O_5 from superphosphate. The Trichy phosphatic nodules may be converted into magnesium-silico phosphates which can profitably be used on the acid soils of the Nilgiris.

Phosphorus-rich sands from the Arabian Sea Islands

There are big deposits of phosphate sands on the beaches of the Minicoy and Lakshadwip islands off the coast of Kerala in the Arabian Sea. This material is of guano origin, fine sand-like grain in size, and contains about 12-16 per cent P_2O_5 most of which is citrate soluble. The estimated deposit is of the order of a few million tonnes. Experiments conducted with this material have shown that this low phosphate material is very good for crop production in acid soils. The material needs no processing or grinding for direct use. The material is loose and there are no mining problems. The only difficulty that is faced is that there are no good port facilities of an adequate nature to bring this material to the Kerala coast.

EDUCATION FOR AGRICULTURAL AND RURAL DEVELOPMENT

From what has been said so far, it is obvious that agricultural technology is rapidly becoming a sophisticated skill. To successfully harness the full genetic potential for yield in a crop variety, an integrated application of intellect, physical inputs and managerial talent is necessary. Where the technology is characterised by great ease of adoption without involving co-operative action on the part of an entire village or watershed community, the impact of the technology can be immediate, as was witnessed in the case of wheat in our country. The scientific advance in extending the yield frontiers has been equally great in rice, maize, *jowar* and *bajra* but in these crops the scientific advance is yet to be reflected in a production advance.

How are we going to extend the results of recent research to such vast numbers of illiterate peasants? In our obsession with university education, we have not given enough thought to the structural changes necessary in our rural educational system. A scrutiny of both our school education and technical literacy will be instructive since our success in eradicating poverty will be directly proportional to the effort we are willing to generate in these areas.

School education

Agriculture as a subject is taught in schools in certain parts of the country where the Board of Secondary Education has accepted it as one of the optional groups of subjects for the high school examination. Agriculture is also accepted as one of the basic crafts in some of the basic and post-basic schools in the country, but is less widely used than desirable. Agriculture as taught and practised now suffers from two defects, which are found at both ends of the spectrum. First, it is not related to the daily life, activities, interests, needs and economic benefit of the surrounding community and second, it is technologically out of date. The main reason for this is that the teachers concerned are not equipped with adequate subject matter content at the appropriate technological level, and they have not been adequately trained to correlate the work with the immediate environmental needs and resources. A new outlook for agricultural education at school level would therefore imply that we set ourselves some of the following aims :

(a) To make primary and secondary education in the rural areas more meaningful and relevant to daily life and environment by relating agriculture to it in a proper manner;
(b) to increase the component of practical work, including manual labour, in education;
(c) to introduce programmes which can be of direct economic benefit to students, and which will enable students to earn while they learn and reduce wastage in education, resulting from economic causes; and
(d) to provide practical avenues for the study at a suitable level, of the biological and social environment, and to provide material and tools for such study.

This should not be done by introducing a new scheme or a new course of study, but by strengthening the existing institutions, personnel, resources and methods in such a way as to bring about a fulfilment of the above aims.

To begin with, such an approach can best be implemented in those schools where agriculture in some form is already being taught or can easily be introduced, that is, basic schools, post-basic schools in which agriculture is a craft, middle and high schools offering agriculture, and other progressive institutions in the rural areas which are interested in such developments. Of necessity, this will restrict it to certain States and areas in the beginning. Again, the technical leadership will have to come from the universities, more especially, from the agricultural universities functioning in the area. The work could, therefore, be undertaken in areas immediately surrounding the universities. The co-operation of the state departments of agriculture and education would be necessary, and the agricultural extension personnel would come both from the department of agriculture and from the agricultural universities. Each university or major agricultural research institution can assume the responsibility for providing the technical help to at least one such school.

The core of the approach would be to undertake projects in agriculture which would be of both economic and educational value. These projects could be of various kinds and could be operated in some of the following ways.

School projects

In the beginning, it would be necessary to create confidence in the new approach, particularly in view of the dismal history of similar projects undertaken in the past without the necessary technical guidance or economic support. A demonstration of the practical feasibility of viable agriculture in the school has to be made first. Without this, such a programme will not prove acceptable. The project should be of an easy type which can attain success, since a successful demonstration is the first step towards widespread adoption. The profit from the completed project should be earmarked for school improvement and should be utilised for some obviously visible improvement. Community support should be sought at every stage. Very little may be forthcoming in the first instance, but whatever there is should be accepted and used to the full, and publicity should be given to the community element. The involvement of community is very important for the later stages of the project.

Individual projects undertaken by the pupils in school

The profit from such projects should accrue to the student concerned, and the teacher should use it for teaching purposes only. Teachers have to be trained in methods of individual and small-group instruction to enable them to handle such projects in a way which will be educationally useful to the student. As a variation, the students may form their own co-operative society and work jointly on common projects, sharing out the profits according to the number of shares. This idea may not catch on until the second or third year for obvious reasons—the demonstration of success mentioned earlier will have to come first.

Individual projects undertaken by students at home on their own land, with the guidance and support of the school teachers as well as the extension personnel

Parents should be involved by being asked to supervise and guide the work of their children. To create further interest, the time spent on this should be recorded and added to school attendance to make up the total requirement of attendance, by a variety of suitable devices which can be worked out; or alternatively, marks may be allotted for this work. The economic value of the work so done will encourage parents to keep the children at school, get them interested in the school and its work, provide additional teaching personnel, and enable them to see the usefulness of school education.

Group or class projects to be undertaken in school

These can be arranged on a competitive basis and for cash profit. The best projects should receive, besides whatever they earn, some additional recognition in the academic sphere.

There are various ways in which such projects can be made educationally useful and meaningful. Without attempting to enumerate them, a few examples of their use are suggested·

(a) For teaching of basic skills, such as reading and writing through descriptions of work done, writing up observations and experiments, preparation of instructions, etc. and numeracy through the need for various kinds of measurement and computation at each step;

(b) for teaching skills of record keeping, observation, comparison, experiments and other aspects of scientific thought;

(c) for teaching practical skills and the relationship of technology to daily work;
(d) for problem-oriented studies in science and social studies beginning with immediate problems suggested by the projects and relating them to social, economic, biological, scientific, environmental and agricultural problems of the community;
(e) for expanding into studies of science starting with the immediate problems suggested, especially in biology; and
(f) for making use of the various mass media, sources of information, resource personnel, etc.

Depending on the location, the projects undertaken may include vegetable production, poultry keeping, seed production, etc. The projects should involve skilled work, so that the educational and learning process gets stimulated.

The teachers concerned with this work will need training in several areas. This can at first be provided through short-term orientation courses, and on-the-spot technical guidance by extension and university personnel, and later, by introducing hanges in teacher training. The training will include :

(a) Knowledge of up-to-date subject matter content in thc concerned areas;
(b) practical skills in the concerned areas;
(c) techniques of group and individual instruction; and
(d) using agricultural projects for teaching and study in correlated areas, project method, etc.

The following kinds of help will be required from agencies outside the school :

(a) Technical guidance from extension workers both of the department of agriculture and from universities;
(b) necessary inputs from the departments of agriculture, such as soil testing kits, pesticides, seeds, etc.;
(c) suitable teaching aids and study kits from the department of education;
(d) suitable literature and appropriately devised programmes from the mass media, such as radio and film, newspapers, journals, etc.;

(e) training as described earlier; and
(f) community support through provision of land, tools, interest and involvement of local authorities, help of parents, supervision and part-time teaching by farmers and other members of the community, etc.

Adult education

The dimensions of our educational problem are truly staggering. In spite of all efforts, the number of illiterates in our country increased by 53 million during the period 1961-71, although the growth in literacy expressed as a percentage showed a rise from 24.03 in 1961 to 29.34 in 1971.

With the spread of the new technology and the dramatic transformation of agriculture in certain areas, new dimensions of adult education also appear. There are new needs for education among farming communities. There is a great hunger not only for new knowledge related to agriculture but also for new skills, particularly technical skills connected with it. The demand for 'techniracy' if one may coin a term based on the idea of technical literacy, is likely to be much stronger and deeper and also more widespread than that for formal literacy, or even for functional literacy. New approaches to adult education must capitalise on this new demand and need for 'techniracy'. Four such approaches suggest themselves.

Agricultural polytechnics as suggested by the Education Commission

These can be organised for young adult farmers who wish to improve their skills and knowledge. Both short-term and long-term residential courses for such people, who may be expected to be middle or high school graduates, can be organised at block headquarters, extension training centres, gram sevak centres, high schools, etc. Janta colleges, especially, would be especially useful for this sort of need-based training.

Short residential courses in 'techniracy'

These are intended for farmers with no formal educational qualification. The courses would be based on real needs, as expressed by the farmers themselves. Skills taught in the short courses would include topics, such as tubewell construction, choice of pumps, motors and implements, care and maintenance of tractors, construction of low cost water storage and conveyance systems, application of fertilisers and pesticides, etc.

Functional literacy for rural people, based on their occupational interests and needs

The literacy course for farmers designed by the Adult Education Department with the technical help of the Extension Division, IARI, and in use as a correspondence course in certain States, such as Haryana and Punjab, is an excellent illustration. It is based not only on the interests and needs of farmers, but is so designed that it is closely related to the cycle of agricultural operations, so that an incentive to continue is built into it. Such courses need to be more widely used in all parts of the country. Similar courses need to be prepared for the use of women.

By-passing the literacy problem

To the extent that the mass media can succeed in (i) transmitting the necessary information, and (ii) demonstrating frequently the necessary skills for daily living and successful farming, the question of formal literacy can be by-passed. Radio and films have to be used more intensively, and of course, television in those areas where it is already or will soon be available. This means that the specifically technical programmes should be still more specific and geared to needs, and frequently repeated. It also requires a more broad range of programmes not concerned with specific information or skills as such, but more closely related to rural life in all its aspects. In the audio-visual world of the future, formal literacy may not be necessary for the vast majority, but only for those interested in pursuing education to higher levels. This is likely to be true for different reasons also for nations at the other end of the technological spectrum. Books soon get out of date. Hence, if we can make the jump from the pre-literate to the post-literate world, without passing through the intermediate phase, we can save enormous resources and time. Planned expansion and improvement of the mass media would hence make a major contribution to the diffusion and correct adoption of new technology.

Challenge and opportunity

At no time in human history, have so few had so much opportunity for service to fellow men as the educated classes in our country have today. If we rise to the challenge, ours can still be the land where science and spirituality can blend to create a truly happy land.

REFERENCES

Datta, N.P. and Motsara, M.R., Evaluation of indigenous basic slag for crop production in India, *Tech. Bull.* (*Agric.*) *ICAR*, No. 26, (1970), pp. 56.

Donald, C.M., The design of a wheat ideotype, *Proceeding 3rd International Wheat Genetics Symposium*, Canberra, (1968), pp. 377-387.

Indian Agricultural Research Institute, A New Technology for Dry Land Farming, *Research Bulletin*, (1970).

Loomis, R.S., A.W. Williams, and W.G. Duncan, Community architecture and the productivity of terrestrial plant community, in *Harvesting the Sun : Photosynthesis in plant life*, (1967), pp. 291-308.

AGRICULTURE ON SPACESHIP EARTH

5

THE EXPRESSION 'Spaceship Earth' was first used by Buckminister Fuller many years ago to dramatise the fact that the resources of earth are finite. Today this viewpoint has become necessary for man. If one looks at it this way, one can see earth as an extra large, very efficient, nature-designed spaceship, carrying its full load of three billion passengers through space at 18.5 miles per second, equipped with its own energy, refuelling, recycling and life-support systems. A thin envelope of air, soil and water around the earth together with energy from the sun provide the major ingredients for the evolution and survival of the large number of living things, including man, on earth, and all are closely interrelated. This complex and delicately balanced web of relationships together constitute, the biosphere within which man has his place. It is hence evident that man can ultimately make only a finite claim on the limited resources of earth.

The utilization of earth's resources as though they were infinite, particularly by the rich nations, has led to the present awareness of an impending environmental and energy crisis, if economic activity is continued on the same path and pace. Brown (1972), for example, has pointed out that in 1950 when the gross world product (GWP) was just over a trillion dollars, eco-catastrophes were few. In 1970, when the GWP became nearly three trillion dollars, rapid eutrophication of lakes, oil spills, fish kills, devastating floods arising from deforestation and similar disasters became more frequent.

Growth in the consumption of natural resources, both renewable and non-renewable, is proceeding at an alarming rate. Petroleum consumption is expanding at 4 per cent yearly, fresh water at 3 per cent, marine protein at 4 per cent and the use of chemical fertilisers at 7 per cent. A 3 per cent annual growth rate means a doubling in every 24 years, while a 7 per cent growth rate leads to doubling every 10 years. In their study, Meadows *et al.* (1972) stressed that the exponential growth in consumption of finite resources, however large the reserves may be, cannot continue indefinitely. Many of their assumptions may be open to question.

Taking agriculture, Meadows and co-workers have calculated that at the present level of productivity about 0.4 hectares of arable land will be needed to feed a person. The total world availability of arable land is about 3.2 billion hectares. As the population grows, more land is not only needed for producing more food, but also for urban-industrial use. Calculations show that in A.D. 2000, the land available for agriculture will fall short of the amount needed to produce the requisite quantity of food for the population at that time, at current productivity levels. This 'doomsday' year will come 25 years later if the productivity can be doubled and 50 years later if the productivity can be quadrupled. There could be a difference of opinion about these dates and calculations but the the basic thesis is clear—we just cannot continue to fondly hope that the earth's resources can be indefinitely exploited on the assumption that some new discovery would always help to open up some hitherto unknown pathway of production.

The *Ecologist* (January 1972) in a much discussed article entitled 'A blueprint for survival' stated the choice available to man as follows :

> The principal defect of the industrial way of life with its ethos of expansion is that it is not sustainable. Its termination within the life time of someone born today is inevitable unless it continues to be sustained for a while longer by an entrenched minority at the cost of imposing great suffering on the rest of mankind.

In the consumption-oriented world of today, the rich nations consume most of the world's products, while within developing nations the richer sections of society, which may constitute only a fraction of the population, consume a large proportion of the goods produced. It is probable that the garbage cans of the richer nations may contain more protein than the total quantity of protein consumed by the poor of the developing world. One-third of the world's people who live in developed lands consume nearly eight times more energy per capita than do citizens in poorer countries. The consumption revolution of the developed world obviously cannot go on at the current pace, particularly since the developing countries also wish to consume more energy now. This realisation is leading more and more thinkers to begin to view the problems of the world as a whole, and not merely consider each part and aspect as an isolated problem. *Only one Earth* by Barbara Ward and Rene Dubos (1972) is an example of this new awareness.

We live in a world of sad scientific ironies and economic enigmas. The regions where man first settled down to cultivate plants and thereby initiated what we now call 'agriculture', are also the regions which contain the greatest number of hungry people today. The regions which scientists designate as the centre of origin of a crop plant are, strangely enough, the areas where the same plant is today giving one of the poorest average yields. The Jeypore tract of Orissa, which is believed to be an ancient centre of origin of rice, is a good example. The regions where technical skills were of a high order in ancient days are today characterised by relatively poor quality of output and workmanship. One need only recall in this connection the past glory of India and China in the production of textiles, pottery, porcelain and metal goods.

This trend needs to be arrested if the developing countries are to accomplish, even partially, their socio-economic goals. This is, however, more easily said than done. The compound interest law of growth rate operates without abatement. We are now in the second United Nations development decade, but by most economic yardsticks the income and consumption gap between the rich and poor worlds is widening. Between 1967 and 1971, developed market economies increased their agricultural-exports on an average by 11 per cent per year, while the developing market economies lost ground by 1 per cent (FAO statistics). Similarly in 1971, agricultural output went up by 9 per cent in North America and 5 per cent in western Europe, while the increase in the developing countries ranged from

1-2 per cent. On the positive side is the fact that we have an opportunity to take to a pathway of development which does not lead to the degradation of both man and his environment. The 'One Earth' concept is vital in any system of planning owing to the many tangible and intangible international linkages which influence national endeavour. However, we must accept the reality of the existence of sovereign nation states and the differences of interests and priorities between the two sharply divided groups in the world—the rich and the poor nations. Hence, within the overview provided by the concept of 'One Earth' it will still be necessary for some time to come to think in terms of planning the rational and best use of resources for each country or region.

POPULATION GROWTH AND FOOD SUPPLY

Elsewhere (Swaminathan 1973), the various projections of population growth and food needs up to A.D. 2000 and also the possibilities for producing the needed quantity of food have been discussed. The population and food requirement projections made in different studies are summarised in Tables 1 and 2. It should be possible for us to achieve the production targets if we systematically adapt and extend the available scientific know-how to the different agro-ecological areas. But what we need from the agricultural sector is not only more food, but also more income and more avenues for remunerative employment. Therefore, we have to develop for each ecological area a land and water use strategy which can through a careful blend of agriculture, forestry, animal husbandry and fisheries, help to diversify the sources of employment and maximise income.

POTENTIAL FOR FURTHER IMPROVEMENT IN YIELD

Crop and fish production may be taken as examples to illustrate current trends.

Crops

It has been estimated by crop physiologists that 12.2×10^5 calories per hectare per day, which is equivalent to 124 tonnes

TABLE 1 : **Population projections in India**

(in millions)

Year	NCAER*	Planning Commission	Registrar General	Dr. Thamarajakshi
1968-69	521	527	—	—
1971	—	—	548	—
1973-74	—	596	—	—
1981	689	690	657	—
1985	755	740	—	703
1991	827	—	—	—
2000	—	—	—	864

*National Council of Applied Economic Research.

TABLE 2 : **Food demand and supply projections for India**

(in million tonnes)

	Gross Foodgrain Demand				Foodgrain Production		
	Demand				Supply		
Year	NCAER	Planning Commission	NCA*	ESD†	NCAER	Planning Commission	ESD
1968-69	99.8	94.4	—	—	96.2	98.0	—
1969-70	—	—	—	102.2	—	—	—
1973-74	--	126.9	—	116.1	—	—	115.6
1975-76	120.3	—	121.9	—	121.5	—	—
1978-79	—	—	—	145.4	—	—	134.8
1980-81	135.7	163.0	146.3	—	137.7	165.5	—
1985-86	150.3	190.0	173.6	—	151.8	192.3	—
1990-91	167.1	—	—	—	168.7	—	—
2000	—	—	228.5	—	—	—	—

Gross Demand : Net demand (for human consumption)+Allowance for seed, feed and wastage.

* National Commission on Agriculture.

† ESD : Economics and Statistics Directorate.

per hectare per year of carbohydrates, can be expected to be the maximum attainable biological yield in the tropics. Assuming a harvest index of 50 per cent in crops, such as wheat and rice, we should expect a yield of 6.1×10^5 calories per hectare per day, or approximately 62 tonnes per hectare per year of carbohydrates in the form of grains. There are reports that yields up to 80 quintals per hectare and 100 quintals per hectare have been obtained in wheat and rice, respectively, in 130 days under intensive agriculture. Due to cloudiness during the growing season, it may be difficult to expect yields exceeding 4.88×10^5 calories per hectare per day in rice. In All-India Co-ordinated trials, energy conservation to the extent of 3.05×10^5 calories hectare per day has been reported in rice, which represents about 60 per cent of the potential.

In wheat, the highest grain yield has reached nearly 1/3 of the potential yield. In oilseeds, the single important factor responsible for poor yield is the low harvest index. Even with one irrigation and 50 kg nitrogen per hectare, it is possible to obtain 80 per cent of the highest yield. Hence, striking improvements in the productivity of these crops is possible in areas with limited water availability.

Improvements in yield in most economic plants have taken place since the beginning of agriculture through small improvements and changes. Occasionally, jumps of larger quanta accelerate the pace of progress. Usually, such jumps are associated either with an important landmark in the genetic improvement of crop plants or in advances in water and pest management. Some significant landmarks in plant breeding during this century with reference to both yield and quality are indicated in Table 3. It should be emphasised that the role of the new seeds in improving yield has been primarily that of a catalyst and that the real yield advance has been brought about by associated changes in agronomy, plant protection and engineering.

Advances have also taken place in improving the yield of plants and animals in semi-arid and arid areas. The yields obtained in trials conducted under the All-India Co-ordinated Research Project for Dryland Agriculture during *kharif* 1972, when widespread drought occurred, indicate that there is much scope for improving production in these areas through an

TABLE 3 : **Some significant landmarks in 20th century plant breeding**

Development	Years of widespread use	Country where originally used	Genetic principle(s) involved
Hybrid maize	1933	U.S.A.	Hybrid vigour
Hybrid sorghum	1957	U.S.A.	Hybrid vigour
Hybrid pearl millet	1959	U.S.A.	Hybrid vigour
Dwarf wheat	1961	U.S.A.	Dwarfing genes from Japanese 'Norin' wheats
Dwarf wheat	1963	Mexico and later India, Pakistan and Middle East	'Norin' dwarfing genes and relative photo-insensitivity
Dwarf *indica* rice	1955	Taiwan	Genes for dwarfing and relative photo-insensitivity, stiff and erect leaves
Dwarf *indica* rice	1965	Philippines, India and other countries in Asia	Genes for dwarfing and relative photo-insensitivity, stiff and erect leaves
'Opaque-2' maize	1965	U.S.A.	High lysine content
Hybrid barley	1969	U.S.A.	Hybrid vigour
'Hiproly' barley	1969	Sweden	High protein and high lysine
Hybrid upland cotton	1970	India	Hybrid vigour

integrated plan for moisture conservation, fertiliser application, pest control and crop and varietal substitution (Table 4). Some imaginative and elegant experiments are now underway in achieving crosses between distantly related species through somatic cell hybridisation, in using pollen cultures for getting haploids, in introducing the genetic capacity for symbiotic nitrogen fixation in non-legumes, and in enhancing the sink capacity or capacity for economic yield through the genetic manipulation of production physiologic processes. It is premature to guess what the ultimate impact of these researches would be on agricultural development. Meanwhile, we have enough work to do in converting the scientific breakthrough which has already taken place in the major crops into production advance.

TABLE 4 : **Yields obtained during the 1972 kharif season**

Rainfall	Yield in q/ha				
pattern and centre	Jowar	Bajra	Setaria	Arhar	Soy-bean
Seasonal rainfall deficient (—20 per cent to —60 per cent from normal)					
Hyderabad	17.8	11.8	16.3	14.1	—
Indore	39.5	—	—	—	29.8
Dehra Dun	—	—	—	—	26.1
Rajkot	3.3	9.0	—	8.9	5.4
Varanasi	—	12.4	14.3	—	7.5
Seasonal rainfall scanty (—60 per cent and below)					
Agra	6.0	19.9	—	11.9	—

Note : Trials conducted under the All-India Co-ordinated Research Project for Dryland Agriculture.

Fish

Among farm animals, fish is the most efficient converter of plant food. World fish production rose from 21.1 million tonnes in 1950 to over 69 million tonnes in 1970. Let us illustrate the position both in marine and inland fisheries in our country.

MARINE FISH PRODUCTION

The realistic estimate of the minimum potential catch per year (both demersal and pelagic) is of the order of 11-12 million tonnes as against the present annual production of about 2.8 million tonnes. From the western part of the Indian Ocean, the total estimate is approximately 6 million tonnes consisting of 3.9 million tonnes of demersal fishes, 1.9 million tonnes of pelagic fishes and 0.2 million tonnes of crustaceans. From the eastern Indian Ocean, 3.2 million tonnes is the estimated potential catch, which include 1.4 million tonnes of demersal fishes and 1.8 million tonnes of other fishes. The Indian Ocean also has a potential of about one million tonnes tuna and tuna-like fishes, of which less than 0.2 million tonnes are being caught, mainly using the longlines. There is, therefore, considerable scope for the development of fishery for tunas, particularly for the skipjack, smaller yellow fin tunas, frigate mackerel and the little tunny.

CONTINENTAL SHELF AROUND INDIA (THE REGION OF THE SEA UP TO 200 M DEPTH)

The minimum estimated potential catch is about 2.4 million tonnes as against the present exploitation of about 1.2 million tonnes. Hence, the scope for increase is of the order of 1.2 million tonnes inclusive of both pelagic and demersal resources.

The break-up for the west coast and the east coast is given here.

West coast of India

The estimated minimum potential catch is 1.6 million tonnes consisting of 1.02 million tonnes of pelagic catch and 0.58 million tonnes of demersal fishes. The present catch on the west coast is about 0.9 million tonnes and hence the new potential available is of the order of 0.7 million tonnes.

East coast of India

The east coast can produce at least 0.8 million tonnes (0.67 million tonnes of pelagic fishes and 0.14 million tonnes of demersal fishes). The present catch is of the order of 0.3 million tonnes.

CATEGORIES OF NEW RESOURCES AVAILABLE IN THE SEAS AROUND INDIA

The new resources available have neither been categorised nor quantified in detail, although some general indications are available. It is now known that the catch from traditional fisheries can be increased provided that the market conditions remain favourable for their utilisation. During the time when the catches are high the prices go down to uneconomic levels, thus forcing the fishermen to exercise a voluntary restraint in landing more fish. The new resources off the Indian coast can be classified as follows :

Pelagic fisheries

Mixed pelagic species

Recent studies have shown that about 200,000 tonnes of mixed pelagic species consisting mainly of anchovies, lesser sardines, ribbon fishes and silver bellies are available in the month of April along the south-west coast in the region extending up to 40 metres depth. These are at present almost totally unexploited. The magnitude of total anchovies resource is probably much greater.

Tunas

In the Laccadive islands, there is a traditional fishery for tunas. However, good concentrations of surface shoals have been noted beyond the traditional fishing range in these islands and also in the region between the islands and the south-west coast. It is also known that the central Bay of Bengal, especially the area near the Andaman and Nicobar Islands, supports a large population of tunas.

Clupeoids off the east coast and off Goa and Maharashtra

There are resources of sardines and other clupeoids available off the east coast and the coasts of Goa and Maharashtra. These have largely remained unexploited.

Cephalopods (squids and cuttle-fish)

Recent work shows that the cephalopods are abundant in the Bay of Bengal and Gulf of Kutch. These are very poorly fished at present. However, the economics of their exploitation and utilisation have not been worked out.

Demersal fisheries

Prawns

Recent studies show that the Gulf of Kutch, south-east coast of India, Gulf of Mannar and Palk Bay and the coastal waters of Tamil Nadu and Andhra Pradesh have very rich grounds of prawns. The fishery in the grounds off the south-west coast has developed considerably, but the other areas are not fished intensively.

Deep sea crustaceans and fishes

Off the south-west coast in the depth range 75-450 m between the latitudes 8° and 15° North (area 43,000 km^2), potential resources of the order of 100,000 tonnes are available. These resources have been discovered only during the last 5 years. Of these, at least 23,000 tonnes are crustaceans (deep sea prawns, deep-sea lobsters and crabs) and the rest are fishes. The crustaceans are particularly abundant in the depth range 180-450 m (the upper continental slope). Rich grounds of deep-sea lobsters have also been found along the upper continental slope of the Gulf of Mannar.

Perch resources

Very good grounds of perches, fishable by hook and line have been found off the south-west coast between 75 m and 100 m depths. The quantification of these resources has not yet been made, but the catch rates are expected to range between 200 kg and 300 kg per 100 hooks per hour, which is considered to be high.

Other resources

Good grounds for sharks, cat-fishes, sciaenids, carangids silver-bellies, pomfrets, and perches fishable by trawls have been found off the Indian coast, up to at least 40 m depth. These are only partly fished at present. Various forms of mariculture offer great opportunities for increasing food production (Table 5). In Japan, seaweed culture is also being widely exploited.

FRESH-WATER FISH PRODUCTION

In terms of quantity the world catch of freshwater fish is only 1/10th of the total fish production, that is about 6.9 million tonnes. Nevertheless, freshwater fish include several varieties of high value which are in great preference in several countries.

TABLE 5 : **Average annual yield of different animal production systems**

Area	Product	Yield (kg/ha)
Pasture land	Cattle	6-308
Inland ponds (India)	Fish	3000
Continental shelf	Ground fish	25-715
Humboldt current	Anchovies	375
Mariculture (Japan)	Oyster	57,500
Mariculture (Spain)	Mussels	300,000

The inland fisheries have been grouped under capture and culture fisheries. Development of capture fisheries is somewhat expensive and has only a limited scope. As against this, culture fisheries can contribute significantly to food production. Freshwater fish culture has its longest history in Asia and the Far East, particularly in China. Stocking of streams, rivers, lakes and reservoirs, has been widely practised for a multiplicity of reasons. Because of lack of adequate data, it is difficult to estimate the inland fish production, especially the quantum of fish produced through culture operations. According to a recent Food and Agricultural Organisation (F.A.O.) estimate based on data from 42 countries, the total world production by aquaculture is over 5 million tonnes. This estimate, however, does not include production of sport, bait and ornamental fishes. In the overall spectrum of inland fishery development, aquaculture plays an important role in the economy of many countries. In countries, such as China, India and Indonesia, nearly 40 per cent, 38 per cent and 22 per cent, respectively, of the total production of fish is accounted for by aquaculture. In land-locked countries, fish culture is developing into one of the important sources of animal protein. Although reliable information on the area utilisable for aquaculture is not available, it is known that in addition to conventional pond culture, there are extensive swamps, estuaries and low-lying areas with assured source of water supply suitable for fish culture. Data so far collected show that only a small part of this is being utilised for aquaculture. With the development of a variety of techniques of fish culture such as closed water ponds, running water ponds, cage culture, paddy-cum-fish culture, hanging culture, culture in lakes and reservoirs, etc., a manifold expansion of aquaculture in most parts of the world is possible.

In many countries, the possibility of substantial increase in yield by the adoption of the technique of composite fish culture has been established. Similarly, it has been proved that integrated culture practices employing a variety of compatible organisms such as prawns, frogs, ducks and even plants, such as *Euryale ferox* and *Trapa bispinosa* along with fish are advantageous in making full use of the three-dimensional aquatic environment. Further, rotation of crops involving fish, soy-beans and rice are also being practised with considerable success by some farmers. The labour-intensive nature of the present aquaculture operations also generates additional employment potential in the rural areas.

Water pollution and water weeds pose some of the greatest threats to fish culture. A concerted attack on both these problems is vital to realise the potential fish offers to improve food supply and promote protein intake.

OUR AGRICULTURAL ASSETS

Sunlight, land and water and plant, animal and human resources form the principal foundations of any agricultural system. The extent of advance made in enhancing both agricultural productivity and stability would depend upon the progress achieved in an integrated domestication of plants, soil and water based on the principles of synergy and symbiosis. In India, domestication of economic plants and farm animals has evoked much interest since ancient days, but an equal interest in the domestication of soil and water was lacking. We see as a result, large areas of eroded land and problems like salinity and alkalinity. Inadequate attention to the replenishment of soil fertility has also led to an impoverished nutrient status in most soils. One of our most urgent tasks, therefore, is to pay greater attention to the care and build-up of soil health and fertility and to the scientific utilisation of water and sunlight. A brief reference will be made to the opportunities we have for better land, water and sunlight utilisation.

TABLE 6 : **Land use statistics (1968-69)**

	('000 *Hectares*)
Geographical Area	328,048
Reporting Area	305,814
	Per cent Area
Forests	20.5
Not available for cultivation, pastures, trees, culturable waste and fallow	34.5
Net area sown	45.0

Source : Fertilizer Statistics : 1970-71

TABLE 7 : **Areas under different soil groups**

Soil Group	Area (10^6 ha)	Mean annual precipitation (mm)	Mean annual temp. (C)
Red soils	72.0	Extensive areas 600-1200	25-28
Red sandy and Red loamy		Small areas in the west and north-east 300 and 4000, respectively	
Black soils (shallow, medium and deep)	64.4	500-1200	25-28
Alluvial soils (coastal, deltaic and plains)	63.3	Extensive area 500-1200 Eastern plains 4000	20-28
Red and yellow soils	33.5	Extensive area 600-1000 Eastern part 3000-4000	20-28
Desert soils	21.9	100-400	25-28 and>28
Submontane soils	20.2	1200-3000	10-20
Mixed red and black soils	14.8	600-800	25-28
Laterite soils	11.7	Extensive areas 2000-3000 small areas 1200	20-25
Grey brown soils	8.9	400-500	25-28
Saline and alkali soils	7.0	200-1200	25-28
Mountain meadow soils	6.6	200-1200	10

Land use

The pattern of use of land for agriculture, forestry and other uses is indicated in Table 6. The soil types are of varied kinds, with red, black and alluvial soils occurring in almost equal proportions (Table 7). Forestry occupies a little less than half the area under agriculture but contributes only 1.4 per cent of the gross domestic product. During 1969-70, the contributions of agriculture, animal husbandry and forestry to the gross domestic product (GDP) were 42.4, 4.1 and 1.6 per cent respectively. The poor contribution of forestry to GDP and the neglected state of this science has been highlighted in an interim report of the National Commission on Agriculture. The Commission has pleaded that we must move away from the concept of mere conservation of natural forests to one of man-made forests. We need a dynamic programme of research in forest tree improvement including imaginative attempts to shorten the duration by accelerating the rate of growth of trees which can provide fuel and raw material for the paper industry. Our ability to promote a better ecological balance and a desirable organic recycling process would depend to a considerable extent upon what happens in the field of forestry research and development in the coming years.

The authors of *Limits to growth* have attempted to quantify the extent of fall in land availability for agricultural use that we will have to be prepared for with population expansion. They have assumed that each additional person would need 0.08 hectares of land for purposes like housing, roads, waste disposal, power lines and other uses and 0.4 hectares for producing the food he needs. If we use this formula in our country, over 5 million hectares of land will be needed every year to meet the requirements of the newborn. Therefore, we have to aim at developing integrated land use systems in agriculture where the productivity of the soil can be continuously improved, without any impairment of its long-term production potential. To achieve this we have to learn both from the successes and failures of the developed countries in the matter of soil care and use. While there are several aspects of this problem, two urgent ones relating to nutrient supply and soil structure may be mentioned.

Soil care and fertility

The recent advances in the genetic enhancement of the yield potential of several economic plants have stemmed from successes in improving their capacity to utilise more nutrients and convert them into the economic product. Thus, for getting a higher output, a greater input, particularly of nutrients, becomes essential. The first question that arises in this context is whether the continuous application of fertiliser is detrimental in the long term. Excessive use of nitrogen and phosphorus has led to difficulties in some countries. Kanwar (1972) has discussed this question with reference to our country. He has shown that our problem is not akin to those of the developed countries for a variety of reasons, among which the following are some of the more important.

We are at present using about 6.15, 1.45 and 0.92 kg N, P_2O_5 and K_2O, respectively, per hectare (according to the 1969-70 statistics), which is about 1/47th of the fertiliser consumption per hectare in Japan. On a per capita basis, the amount is about 2.6 kg. Even if a fraction of this fertiliser is lost through leaching or other biological activities, the effect on the environment will be hardly measurable. However, in the monsoon season the loss of N can be high in rice. Drainage studies in heavily manured paddy fields at the Central Rice Research Institute, Cuttack, have revealed that during the *kharif* season, 42 kg N, 29 kg, P, 38 kg Fe. and 17 kg Mn were lost per hectare. No separate record is available on the nitrate content of the water. There are very few studies about the quantitative estimation of N losses in the gaseous form from submerged condition in paddy cultivation. Datta and associates using N^{15} technique concluded that gaseous N loss was 24.1, 30.2 and 53.7 per cent in case of tagged ammonium sulphate, nitrophosphate (high water solubility) and nitrophosphate (low water solubility), respectively.

The loss of nutrients in gaseous forms as well as in drainage from heavily fertilised rice fields requires critical studies. Also, more studies are needed of the nitrate content of underground water in areas of intensive fertiliser application such as the grape gardens of Hyderabad.

From the available data, fertilisers do not seem to be significantly involved in raising the P levels in surface and

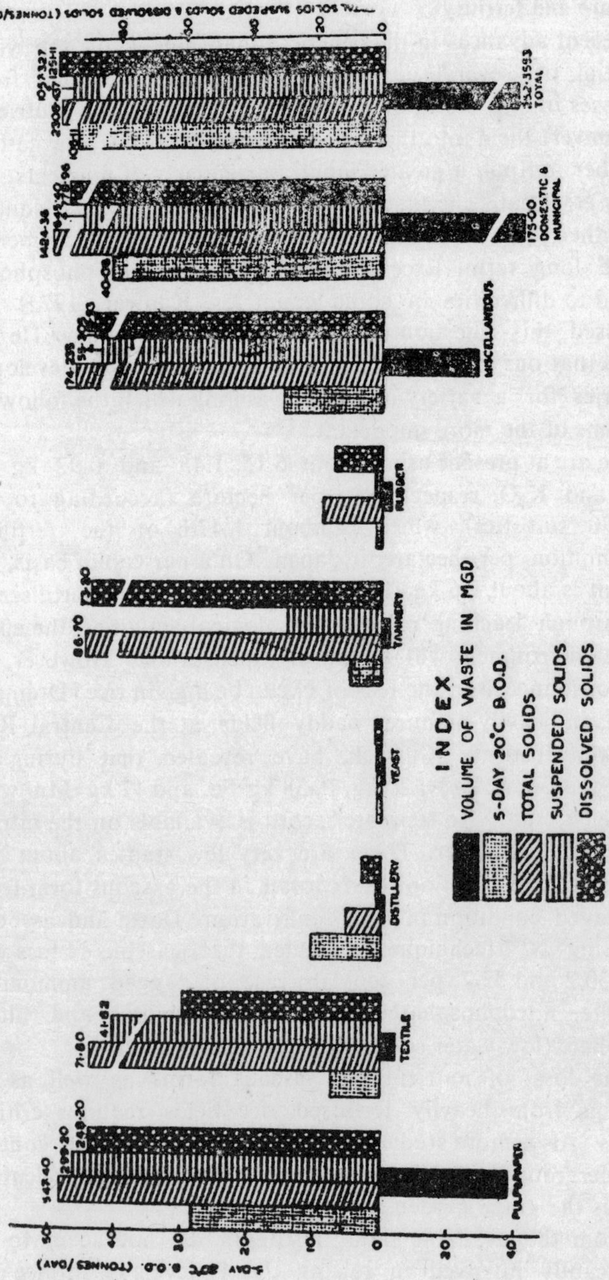

FIG. 1 : *Pollution load contributed by the various industries, estates and municipalities located on the banks of the Hooghly*

ground waters. On the other hand, by promoting the growth of vegetation they help in reducing erosion and thus reduce the loss of P to waters. The contribution by human, animal and industrial wastes and detergents to P content of streams, lakes and marine and also inland waters may be substantial as studies by the Central Inland Fisheries Research Institute, Calcutta, have revealed (Fig. 1). Thus, organic sources of phosphorus may be a source of pollution in some areas.

Kanwar has stressed that the most important cause of pollution from the agricultural lands is soil erosion. This process not only leads to the loss of millions of tonnes of nutrients every year, but it is threatening our irrigation projects and cities. It is estimated that we are losing annually about 6,000 million tonnes of soil from 91 million hectares, which are reported to be suffering from problems of erosion. Assuming that from a soil of 0.5 per cent slope, the loss of nutrients is of the order of 5.8 kg N., 10.7 kg P_2O_5 and 42.8 kg K_2O per hectare the annual total loss from Indian soils could be as high as 2.5 million tonnes, 3.8 million tonnes and 2.6 million tonnes of N, P_2O_5 and K_2O respectively. This quantity is much greater than the present total consumption of N, P, K from fertiliser as well as organic manure sources. Moreover, there are millions of hectares which lose many times more nutrients per hectare because of greater slope and erodibility. Obviously, such losses cannot be totally avoided, but we can certainly minimise them. Fortunately, a part of these leached nutrients must be going back to soil through water.

We have to assess the quantity of nutrients we need to produce about 228 million tonnes of foodgrains by A.D. 2000. We need nutrients not only for food crops but for all domesticated plants and for fish production. Research carried out under the All-India Co-ordinated Project on the correlation between soil test values and response of crops to fertiliser has shown how we can maximise the return from fertiliser application. Based on this data, Ramamoorthy *et al.** have calculated that to produce the food and other products we need by A.D. 2000, we may need a minimum of 4.60, 3.94 and 1.92 million tonnes of the nutrients N, p and K, respectively. These

*Personal Communication

calculations are based on the assumption that the efficiency of fertiliser application will be very high. The present installed capacity for fertiliser production is of the order of 1.46 and 0.50 million tonnes for N and P, respectively.

What pathways of nutrient supply should we take? The plant cannot give more yield from hungry soils. It is obvious that we should apply fertilisers judiciously and economically making full use of the research data relating to the potential for synergistic interactions. It is equally obvious that we should not use synthetic fertilisers as the sole means of nutrient supply. We have to evolve an integrated nutrient supply strategy for each cropping system, involving an appropriate combination of organic and inorganic manures and ensure that legumes find a place in the crop rotation.

In its research bulletin on 'Towards self-reliance in agriculture', the Indian Agricultural Research Institute (IARI) has advocated the tapping of the following sources of P to the maximum possible extent:

(a) Basic slag, a by-product of the steel industry wasted at present;
(b) rock phosphate deposits in different parts of the country; and
(c) phosphorus-rich sands of the Arabian Sea islands;

The following are some of the major sources of organic manure which deserve widespread conservation and use:

(a) Urban solid wastes, such as garbage, night-soil, sludge and slaughter house wastes;
(b) urban liquid wastes, such as sewage, sullage and urine;
(c) industrial wastes;
(d) all farm and crop wastes;
(e) weeds, particularly water weeds, such as water hyacinth;
(f) cattle-shed sweepings and all animal wastes; and
(g) inedible oil cakes.

If we are to conserve cowdung and bones for manurial purpose, we should popularise the widespread use of cowdung gas plants and bone digesters. If quick-growing fuel trees can be developed, the rural population need not have to rely so heavily on cow dung for fuel. In addition to the use of all such wastes, the cultivation of pulse and green manure crops both as a pure and as an intercrop in rotation in irrigated areas will be very helpful both to get more pulses and to fix more nitrogen biologically.

There is a super abundance of nitrogen in nature, with about 87,000 tonnes in the atmosphere above each hectare. The contribution of legumes to nitrogen fixation in the soil is highest in Australia and least in India (Table 8). Of more than two thousand million hectares of meadows, pastures and rough grazing in Australia, much of it arid, about one hundred million hectares have been improved by introducing legumes such as *Trifolium subterraneum* inoculated with bacteria and usually sown with superphosphate, and sometimes with lime and minor elements. In the United States also, legumes provide the largest amount of nitrogen for primary production, soy-beans alone contributing approximately 1.4 million tonnes of nitrogen. We will do well to emulate these examples.

TABLE 8 : **Nitrogen balance 1969 (1000 Metric tonnes N)**

	U.S.A.	Australia	India
I. N in Yields			
Non-leguminous crops	4518	365	2841
Leguminous crops	1996	6	460
Forage and pasture	5180	10,700	300
II. N Input			
Legume crops and forage	8610	12,840	912
Free-living N-fixation	1400	1000	650
Fertiliser N	6313	172	1222
Difference II-I	+4629	+2941	−816

In contrast to our country, where interest in organic recycling of all wastes has been generally poor, much attention has been paid to the conservation and use of all wastes including human excreta in China.

In Europe and North America also, human waste recycling systems are now under development and alternative methods which do not involve water to flush excreta, are rapidly being standardised. It is high time we also start seriously working on the development of efficient recycling and nutrient supply systems which will lead to the proper maintenance of soil structure and fertility.

POLLUTION FROM PESTICIDES

As in the case of fertiliser, the average consumption of pesticides is so low that there does not appear to exist a situation akin to those of some of the developed countries. However, a good proportion of the pesticides used by us has the property of persistence in the plant material. Therefore, a more extensive surveillance and monitoring system is necessary. Also, the right combination of pesticides is necessary for each region, as otherwise the pest which is not sensitive to the particular chemical used, would tend to survive preferentially and cause much damage. Entomologists now advocate the use of integrated pest control methods involving an appropriate admixture of genetic, chemical, biological, agronomic and other techniques. It is planned to get such an approach tested at the field level shortly in rice. So far we have not gathered operational experience in this field.

WATER REQUIREMENTS

On an average, we receive an annual rainfall of about 112 cm for 370 million hectare-metres. It has been estimated that about 120 million hectare-metres seep into the soil and about 170 million hectare-metres remain in the top layers and contribute to soil moisture which supports crop growth. The Irrigation Commission has made detailed projection of both water availability and scope for planned exploitation. It appears that the total ground water recharge available for utilisation may be of the order of 26.75 million hectare-metres per annum, in contrast to the current utilisation of about 10 million hectare metres. Major, medium and minor irrigation works have gradually expanded the irrigated area. The states which still have less than 15 per cent of the net cultivated area with irrigation facilities are Madhya Pradesh, Maharashtra, Karnataka, Gujarat and Rajasthan. The Irrigation Commission has made a broad assessment of the irrigation potential in the different States (Table 9).

TABLE 9 : **Ultimate irrigation potential in different States**

(*in million hectares*)

State	Area	
	Ultimate potential	Irrigated (1966-67)
Andhra Pradesh	10.3	3.9
Assam	2.2	0.6
Bihar	8.0	2.0
Gujarat	3.8	1.1
Haryana*	0.85	1.8
Jammu and Kashmir	0.6	0.3
Kerala	1.5	0.5
Madhya Pradesh	8.0	1.1
Maharashtra	4.5	1.4
Karnataka	3.4	1.2
Orissa	4.0	1.1
Punjab	6.1	3.4
Rajasthan	5.0	2.1
Tamil Nadu	3.6	3.4
Uttar Pradesh	15.1	7.2
West Bengal	4.3	1.5
All-India	81.7	32.8

* Area under major and medium projects included under Punjab.
Source : Data from the Report of the Second Irrigation Commission.

The total water requirements of crops, animals and man and of industry up to A.D. 2000 have been calculated by Michael *et al.** of the Water Technology Centre, IARI, using the projections for domestic and industrial use made by Kathpalia and Varadan (1971) and by the Planning Commission. These studies show that at present there is a big gap between the net available water supply and the amount

*Personal communication.

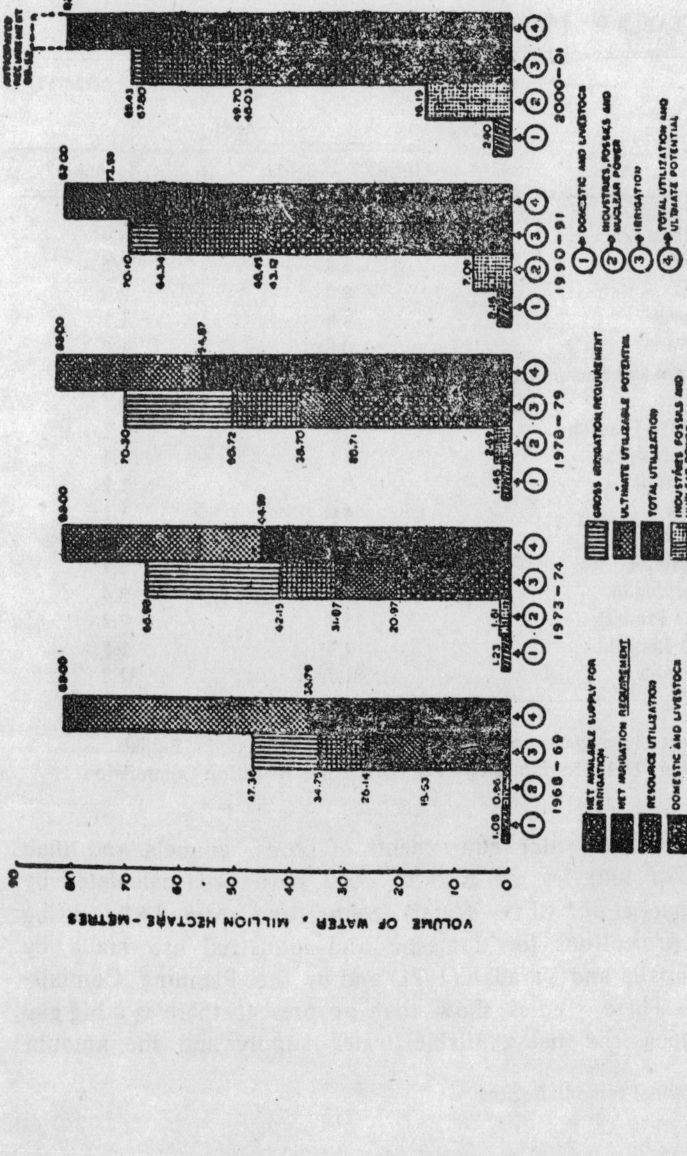

FIG. 2 : *Progressive demand, availability and utilisation of India's water resources*

required for intensive cropping. The demands on water resources, possible supply and progressive exploitation during the period 1968-69 to 2000-01 are shown in Figure 2. It appears that if the available resources can be tapped and husbanded properly, particularly through intensive efforts to increase the efficiency of water conveyance and use, we may be able to manage up to A.D. 2000 without having to go in for new sources of water such as desalination of sea water. However, such an over-all analysis of water budgeting hides the fact that even today there are considerable locational and regional gaps in the water demand-supply position. Rapid technological developments are taking place in areas, such as desalination of brackish water and weather modification and obviously, in the choice of areas for conducting feasibility studies in the use of the new sources of water supply, the regions where the water budget shows greater deficit thereby causing much human hardship, should receive priority. There is, however, immediate scope in all parts of our country to capture more water through better watershed management by introducing water-saving concepts, such as design of houses which collect rain water, development and use of waste disposal systems which do not involve the use of much water, and by the adoption of improved methods of water conveyance and by distribution (IARI 1970).

UTILISATION OF SUNLIGHT

The need for using productively sunlight, which is one of our greatest endowments, has been stressed repeatedly by many research workers but little has so far been done in tapping for human use more of this valuable energy. Multiple cropping and intercropping provide an effective agricultural method of solar energy (1972). Green plants can be made to harness sunlight throughout the year, wherever there is water to sustain crop growth. There is a vast potential for using solar energy in arid and semi-arid areas for household purposes, thereby saving the valuable organic matter for the soil. Garg and Krishnan* have shown that a flat plate collector of two square metres at Jodhpur and three square metres at Delhi can help to heat 140 litres of water up to 55°C in the afternoon of

*Personal communication.

January. This can provide sufficient hot water for a family of 5 persons. Such techniques should not remain only in the research laboratory.

GLOBAL ECOLOGICAL BALANCE

It, however, hardly needs mention. that technological changes, particularly those which affect the planet's balance of energy, could trigger off catastrophic changes. For example, there is evidence to suggest that over the last decade, the release of CO_2 into the atmosphere, as a result of man's burning of fossil fuels and of deforestation, has been increasing by 0.2 per cent a year. If this trend continues, the earth's temperature could rise by 0.5°C by A.D. 2000. Industrial emission of dust, soot and gas as well as the development of supersonic transport may all influence earth's climate. Barbara Ward and Rene Dubos have hence pleaded for concerted world action in this field. According to them,

> These concerns with global air pollution lie beyond the effective protection of individual governments. It is no use one nation checking its energy use to keep the ice caps in place if no other government joins in. It is no use the developed nations suggesting lower energy use just at the moment when the developing nations see increased use as their only exit from the trap of poverty. Man's global inter-dependence begins to require, in these fields, a new capacity for global decision-making and global care.

DOS AND DONTS

The environmental policy advocated in the richer nations is designed to protect the high standard of living resulting from the unprecedented growth in the exploitation of natural resources during the last century, from serious damage by the very processes of such growth. It is of necessity a policy based on a series of 'donts'. This is inevitable, since the aim is to undo some of the damage already done or to prevent further damage along the same lines. Thus, there is an outcry against some of the potent agents of improved agricultural productivity such as fertiliser and pesticide.

The poorer nations, however, are faced with the desire and need to produce more food from hungry soils, more clothing and more housing. They are aware that, historically, a rising standard of living has depended on the ability of agriculture to release manpower to other more industrial pursuits. They hence naturally wish to develop more industries and to find productive and remunerative employment for their growing population. For them, conditions of poverty and inadequate arrangements for human and other waste disposal may be greater causes of water and air pollution than the effluents from factories or fertiliser from the fields. Since the causes of pollution are by and large different, the solutions also will have to be different, and it would be a grave mistake to attempt to copy the policies now being propagated in the developed world.

We are fortunately in a position to build a positive policy of economic ecology based on a series of 'dos' rather than 'donts'.

Hutchinson (1972) spoke about the need for breeding soils for sustained high productivity, and has in a recent book (1972) explained the part that farming as a way of life has played in the preservation of good rural environments and the extent to which the future depends on this precious feature of agriculture. To the farmer, he says, the farm and family are one integrated unit. He remains poorer than his urban cousins who not only want him to produce cheap food but accuse him of destroying the amenity of the environment, if with purely economic motive he removes his hedges or uproots a tree. Too often his critics want it both ways. To Hutchinson the only hope for the future is that there are still many people who are prepared to live with less of the world's goods than they could acquire in an urban occupation.

Borlaug (1972) carried this theme further and reminded us that well-fed and over-fed human beings have no right to impose conditions which will preserve hunger and starvation for the majority. There is no time to relax, in our efforts to eradicate malnutrition and poverty and as an illustration of choice of priorities and options in action programmes, he said that if he were faced with the choice of having to watch the death of a few birds or the slow death of starving millions, he would 'vote for the survival and feeding of man'.

It is clear, that only integrated land use involving a relevant combination of agriculture, forestry, fishery and animal husbandry, integrated strategies of nutrient supply and pest control, greater attention to organic recycling and water conservation and extensive tapping of sunlight through the agency of green plants and simple heat collectors that can help us to improve rural economy without ecological harm. We have an unique opportunity to evolve a policy for natural resource utilisation based on the principles of economics and human welfare. To do this we have to learn how to deploy two of the most potent tools employed by Nature—synergy and symbiosis. Can we do this?

We can, but for this there are three prerequisites. First, we have to shed single-discipline-oriented and one-sided thinking and develop a problem-solving and integrated approach. Integration is needed not merely in the planning process, but more urgently at the action level. Second, we must launch a 'techniracy' (technical literacy) programme aimed at imparting technical skills to illiterate peasantry. Third, we must shun the band wagon and aping approach and generate a *do* rather than a *don't* atmosphere. We must help our farmers to apply fertiliser, pesticide, water and other inputs wisely and should not try to create confusion about the basic truth that inputs are needed for output. A *swadeshi* approach is even more relevant today than when Mahatma Gandhi first advocated it.

REFERENCES

Barbara Ward, Rene Dubos, *Only One Earth*, Penguin Books Harmondsworth, Middlesex (1972), p. 304.

Brown, L.R., *World without Borders*, New York : Random House, (1972), p. 395.

Kanwar, J.S., Are fertilisers pollutants? *Fertiliser News*, 17, (1972), pp. 17-22.

Kathpalia, G.N., N.S. Varadan, Need for national water policy, *Symposium on Integrated Development of Surface and Sub-Surface Water Resources*, New Delhi, (1971).

Meadows, D.H., D.L. Meadows, J. Randers, and W.H. Behrens, *The Limits to Growth*, New York : Universe Books (1972), p. 205.

"Recent Research on Multiple Cropping", *IARI Research Bulletin*, 8, (1972), p. 148.

See Handbook of Farm Irrigation Structures, *IARI Research Bulletin* (New Series) (1970), p. 82.

Swaminathan, M.S., Population and food supply, *Yojana*, 17, (1972), pp. 7-15.

AGRICULTURAL PROGRESS, EDUCATION AND RURAL DEVELOPMENT

6

OUR AGRICULTURAL PROGRESS DURING THE LAST 30 YEARS

THE TIME is opportune to look back over the last 30 years and critically assess our successes and failures. The most striking success is in the field of infrastructure development, whether in education, industry, commerce or agriculture. We occupy an enviable place in the developing world in our educational and technological capabilities. In addition to a national grid of scientific laboratories, we now have more than 120 universities, 4,500 affiliated colleges, 40,000 secondary schools and 600,000 elementary schools. There are about 3.5 million teachers and 100 million students in the country. In industry, we are the tenth largest industrial nation. In agriculture, we have achieved a greater capacity to produce food in the last 30 years than in the preceding 10,000 years. The 10,000 year evolutionary history of agricultural systems in our country gave us the capacity to produce annually about 50 million tonnes of foodgrains in 1947. In 1978 this figure was expected to reach about 125 million tonnes. Many more such figures can be given which indicate the commendable progress we have made in statistical terms.

However, when we measure progress in human terms, the deficiencies of the pathway of progress adopted so far become apparent. Our Gross National Product (GNP) and per capita income are among the lowest in the world. We have, in absolute numbers probably more people going to bed hungry, more persons who are illiterate, more children who are drop-outs from the school system and more numbers of unemployed than there were in 1947. There has been a drain of both brain and resources from the village to the town. As a result of this, the towns and cities experience a severe strain on their public utility services, particularly sanitary arrangements owing to the growing influx of the rural poor to the urban areas. University campuses are in many instances the centres of the origin of unrest and disillusionment. When adults cry for help there is little time to attend to the needs of preschool and primary school children although this age-group needs the greatest attention. Women, particularly in rural areas, have been mostly bypassed by extension agencies, although both by nature as well as because of economic compulsions, women are no more inclined to limit themselves to motherhood than men are inclined to limit themselves to fatherhood. The report of the Committee on the Status of Women drew attention to the fact that while according to the 1971 census there are over 31 million working women, 20 million of whom belong to the most needy sections of the society, yet day-care facilities for the children of these working mothers are scanty.

We can go on enumerating the positive and negative aspects of our socio-economic evolution since independence. Statistical figures, however, hide the deep human dilemma we are faced with. An example may be cited here from one of the most crucial tests of human behaviour faced during the last 40 years, namely, the Bengal Famine of World War II. Amartya Sen (1978) in an article. "The statistical chickens" makes the following remarks about this famine:

> I have a harrowing memory of an endless procession of emaciated men, women and children—more like skeletons than human beings—trekking in search of food. And of roads littered with corpses. One recalls families of labourers, fishermen and craftsmen—all of whom had lost their means of livelihood. Today, when I look at the statistics of that period, I can see them in the tables of destitution and mortality. Also, in the charts on the epidemics that followed the famine. But I don't see them in the table on food availability per unit of population. The index of per capita food availability with 1941 as 100 had a value of 109 in 1943. While that figure stood high people fell and perished and that general problem is with us even today.

Today, we are fortunate in having in our country a large grain buffer. Yet we know that many Indians go hungry. This emphasises the need for social security measures which can insulate the economically handicapped sections of the society from want in the basic needs of man, such as food, clothing, energy and shelter.

What can educational institutions do to assist in achieving our socio-economic goals? Two important contributions can be made. First an interdisciplinary analysis of the attitudinal and organisational changes needed for promoting growth for social justice can be made in each area at the micro-level. Second, there could be direct participation in action plans designed to demonstrate how the goals can be achieved.

It is clear that we have not benefited so far from two of the most potent instruments used by Nature, both in the origin and evolution of life and in the organisation of biological systems. The first is the principle of synergy. This subject has been mentioned earlier (Swaminathan, 1973). Synergy means behaviour of whole systems unpredicted by the behaviour of the parts taken separately. It involves the generation of multiplier effects among the components of a system, so that the ultimate product is something more than the sum of the parts. Buckminster Fuller (1975), who has utilised this principle in his engineering creations very effectively has dealt with this phenomenon at length in his book on *Synergetics: Explorations in the geometry of thinking*. An explanation of the rationale of synergetics from his book is cited here:

> By conventional arithmetic, one triangle plus one equals two triangles. But in association as left helix and right helix they form a six-edged tetrahedron of four triangular faces. This illustrates an interference of two events impinging at both ends of their actions to give us something very fundamental: a tetrahedron, a system, a division of Universe into inside and outside. We get the two other triangles from the rest of the Universe because we are not out of this world. This is the complementation of the Universe that shows up time and again in the way structures are made and in the way crystals grow. As separate actions, the two actions and resultants were very unstable but when associated

as positive and negative helixes, they complement one another as a stable structure.

Our two triangles now add up as one plus one equals four. The two events make the tetrahedron, the four-triangular-sided polyhedron. This is not a trick; this is the way atoms themselves behave. This is a demonstration of synergy. Just as the chemists found when they separated atoms out, or molecules out, of compounds, that the separate parts never explained the associated behaviour; there seemed to be 'lost' energies. The lost energies were the lost synergetic interstabilisations.

The compartmentalisation of institutions and individuals who are to perform specific tasks in a development project denies us the benefits of synergetic interactions, which alone can help to give a larger end-result from limited inputs. Our project working model not only fails to derive benefit from potential multiplier effects, but does not often generate even additive effects. This explains our low growth rates. In fact, we have come to a stage in our agricultural advance where the absence of social synergy in terms of land-use planning and water and pest management is becoming a serious handicap to further progress.

"What is social synergy? Ruth Benedict, one of the earliest anthropologists to apply the concept of synergy in social sciences, says;

> Societies where non-aggression is conspicuous have social orders in which the individual by the same act and at the same time serves his own advantage and that of the group...... Non-aggression occurs in these societies, not because people are unselfish and put social obligations above personal desires, but because social arrangements make these two identical.
>
> Cultures with low social synergy are those in which the social structure provides for acts which are mutually opposed and counteractive and cultures of high synergy where it provides for acts which are mutually reinforcing.... In cultures with high social synergy, institutions ensure mutual advantage from their undertakings, while in societies with low social synergy the advantage of one

individual becomes a victory over another, and the majority who are not victorious must shift as they can.

According to Abraham Maslow: 'The high synergy society is one in which virtue pays.... High synergy societies all have techniques for working off humiliation, and the low synergy societies uniformly do not'.

It is evident that our society as at present organised is a low synergy society. The joint-family system, an experiment in social synergy, is vanishing. The exceptions are to be usually found in tribal communities. Strangely enough, much of the developmental planning for tribal areas stresses individual rather than group effort and thus will lead to these societies also becoming low synergy ones. What steps can we take to ensure that we move from this to a better state of affairs?

The second important missing ingredient of the pathway of progress we have chosen so far is adequate attention to the problem of self-replication of programmes. The secret of success of the chemical substance of heredity, the deoxy ribo nucleic acid (DNA) molecule, lies in its ability to make an interminable number of copies of itself. If we wish to have a self-replicating movement, the project should promote self-help. The external input should have a catalytic role and not a self-perpetuating role. Unfortunately, we have very few projects, particularly in the rural areas, which have grown under their own momentum when the external input is withdrawn. This is true of projects in the field of nutrition, health care, malaria control and soil conservation. This is why government aided programmes do not usually trigger self-propelling growth, that is, enable small government programmes to become mass movements. Yet, there are examples, such as our wheat revolution, which give us insight into the making of a developmental symphony. The wheat revolution became a self-propelling movement, because of the synergy generated by matching a package of economically viable technology with appropriate packages of services and public policies.

We often identify maladies but refrain from applying the appropriate remedies. Thus, the malady analysis becomes a sterile one and gives only psychological satisfaction to those who make it. While time passes by, we find that the emerging technology, whether in agriculture or industry which is appropriate to our ecological and sociocultural milieu, demands, for its success, a social infrastructure which can promote and sustain group action. Water harvesting in dry areas, crop planning to suit different weather models, pest management and post-harvest technology, all demand the efficient adoption of community action on the part of a village or watershed community. If we continue to neglect this aspect of social engineering, the cost of production will rise to uneconomic levels, productivity will remain low and social disparities will widen.

Appropriate post-harvest technology at the village level is a potent method of increasing the wealth of the village through the production of value-added products from agricultural raw material. A rice- or *jowar*-based farming system can become the base for animal husbandry programmes for the rural poor through the introduction of fortification procedures which make the straw or stem into a complete animal food. During 1976-77, about 5.8 million tonnes of cattle feed were exported. This included about 4.5 million tonnes of oilcakes. Our dairy experts calculate that in contrast to the earning of about Rs 210 crores through the export of oilcakes, dairy products worth over Rs 1000 crores could be produced within the country by utilising them in well-planned dairy enterprises. Fostering mixed farming in ravine and degraded lands can also stimulate interest in sylvi-pastoral systems and in planting leguminous shrubs and trees which can enrich soil fertility through biological nitrogen fixation, supply fodder and feed and provide fuel. We still have the opportunity to achieve self-sufficiency in energy requirements, thus bypassing the pathways which lead to an increasing consumption of non-renewable forms of energy. Under tropical conditions, both growth and decay are accelerated. Hence, if the principle of recycling is used effectively, current liabilities, such as leaching of nutrients, mineralisation of organic matter and loss of run-off water can be converted into assets.

To help farmers with low risk-taking capacity, we need crop and cattle insurance based on an area approach. If small and marginal farmers are insulated against risk, the diffusion of technological benefits will be more rapid.

There is a vast untapped yield reservoir available even at current levels of technology in most production systems. The highest priority in the allocation of resources should go to deriving benefits from this reservoir. To do this, however, we shall need precise information on the constraints responsible for the gap between potential and actual yields. An interdisciplinary constraint analysis undertaken jointly by biological and social scientists and students would help in developing programmes designed to elevate and stabilise yields.

To summarise, our experience during the last 30 years of agricultural growth has shown that :

1. Our farmers are prepared to adopt economically viable new technology provided that the technological package is supported by appropriate packages of services and public policies.

2. By and large, advance in production has arisen from an increase in area rather than an increase in productivity.

3. There has been a differential rate of progress between regions, between crops and between different farming systems. Also, crop-livestock-fish production systems have not received the attention they deserve.

4. Unirrigated areas have by and large been neglected, since the earlier strategies relied heavily on irrigated areas to produce the food we needed.

5. Rural women as a class have generally been bypassed by most extension programmes, though they play a key role both in the production and post-harvest phases of agriculture.

6. Though we have developed some capacity to grow more food, we are yet to develop the capacity of the entire population to purchase and eat food. This disparity between the ability to grow and the ability to consume has resulted in severe problems of marketing, pricing and storage. Even a 5 per cent increase or drop in production, hence, tends to create all the difference between an uncomfortable glut and acute scarcity. Because of the relative high cost of production of most agricultural commodities, owing to the poor management of small holdings, the global cost-competitiveness of our agricultural products is poor. To promote agricultural trade we cannot count on the exceptional circumstances which prevailed for a few years in the case of sugar.

Our agriculture is now at the cross-roads. We cannot follow the same path hereafter. If we do so, we stay where we are and will find it very difficult to increase production, except by a few million tonnes in good seasons. What we need now is complete reorientation so that we can use the infrastructure for growth already created for the following purposes :

(a) To improve production through increased productivity of both terrestrial and aquatic farming systems and the development crop-livestock-fish integrated production systems;

(b) to make agricultural growth an important instrument of generating more income and employment by linking production and post-harvest technologies in the form of an integrated chain;

(c) to organise agro-industrial complexes in every district for the purpose of linking agriculture and rural industries in such agro-industrial complexes, labour should get every encouragement to become agents of production, since it has been estimated that a majority of over 100 million severely malnourished people in our country belong to the households of landless labour, it is essential that some of the landless labour is withdrawn from the routine operations of farming; and

(d) to introduce farmer-cum-area centred planning and intensify location-specific research and extension facilities.

The major components of agricultural advancement are : (i) technology development; (ii) technology transfer; and (iii) technology substance. In each of these components there has to be an integrated approach to agriculture, animal husbandry, fisheries and forestry. Those responsible for each aspect should therefore have appropriate technical support in the fields mentioned. The different aspects will also need to be co-ordinated in such a way so as to function as an organic whole.

Monitoring of agricultural progress will have to be done, not only by the current yardsticks of production and expenditure, but also by additional yardsticks, such as the increased income which has accrued to those below the poverty line, the additional man-days of employment generated, the impact of new technology on the ecological, infrastructure necessary for sustained agricultural progress and the cost competitiveness of our products in the world market.

INTEGRATED RURAL DEVELOPMENT: PROBLEMS AND OPPORTUNITIES

The greatest challenge before us now is achieving self-replicating economic growth which can provide gainful employment to everyone. Sukhatme (1977) has given estimates of the incidence of malnutrition in India. According to him, 'there are close to 100 million in the country who are chronically malnourished and poor . . . . the majority of them are labour households with little or no land of their own, depending almost exclusively for their earnings on the casual work they obtain'. He goes on to point out that these are the people who for want of adequate food, are unable to attain their full potential and who are particularly vulnerable to disease and natural calamities and live a precarious life for lack of gainful employment and food at prices they can afford. This human tragedy becomes even more painful in the context of recent increases achieved in grain reserves. On the one hand we are finding it difficult to build up adequate storage capacity for foodgrains, and on the other we cannot banish malnutrition by increasing the purchasing power of the rural poor through productive employment.

Faced by this dilemma, one can see that political will and professional skill must combine effectively to provide an urgent break-through. It is here that professional scientists and technologists have a vital role to play in achieving rural transformation. Their first step is to prepare a scientific balance sheet of the developmental assets and liabilities of a selected rural area. An analysis of this rural balance sheet will help to identify the developmental opportunities that exist and the bottlenecks that have to be removed. The next step is to convert these developmental opportunities into a portfolio of economically viable projects, in consultation with bankers and administrators. It is at this stage that the *antyodaya* concept becomes especially relevant. Only those projects which will help to increase the purchasing power of the rural poor should be taken up by government and voluntary agencies, for immediate implementation. The better-off sections of the rural community must be left to depend upon their own initiatives. It is in establishing this new system of priorities for the benefit of the rural poor that we need a radical departure from previous tradition (see also Swaminathan 1974, 1975).

Employment generation programmes based on scientific resource utilisation strategies can be of two major types:

(a) Employment generated by government through developmental projects; and
(b) employment generated through projects based on self-help and group initiative.

In the immediate future, the government can help to provide a minimum wage to rural labour by taking up a massive programme for irrigation, supply of drinking water and communications sectors with significant employment potential. The national irrigation plan now (1978) under development envisages bringing 57 million hectares under major and medium irrigation projects and 50 million hectares under minor irrigation projects. The allocation for irrigation projects in the year 1977-78 alone is expected to exceed Rs 10,000 million, the highest outlay ever, and create 1.3 million hectares of additional irrigation potential. Investments on this massive scale will call for the preparation of detailed area plans for minor irrigation schemes and the efficient use of water available from the irrigation system. Development of this basic infrastructure will increase the opportunities for self-employment through multiple cropping and mixed farming.

Government projects for the development of communications and supply of drinking water in the rural areas will also help to increase the purchasing power of the rural poor and to develop the rural infrastructure.

In the long run, however, the real solution lies in generating employment through projects based on self-help and group initiative. It is these projects which have a special relevance to countries in the Asian region with their own distinctive patterns of social organisation and massive man and woman-power resources. Perhaps, at this stage one may think of setting down certain basic guidelines for developing employment generation programmes :

1. The conversion of human energy into a specific output should be enhanced by the application of appropriate technology. Human drudgery should not be perpetuated and the best use should be made of the delicate finger-skills so wide-spread in the Asian region.

2. The role of women in the rural labour force should be given specific recognition. Agricultural extension programmes should be so designed as to reach out to them, and wherever possible, agro-industries should be organised to provide for both part-time employment and for home-based functioning.

3. Children should be relieved of full-time income-earning responsibilities so that they can attend school :

4. Wherever possible landless labour should be helped to become owners of production units. Increasingly in the entire Asian region, land will become the most priceless possession. It will be almost impossible to ensure that everyone owns a viable plot of land, and so animal husbandry, fisheries and rural industries will have to be developed as alternative production units to be owned by landless labour. It is here that basic public policy issues are involved. For example India has a coastline of about 6000 km which at present supports only 3.5 million fishing families. When scientific sea farming practices are developed through a blend of culture and capture fisheries, the potential employment will be increased considerably. It will be necessary to decide, immediately, that landless labour should get the first priority in allocating sea space for mariculture. New settlements combining mariculture with the plantation of casuarina, cashewnut and coconut can provide the basis for prosperous coastal communities.

5. In order to hasten the process of combining intellect with labour, all educational, scientific and technological institutions should be asssigned well-defined responsibilities for undertaking resources analysis for selected areas, and preparing portfolios of viable projects in consultation with the people of the area.

6. State governments, political parties, voluntary agencies and local self-governing institutions should accept the

responsibility for motivating the local community to implement these plans.

A core group on integrated rural development working in the Indian Council of Agricultural Research (ICAR) has developed the following guidelines for organising a scientific upgrading of rural economy :

(a) The action plans must provide gainful employment and increase the purchasing power of the rural poor, in particular, landless labour, marginal farmers, artisans, women and children;
(b) employment generation programme must spring from scientific resource utilisation strategies; and
(c) the programmes should be simple in operation and economically viable so that they are quickly capable of achieving self-reliance and self-replication.

It has been emphasised that the programmes should have no rigid structure; instead, each action plan should be tailored to suit local needs, resources and priorities based upon participation of the local community.

The planning phase was accordingly divided into three steps :

(a) Compilation of an integrated resource inventory that will identify natural resources, infrastructure and participants drawn from the rural poor;
(b) undertaking a malady-remedy analysis and preparing draft action plans indicating major break-through points; and
(c) vetting the draft action plans with the help of the local community.

Examples of the kinds of developmental opportunities revealed by the analysis of resources inventories in the Chandrapur and Cannanore districts are given in Table 1.

At this point it will be helpful to present some concrete illustrations. Thus in the rice-growing delta of the Cauvery river in Thanjavur district in Tamilnadu, it appears possible

TABLE 1 : **Examples of development opportunities identified by resources inventory**

Developmental opportunity	Projects to be taken up	Participants
(1)	(2)	(3)
Chandrapur District (Maharashtra)		
This region suffers from low yield of rice, *jowar* and other principal crops. There exists a good untapped yield reservoir. There is also considerable scope for horticulture.	Steps to close the resources-cum-extension-cum-crop management gap.	Marginal and small farmers and women.
The largest cattle population in Maharashtra State with huge forests and ample grazing facilities together with low milk yields (0.5-2 litres per day).	Integrated programmes involving genetic upgrading, health care, conventional and non-conventional nutrition sources, and processing and marketing facilities.	Marginal farmers and landless labour.
A waterspread area of 24,000 hectares of which 12,000 hectares are suitable for developing fisheries. The present fish landing of the district is as low as 700 tonnes per year against a potential of about 50,000 tonnes.	Improved management of tanks and development of fisheries involving establishment of fish seed banks; composite fish culture; and fish processing, storage and marketing facilities.	Fishermen communities and landless labour.
An estimated ultimate irrigation potential of 318,000 hectares of which only 115,345 hectares	Development of medium projects involving storage and diversion works and	Immediate employment opportunities for landless

have been developed. Thus, nearly 60 per cent of the irrigation potential is unexploited.	allied canal networks including minor irrigation projects, through a large number of lift-irrigation projects and intensive utilisation of ground water resources.	labour. Increasing the irrigation potential would benefit all farmers.
A major part of the ground water potential of the district remains unutilised. There are 17,300 irrigation wells in the district, and another 72,000 wells could be constructed in areas identified by the State Ground Water Organisation, mainly in the predominantly sandstone regions.	Scheme for construction of dug-cum-bore wells organised preferably on a co-operative basis to provide irrigation facilities to small and marginal holdings; organisation of community nurseries around these wells.	Small and marginal farmers and agricultural labour.
The irrigation facilities provided in the district at present are mainly for supplementary irrigation in the *kharif* season, while there is very little provision for *rabi* irrigation. A careful analysis of the rainfall characteristics and soils of the district has revealed that the amount and distribution of rainfall in the district is almost adequate to raise good *kharif* crops without irrigation, if suitable soil and crop management practices are adopted. Thus, the irrigation requirement during the *kharif* season could be	Suitable regulation of canals and the creation of additional storage capacity of tanks to store the monsoon rain and release it for irrigation in the *rabi* season. Building of run-off ponds in watersheds.	All farmers.

TABLE 1—*Contd.*

(1)	(2)	(3)
substantially reduced and the water saved could be used for *rabi* irrigation and help in intensifying the cropping pattern in the district.		
The rich forest areas provide considerable opportunities for organising woodbased industries by the tribal people themselves. Similarly, there is potential for sericulture.	Formation of suitable organisations of tribal people, who now work as labourers with a view to making them owners of production units.	Rural artisans and all classes of rural poor.
Cannanore District (Kerala State)		
About 76 per cent (2.47 lakhs) of the total land holdings in Cannanore district are below the size group of one hectare. Traditional cropping involving uneconomic plantations are predominant in the district. There is great scope for introducing mixed, multilevel and multiple cropping on scientific lines, involving appropriate blends of annual and perennial crops and animal husbandry.	Introduction of cropping patterns involving multilevel cropping and use of hybrid and other high-yielding varieties of crops. Expansion of seedling multiplication programmes in view of the acute shortage of seedlings of suitable varieties of cocoa, coconut, cashewnut and other plantation crops.	All classes of rural poor.
Very low productivity in the 0.4 hectare plots distributed by the government to 13,000 landless labourers.	Organisation of farmers' co-operatives; integrated land development works; and introduction of multiple cropping and scientific farming practices.	13,000 rural families.

The ultimate irrigation potential of the district is estimated at 1.5 lakh hectares of which only 27,200 hectares have been developed. The following are the kinds of opportunities which exist. (i) Lift irrigation	Opportunity exists for a major effort in lift irrigation development. Lift irrigation potential of the district is estimated at 17,000 hectares of which the present utilisation is only 1.158 hectares. The project would cover small and medium lift irrigation schemes using floating barges wherever required. There are also numerous hillside streams with lift irrigation potential. These are ideally suited for being operated by co-operatives or may perhaps be State owned.	Small and marginal farmers and agricultural labour.
(ii) Ground water surveys by the Central Ground Water Board have revealed the availability of suitable water bearing formations for shallow tubewells and open wells in distinct belts of the district. There is scope for sinking large-diameter irrigation wells at specified locations in the lower and midland regions of the district.	Filter point wells provided with diesel or electric pump sets can be installed in the region. Formation of farmers' co-operatives and initiation of minor irrigation programmes through filter-point wells and introduction of efficient methods of water conveyance and distribution.	All farmers.
(iii) Development of small diversion works in the hilly areas. Streams and springs predominate in the north Wynad taluka, and	Minor irrigation projects including small diversion works coupled with efficient water management.	All farmers.

TABLE 1—*concld.*

(1)	(2)	(3)
many of them could be harnessed for irrigation through suitable diversion works.		
(iv) Potential for irrigation development in the district for an additional area of 67,000 hectares through major and medium irrigation projects has been identified.	Planning and initiation of major and medium irrigation projects coupled with schemes for efficient water management of the command areas.	Landless labourers and farmers.
Extremely low per capita consumption of milk (43 per day per head) although a pasteurisation plant with a capacity of 42,000 litres per day is available in Cannanore town. The existing level of milk production is inadequate for the optimum functioning of this plant. Hence, milk production needs to be augmented by increasing the number of milch animals who could be owned by marginal farmers.	Organisation of co-operative milk production units involving the distribution of milch animals (cows and buffaloes) to marginal farmers and the organisation of a centralised marketing system for the supply of inputs. The project will involve adequate health cover facilities and cattle insurance schemes. Mixed farming by raising hybrid fodder grass in the interspace of coconut and rearing of hybrid cows.	Marginal farmers and landless labour.
The district has a coastline of 150 km with rich fisheries potential. Only a small part of the potential is being utilised at present. There is scope for a major increase in marine fisheries development through coastal and offshore fishing.	Introduction of integrated sea farming techniques involving a proper blend of culture and capture fisheries; establishment of fish curing and drying on hygienic lines; setting up of repair and	Fishermen and their families, and landless labour.

The extremely low income of the fishermen owing to exploitation by middlemen and poor marketing system are major maladies. The womenfolk of fishermen families are engaged in household chores, only a few of them are engaged in fish drying, curing, selling and mending of nets.	maintenance workshops for fishing crafts; net weaving and mending supported by training would provide employment to the women of fishing families.	
Scope exists for poultry farming and pig rearing.	Development of backyard poultry supported by proper distribution of poultry feed and provision of health cover. Introduction of pig rearing, specially among the settlers of north Wynad Taluk.	Rural poor.
There is a reserve of 13 million tonnes of china-clay, an important raw material in ceramic industries. Only about 20,000 tonnes of china-clay is processed annually, at present. There is scope for setting up small industries for manufacturing crockery, pottery and a wide range of ceramic products.	Co-operative industrial complex with a common facility for the supply of processed ceramic material and provision of kiln facilities for firing final products.	Landless labour and rural artisans.
Traditional industries such as handloom and *beedi* rolling dominate the industrial scene of the district. However, the limiting factor in these industries is the periodic non-availability of raw materials, such as yarn, dyes and chemicals; high cost of production; and lack of organised marketing and credit facilities.	Augmentation of credit facilities and provision of assured supply of quality raw material.	Landless labour and rural artisans.

to provide additional employment and income for families of landless labour and marginal farmers through the introduction of a relevant package of post-harvest technology. This package involves fortification of rice straw with urea and molasses for use as cattle and goat feed; extraction of rice bran oil and use of deoiled bran and rice husk. For this purpose, suitable animal husbandry programmes have to be organised side by side with a fodder bank and a co-operative service society. This approach can be adopted in every major cereal-based farming system.

In a totally different milieu, families of fishermen engaged in capture fisheries at Kovalam village in Tamilnadu, will be taught open-sea culture of mussels on simple rafts and poles made from locally-available raw materials. The seed mussels and technical supervision will be provided by the local laboratory of the Central Marine Fisheries Research Institute. This approach can again be replicated all along the coast.

There is a detailed list of small-scale industries, khadi and village industries, handicrafts, sericulture, etc. that also possess considerable potential for self-employment. It is important that these activities should be helped to quickly achieve self-reliance and to restrict the element of subsidy. However, their real success will depend upon the organisation of the following vital ingredients : (i) steady supply of raw materials of the right quality and at economic prices, (ii) provision of designs that can be adapted to keep pace with change in consumer demand, (iii) maintenance of strict quality control on the end product, and (iv) organisation of producers' marketing societies that leave them with the maximum share of the profit.

A special effort has been made to get research scientists to suggest how best the technology developed in their laboratories can be used to help develop operational projects, economically viable and capable of replication. Some of the ideas thrown up by the scientists include (i) the cultivation of geranium and pyrethrum flowers; (ii) upgrading of local nondescript goats; (iii) systematic programme of coconut replanting combined with schemes for intercropping; (iv) mixed farming; (v) schemes for growing fishes in fresh water reservoirs and paddy fields; and (vi) a scheme for developing an industrial estate based on marine fisheries. This last scheme is really intended to help fishermen and their families to catch more fish, to improve their processing methods and to develop new by-products. All along, the effort has been to get scientists and technologists interested in the late Professor Schumacher's idea that 'small is beautiful'. It is only by insisting on the design and implementation of small replicable projects that the integrated rural development programme can develop the dimensions of a mass movement.

A portfolio of well-defined and carefully costed projects can be drawn up for each target area. These projects can then be entrusted for implementation to the most appropriate non-official or official agency in the area. Such a 'task adoption' approach will enable each of these agencies to monitor its own contribution in qualitative and quantitative terms, according to a well-defined milestone chart. At present, there is a trend towards adopting the village as a whole which confronts the implementing agency with a universe of problems and leads in the end to dissatisfaction and despair. Instead, each agency will adopt only that task for which it possesses the necessary expertise, that is medical, educational, agricultural, veterinary, industrial, etc.

The success of the programme will depend primarily upon the calibre of the staff deployed for its implementation. Apart from a small core of staff permanently posted in the project area, the rest will consist of specialists deputed to handle specific short-term assignments. However, it is felt that the field of rural development holds out great promise for the organisation of a rural resource corps manned by young professionals who have volunteered to serve in the rural areas for a minimum period of 2-3 years. Experience has shown that there are many young persons with a sense of idealism and dynamism who would be willing to give some years of their life to rural development before entering upon their regular careers, young doctors, engineers, agricultural scientists, veterinarians, social or home scientists, etc. who could function as professional interns, working under supervision in completing clearly-defined assignments. This period of rural service will help them in acquiring greater professional maturity and experience and greater insight and sympathy in understanding the realities of life in rural communities. These volunteers will not receive a regular salary during the contract period; instead, they can be paid a consolidated fellowship linked with their individual levels of professional training.

Apart from a careful scheme of recruitment and training, these volunteers should be deployed in selected villages in carefully chosen groups of 3-4 persons in order to provide a blend of expertise and to help each other in the unfamiliar rural environment. These volunteers have a specific contribution to make in spreading the latest scientific and technological developments in the fields of agriculture, agro-industries, nutrition, supply of drinking water and primary health care. They can help in training a cadre of soil health care workers drawn from local educated youth. Simple kits can be designed for taking regular soil samples and a link can be established with specialist staff working outside the project area in well-equipped laboratories. Similarly, volunteers can help in building up a cadre of animal and plant health care workers, introducing improved practices for conserving and using water resources, new techniques of fish culture, energy supply, recycling of waste products, etc. Volunteers can also help in building up local farmers' organisations so that group initiative can be used in handling common management tasks, for example, crop planning, varietal choice, soil, water and pest management, grain drying, storage and marketing. Young married couples would be ideal for serving as members of the rural resource corps.

In conclusion, the aim of the integrated rural development programme should be to promote the generation of opportunities for gainful employment through the optimum use of locally available resources. The programme will have to be developed with the help of the participant groups and its success or failure should be measured by human rather than strictly economic yardsticks. *Antyodaya* or benefit to the poorest sections of the community should be the sole criterion for determination of priorities. Further, the methodology of implementation should provide opportunities for a confluence of efforts with opportunities for everyone interested in rural development making a contribution through the adoption of well-defined tasks.

The guiding principles of a scientific rural regeneration movement may be summed up as follows :

1. Improvement in the quality of life and purchasing power of the most underprivileged sections of the rural poor will be the sole criterion in the determination of priorities in programme formulation and implementation.

2. Contribution to productivity rather than receipt of a dole will be the mechanism of improvement in purchasing power.

3. The creation of unique show-pieces involving massive external inputs of money, manpower and technology will be avoided. Instead, programmes which will catalyse self-propelling and self-replicating growth, leading to the conversion of a small programme into a mass movement, will be developed with the help of the people concerned.

4. The techniques of science introduced will be based on low-cost, relevant and small-scale technology using sound principles of ecology and economics.

5. The reversal of the drain of brain and resources from the village to the town will have to be brought about by providing organised opportunities for educated youth and young professionals to participate in the process of development. Through the deployment of a rural resource corps of young professionals, a cadre of trained local youth can be built up to take the tools of science to the rural areas.

6. The immediate task of all universities, scientists and technological institutions should be the compilation of integrated resource inventories bringing together data on the developmental assets and liabilities of each area. This will enable the preparation of a portfolio of projects which can help to convert the endowments of each area into wealth, meaningful to the rural poor.

7. The developmental opportunities revealed by the resource inventory should be further classified into those which lend themselves for government action, such as irrigation, supply of drinking water, communications, etc. and those which can lead to self-employment. Priority should be accorded in the choice of projects to those which can help persons below the poverty line.

8. The pattern of administration of the project should be such that it will provide opportunities for every agency—official and non-official—to make a contribution.

REQUIREMENTS OF EMERGING AGRICULTURAL TECHNOLOGY IN THE AREA OF SOCIAL AND VILLAGE ORGANISATION

The emerging agricultural technology is increasingly based on integrated approaches to production systems. Since energy will be the most critical limiting factor in improving productivity at a rate essential for both increased production and accelerated economic growth, the new technology will have to rely heavily on recycling principles and renewable sources of energy. Integrated energy supply systems will have to be developed in each village, based on a blend of renewable and non-renewable forms of energy. Integrated nutrient supply systems involving organic, inorganic and biological sources of fertilisers will have to be developed and introduced. Integrated pest management, based on crop and field sanitation, cultural practices, biological control, genetic resistance and chemical pesticides will have to be popularised. Because of unfavourable chain reactions, the use of chemical pesticides will have to be kept to the minimum.

To ensure that water becomes a boon and not a curse in crop production, scientific water management and land use patterns have to be introduced. To stabilise production in rain-fed areas and to delink our agricultural fortune from the vagaries of the weather, water harvesting, crop life-saving techniques and alternative cropping strategies based on weather conditions will have to be introduced in semi-arid and arid areas. Above all, the ecological infrastructure, essential for sustained agricultural progress, will have to be continuously protected and improved. The community as a whole should be made aware of the fact that there should not only be no depreciation in agricultural assets, but that there should be a continuous appreciation of our soil, water, plant and animal wealth.

Small holdings are ideal for the adoption of labour-intensive technologies based on recycling principles. Mixed farming involving suitable blends of agriculture, animal husbandry and aquaculture can help to increase income and reduce unemployment and underemployment. We have a vast coastline, and there is great scope for introducing integrated sea farming techniques involving a blend of capture and culture fisheries. With a 322 km economic zone, our ocean surface is nearly 1/3 of our land surface. Hence, the soil and the sea and the farmer and the fisherman deserve equal attention. Thriving coastal communities can be promoted through scientific planning of the use of sea and coastal space.

There is considerable amount of data available now on the efficiency of utilisation of land judged by yardsticks, such as productivity per hectare and intensity of use of human labour. Field data generally available from developing countries like Bangladesh, India, Indonesia, Malaysia, Pakistan, Philippines, Sri Lanka and Thailand, lead one to conclude that employment per hectare rises and yields and value per hectare rise, as the average size of farm declines. This is because, in general, small farmers tend to adopt more labour-intensive techniques whether it is with reference to cultivation, crop composition or livestock. Land is also used more intensively, at times exhausting soil fertility. Again, it is observed that proportionally more land lies fallow or becomes pasture land as the size of farm increases.

Invariably, success in deriving the maximum benefit from the untapped production reservoir available at current levels of technology comes from concerted efforts in social engineering and organisation.

There are certain aspects of technology where success or failure will depend entirely on an individual farmer's own efforts. An example is the new technology of dwarf wheat cultivation. Here, the rate of diffusion of technology is solely determined by economic and ecological factors. The success of such technologies tends to become independent of efforts in social engineering. However, there are several other areas of technology where, for effective adoption, community action is a must under conditions of small and often fragmented holdings. So far, we have been able to make progress largely through individual action. Further progress will depend on the extent of group and community action we are able to generate. What is necessary, now, is the integration of technical know-how with social organisation as has been done in the case of dairy development in Gujarat.

Seen in the above context, there is an urgent need for restructuring the *gram panchayats*. If the *panchayat* has to become an effective instrument of development and accelerated agricultural advance, it will have to have a structure which is suited to its functions. Each *panchayat*, depending upon the agricultural balance-sheet (i.e. assets and liabilities) of the area covered by the *panchayat*, will have to develop social instruments for generating group action. For example, in rain-fed and semi-arid areas, one member of the *panchayat* will have to be in charge of watershed management and water harvesting. It will be his duty to stimulate group action on the part of farmers in a watershed in the area of land levelling and run-off recycling. The water harvested will have to be equally shared. The technical know-how will have to come from technical extension personnel. The *panchayat* member in charge of water harvesting and management will be concerned mainly with mobilising the necessary community action. Similarly, another member of the *panchayat* will have to assume the responsibility of canalising community action for pest management. For example, the operational research project in pest control in cotton in the Coimbatore district has shown that past damage to cotton can be greatly minimised provided that proper field and crop sanitation procedures are adopted, and the alternate hosts of pests, which are usually weeds, are removed. Spraying of chemical pesticides should be done on the basis of a surveillance system.

Post-harvest technology involving drying and processing of the produce is another area where community endeavour can help to produce value-added products before the commodity is sent out of the village. Unless production and post-harvest technologies are linked in the form of an integrated chain, the producer as well as the consumer will not be able to derive full benefit from the production effort. One member of the *panchayat* will have to deal with the social aspects of processing, storage and marketing. Therefore, the structure of the *panchayat* will have to be designed depending upon the developmental opportunities available in a village.

The proposed reorganisation of *panchayats* should be based on two major sets of principles :

(a) Certain universal principles of *panchayat* organisations based on the effective participation of all members of the village community in promoting a self-reliant and self-propelling economy; and

(b) certain unique principles and procedures based on the specific needs and developmental profile of the village.

It is only through a union between the universal and unique that we can end the lack of co-ordination and develop a dynamic system of village management which can help us to achieve the desired social goals.

THE ROLE OF FARMERS' ORGANISATIONS IN RAPID AGRICULTURAL ADVANCE IN A FEW ASIAN AND LATIN AMERICAN COUNTRIES

Several countries in Asia and Latin America have made rapid progress in increasing production and productivity in agriculture. Some examples are given here.

Taiwan

Taiwan has three distinct systems of farmers' organisations dealing with rice production, namely (i) farmers' associations, (ii) irrigation associations, and (iii) joint farming operations and land consolidation.

Farmers' associations

Only one person in a household engaged in agriculture can become a voting member of a farmers' association; those interested in the association, but not engaged in farming can become associate members, but without voting privileges. At present, about 95 per cent of all Taiwanese farmers belong to such associations and in 1975, there were 650,000 farmer members and about 200,000 associate members.

These farmers' associations are controlled by farmers and supervised by government agencies serving the economic needs of the farming community. The organisational structure is given in Table 2.

TABLE 2

Name	Number	Functions
Provincial association	1	Supervisory and organisational
Country/city level associations	20	- do -
Township-level associations	273	Major functions
Small agricultural units located in villages	4,500	Provides link between farmer members and township association and serves as voting station for election of office bearers

The services provided by the associations are :

Agricultural extension service. Each township association has an average of six extension agents who advise farmers and organise farm study groups in the village. Currently, there are over 1,600 full-time extension workers employed by these associations.

Credit service. The associations accept savings deposits from their members and make production loans to farmers. At the end of 1975, savings deposits were estimated at US $ 471 million, and total credit extended to farmers was US $ 359 million (about 73 per cent for farming use only). About 90 per cent of farm credit comes from these associations.

An elected committee of representative farmers decides on the credit rating of each member and the maximum loan that can be made to each person.

Marketing and purchasing services. The Government Food Bureau enters into contract with the farmers' associations for the distribution of chemical fertilisers and for the storage and milling of about 1/3 of the entire rice crop (the amount purchased by the government).

The associations own the following infrastructure that provides certain services :

(a) 1,587 rice warehouses with a storage capacity of 850,000 tonnes;

(b) 823 rice fertiliser warehouses with a capacity of 437,700 tonnes; and
(c) 423 rice mills with an average milling capacity of 10,500 tonnes per day for each mill.

The association also arranges for the sale of seeds, agricultural machinery, pesticides, etc. to its members.

Thus, through the association, a farmer can get his requirements of agricultural supplies, credit, technical advice and assistance with the full support of official agencies.

Irrigation associations

The irrigation associations are self-governing corporate bodies of farmers for the administration of irrigation facilities and the construction of new watering systems.

Today, Taiwan has 16 irrigation associations which function through an elected assembly headed by a chairman, and assisted by a general manager who supervises the working of four broad divisions, namely, engineering, management; finance and administration. The structure of a typical irrigation association provides for :

(a) A number of working stations for the maintenance of irrigation facilities and the regulation of water in each canal; and
(b) a working group made up of several teams assigned to each canal who maintain irrigation laterals and drainage ditches, regulate the use of irrigation water, and set up common seed farms.

In 1975, the irrigation network had a length of over 36,000 kilometres and during drought years, the associations have been able to conserve about 25 per cent of water resources.

While the government subsidises the construction of major irrigation projects, between 30-50 per cent of the costs are financed by irrigation associations through membership fees. These fees are calculated on the basis of land productivity, source and costs of water and ranges between U.S. $ 1.50 to $ 25 per hectare per annum.

The government has recently decided to exercise more control over the irrigation associations by nominating the chairman (until-now an elected representative), by strengthening the staffing pattern so that one person is employed for every 150 hectares of irrigated land, and by increasing the rate of subsidy for new construction and maintenance.

Joint farming operations and land consolidation

This is a relatively recent programme designed to raise the efficiency of farming. In Taiwan, the size of an average rice farm is a little less than one hectare (about 40 per cent are less than half a hectare). The mechanisation of such small farms is not economical, and farm workers are increasingly being diverted to industry.

In 1968 a strong effort was made to get 30-40 farm families to combine their land into a 20 hectare block. Existing manpower and farm equipment were pooled to run the block more efficiently.

As far back as 1959 a programme was started for the consolidation of small land-holdings by rearranging them into larger rectangular plots in irrigated areas. By 1971 over 260,000 hectares of land had been consolidated.

These two programmes have encouraged mechanisation of rice production. In the decade 1966-76, the number of power tillers rose from 9,300 to 45,000. In recent years, the number of rice transplanting machines, combines and four wheeled tractors have grown at the rate of 30-100 per cent each year.

Republic of Korea

Agricultural productivity in Korea has received a spectacular boost through a combination of the New Village Movement (*Saemaul Undong*), organisation of co-operative farming and strengthening of agricultural extension.

The New Village Movement is a joint effort of the government and the people to attack the causes of rural poverty through a self-help programme. The government contribution has been primarily in terms of road building, improvement of irrigation and drainage ditches, sinking of wells and construction of public buildings. However, the self-help component has meant that the value of the completed projects was much greater than the government contribution. Thus in the years 1975 and 1976, while government contributed annually U.S.

$ 330 million to the programme, the estimated value of the completed projects was U.S. $ 592 million and $ 645 million, respectively.

The number of co-operative farming units rose from 22,000 in 1972 to 52,000 in 1977, which made it possible for farmers to pool manpower and equipment and to cultivate larger farms more efficiently.

In 1972 the agricultural extension programme was intensified, about 1,800 additional extension specialists were recruited and by 1976, there were 7,500 extension workers deployed in rice growing villages. Special training courses were organised for extension workers in order to equip them to advise and motivate farmers. In the winter season, training courses were organised for farmers and in the year 1976, as many as 2.84 million farmers attended short-term winter courses. Villages and individual farmers in each village, that did not measure up to expectations were singled out for special attention by extension workers.

The Philippines

In May 1973, President Marcos announced an all-out effort to reach self-sufficiency in rice production through a programme named *Masagana 99*. (The word *masagana* in Tagalog means beautiful and the figures 99 stands for the goal of producing *99 cavans*—44 quintals per hectare). The four important elements of the programme are (i) credit, (ii) transfer of the new technology (supported by a massive publicity programme), (iii) price support for rice, and (iv) provision of low-cost fertilisers.

Credit

It was clear that most farmers needed credit to purchase the inputs required for expanding rice production. A further complication was that most of them were tenants or leaseholders without the collateral needed for securing loans.

Accordingly, in 1973-74 the government set up a new credit system with the support of 420 rural banks, 102 branches of the National Bank and 25 offices of the Agricultural Credit Administration. The government guaranteed 85 per cent of loans advanced by banks to farmers enrolled in the *masagana*

99 programme, without collateral. Bank representatives and field technicians were authorised to process loan applications in the field. The National Bank used a fleet of 100 jeeps to deliver money at the farmers' doorstep. Extension workers helped the farmer to draw up farm plans and budgets that would be acceptable to the bank. Farmers were organised into small groups of 5-15 persons with joint-responsibility for group loans. In 1974, 6,43,000 loans had been granted valued at U.S. $ 80 million; and another 257,000 farmers managed to share in the programme without recourse to loans.

The credit limit was set at U.S. $100 per hectare, a part of which was given in cash to cover labour costs and the rest in the form of purchase orders for fertiliser, pesticides, etc.

Transfer of the new technology

Technical advice and guidance was supplied by a field force of 3,200 trained technicians, all agricultural graduates, in the following areas :

1. Trials of new varieties and management practices were carried out in farmers' fields.

2. Field technicians visited the farmers regularly to advise them on the use of new varieties, use of fertilisers and pesticides, etc. They also helped farmers in making loan repayments.

3. The mass media was used extensively to spread information. Three of every four Philippine farmers own a radio so a massive broadcasting campaign was launched with a series of spot announcements, skits and jingles in six principal dialects. Each day, farm technicians broadcast 50 one-hour programmes on rice production. In addition, hundreds of thousands of pocket-size primers, leaflets and brochures were presented in the six principal dialects. Membership flags were also distributed.

Price supports

The government support price for paddy was raised from U.S. $ 57 per metric tonne in 1965 to US $ dollars 140 in 1975.

Low-cost fertiliser

The subsidy for urea was raised from 21 per cent in 1974 to 25 per cent in 1975, and a fall in world prices of fertiliser encouraged farmers in 1976 and 1977 to continue with fertiliser application. Studies have shown that the reasons for low rice yields in the Philippines can be listed as inadequate irrigation, inappropriate fertiliser use and poor pest and weed control. Many irrigation canals and ditches are poorly maintained and water deliveries are not properly managed. Inadequate capacity of the irrigation systems has meant that water is provided only for short periods after the end of the rains.

It has been suggested that irrigation associations, on the Taiwan pattern, should be formed in the Philippines, as direct participation would help in improving water-management practices.

Colombia

Colombia has an efficient organisation, Fedearroz, serving the rice grower. Started by the rice growers themselves in 1947, the organisation now receives its major funds from a tax law passed by Congress in 1963, which levies a cess of one cent per kilogram of rice sold by the rice grower. Fedearroz uses the cess fund to support rice research, organise regional variety testing, publish technical bulletins, conduct training courses for field agronomists, and meet the expenses of its technical division.

In addition to providing technical services, Fedearroz produces and sells certified rice seed, and is also engaged in the sale of fertilisers, pesticides, herbicides and farm machinery at reasonable prices. It runs as a non-profit agency that provides supplies and services to farmers and has a well-trained technical advisory staff.

In conclusion it may be stated, that rapid integrated rural development is the only answer to our socio-economic problems. This is the only pathway that can help us to develop that most precious of our assets, the human resource. If, however, we continue on the current path, we will meet with the same fate as that described by Dr Astroff in Chekhov's play, *Uncle Vanya*.

> We have the same swamps and mosquitoes; the same disease and want; the typhoid, the diphtheria and malaria. We are confronted by the degradation of our country, brought on by the fierce struggle for existence of the human

race. It is the consequence of starving, shivering, sick humanity that, to save its children, it instinctively snatches at everything that can warm it and still its hunger. So it destroys everything it can lay its hands on, without a thought for the morrow. And almost everything has gone and nothing has been created to take its place.

REFERENCES

Fuller, R. Buckminster, *Synergetics : Explorations in the Geometry of Thinking* (1975), Macmillan Publishing Company Co., Inc. New York, 1975. pp. 878.

Sen, Amartya, The statistical chickens, *Ceres*, (1978).

Sukhatme, P.V., Nineth Lal Bahadur Shastri Memorial Lecture, New Delhi (January 1977).

Swaminathan, M.S., *Our Agricultural Future*, Sardar Patel Memorial Lectures, New Delhi : All India Radio, (1973).

Swaminathan, M.S., *Agricultural Evolution Productivity Employment and Rural Prosperity*, Princess Leelavathi Memorial Lecture, Mysore (1974), pp. 49.

Swaminathan, M.S., *Education and Agricultural Progress*, Zakir Hussain Memorial Lecture, New Delhi (1975), pp. 14.

ADULT EDUCATION FOR AGRICULTURAL PROGRESS

7

AN EDITORIAL entitled, 'Not form but content' in an issue of the *Indian Journal of Adult Education* (1974) underlines the dilemma of our educational programmes and efforts. The late Dr Zakir Husain referred to the same problem in the Sardar Patel Memorial Lectures delivered in 1958, when he said :

> We have turned the so-called intellectual book-school into a mechanical memory training school and succeeded in making our Work School, the Basic School, a place of mechanical work. The work is extraneously and uniformly prescribed; there is no semblance of a spontaneous motivation in the child and he is supremely ignorant of any personal or social purpose behind his work. Work which is mechanical, work in which no mental exertion is involved, work in which one is satisfied with just any result and there is no constantly prodding urge to aim at its possible perfection, work in which there is no self-criticism and so no real progress, is in no sense educative. Schools that have such work are not Work Schools in any sense.

In 1970, Swaminathan (1970) pointed out that the only feasible way of marrying intellect and labour, was to take advantage of the new opportunities which recent agricultural progress has provided for bringing about a 'learning revolution' and pleaded for the involvement all university students in developmental and rural educational projects for at least two months in a year through a suitable built-in provision in Plan projects. With an understanding of the basic principles of biological productivity, a whole new world can be opened up for both school children and adults in villages. Appropriate projects involving the study of birds, the identification and eradication of weeds, the detection of acidity, salinity and alkalinity, the harvesting of water, the prevention of damage by rats and pests both in the field and in the store rooms, the more efficient use of solar energy, organic recycling, social and man-made forestry, crop-livestock integration, coastal and inland aquaculture would all have immense educational and practical value. The equipment needed for such studies is simple and inexpensive and mostly requires only a well informed teacher who does not curb the questioning mind and is not afraid of long walks. With a little training, this is one field where all university students of agriculture and science can render great service.

India is a land of the youth and the poor, who constitute the two genuine majorities in the country. Fortunately, we have extensive programmes for the education of youth (Ministry of Education and Social Welfare, 1974). It must however be confessed that a considerable proportion of children belonging to landless peasants and migrant labour are missed from the educational umbrella. Serious thought needs to be given to this problem.

The dimensions of our educational problem are indeed staggering. In spite of all efforts, the number of illiterates in absolute numbers tended to increase during the period 1961-71, although the growth in literacy expressed as a percentage showed a rise from 24.03 in 1961 to 29.34 in 1971. Growth rate in population is yet to show a marked fall. Therefore, as suggested, in the editorial referred to earlier, we have to give more thought to the question of what we wish to achieve through adult education. With the beginning of the scientific transformation of agriculture in certain parts of our country, new dimensions of adult education also appear. There are new needs for education among the rural communities, since there is hunger not only for new knowledge related to agriculture but also for new skills, particularly technical skills, connected with it. The demand for 'techniracy' (Swaminathan, 1972) a term used to denote mastery over technical skills relevant to the individual's needs—is likely to be much stronger and deeper, and also more widespread than that for formal literacy, or even for functional literacy. New approaches to adult education must capitalise on this new demand and need for 'techniracy'.

A brief reference should be made here, to some recent global developments in food and agriculture, to indicate both the urgency of developing and promoting educational approaches for speedy agricultural progress and the new possibilities which technological development has opened up in the area of adult education.

GLOBAL FOOD PRODUCTION OUTLOOK

The world has been going through cycles of optimism and pessimism on the question of population—food supply balance. At the current annual growth rate in world population of 2 per cent, it is generally agreed that food production must be expanded from the present annual growth rate of 2.6 per cent to at least 3.6 per cent in the next 12 years. In our country, the average growth rate has been about 2.8 per cent since the beginning of the First Plan. We however reached a growth rate of 4.5 per cent per annum during 1967-68 to 1970-71, thanks to the striking progress made in wheat production. Since more equitable distribution of the food produced seems to be still a dream, average projections of growth rate have little meaning to areas of dense population, great poverty and widespread under-nutrition and malnutrition. Here, not only the growth rate in food production needs to be much higher than the postulated global average of 3.6 per cent but there also has to be a simultaneous rise in the purchasing power of the population. Agricultural growth in such areas has to ensure increased food production as well as income and employment generation. Employment guarantee schemes have to be dovetailed to food production drives. Thus, food production strategies have to be tailored to each socio-economic and agro-ecological milieu in such a manner that both food availability and the capacity to purchase food are concurrently assured.

FOOD PRODUCTION MODELS

Taking the various parameters which regulate food production, different groups of scientists have been constructing models which provide a glimpse into the future production possibilities. Thus, the University of California group headed by Kenneth

Watt has proposed a model termed 'speculater' to indicate a simulation programme for examining the casualties underlying land, agriculture, transportation and energy relationship. In the second report to the Club of Rome, Mesarovic and Pestel (1974) have constructed a model which divides the world into 10 regions in terms of its environment technology, demographic-economic characteristics, institutional and societal processes, and psychological and biological make-up. The output of the model has been structured to show the relative price of various policy options as well as the cost of delaying various actions.

Applying their model to South Asia's food and feed needs on the basis of what they term somewhat optimistic assumptions about growth, fertiliser utilisation and bringing the uncultivated land into production, Mesarovic and Pestel have estimated that the annual protein deficit of the region would be equivalent to that of 500 million tonnes of grain by A.D. 2025. If the production and consumption gaps in developing countries are not closed either by accelerated domestic production or imports, they predict that 500 million children may die by 2025.

In spite of such grim predictions and in spite of the efforts of some experts to revive the 'triage hypothesis' which would lead to the writing off of large sections of humanity to death by hunger and starvation, the World Food Conference held in Rome in November 1974, adopted a resolution setting forth the following goal:

> Resolves that all Governments accept the removal of the scourge of hunger and malnutrition which at present afflicts many millions of human beings, as the common responsibility of the international community as a whole and accept the objective that within a decade no child will go to bed hungry, that no family will fear for its next day's bread, and that no human being's future and capacities will be stunted by malnutrition.

Are these empty words or do they represent realisable objectives? The goal can surely be achieved, but this will need intensive and co-ordinated effort within developing countries as well as between developed and developing nations on a scale and quality only rarely seen so far. It will involve steps, such as soil and water-conservation measures and ecological regeneration through tree planting on an unprecedented scale, integrated irrigation and power schemes, spread of improved genetic strains of plants and animals, conservation and effective use of all available nutrients, co-ordinated systems of pest management, detailed attention to all aspects of post-harvest technology, voluntary restrictions on the consumption of animal products in affluent nations, promotion of co-operative systems of plant-animal-man food chain, harnessing the resources of inland and sea waters, promotion of recycling and energy conservation principles, and mobilisation of human resource. Among these, the mobilisation of the human resource through extension and educational efforts and through matching economically viable technological packages with appropriate package of services and public policies, is the most important as well as difficult task and should consequently receive the greatest attention.

It is clear, whether we look at the productivity of crops, farm animals or fish, that the gap between what is immediately possible and what is being achieved is very great, particularly in several countries of South Asia and parts of Africa. Our first task is to narrow this gap. The precise methods of doing this will naturally, vary from area to area. Many limiting factors will have to be overcome—lack of appropriate extension manpower, deficiencies in technology, inappropriateness of institutional structure, inadequate inputs, excess or poor water availability, fragmented holdings and absence of organised human efforts—one or more such factors may limit productivity in different parts of our country. The various steps necessary for converting a technological breakthrough into a production advance and a production advance into a prosperity advance hence need to be identified and initiated by each state government.

FURTHER POSSIBILITIES FOR INCREASING BIOLOGICAL PRODUCTIVITY

During recent decades and particularly during the 1960s much progress has been made in raising the ceiling to yield levels in major cereals and millets. By and large, the principles used are the improvement of the harvest index (i.e., the proportion of economic yield to the total biological yield) as well as the ability to respond to good management, through a restructuring of plant architecture and developmental rhythm, the exploitation of hybrid vigour and the enhancement of per day productivity through the introduction of insensitivity to photo-period, thereby facilitating multiple cropping. At the International Rice Research Institute in the Philippines, over 20 tonnes of grain have been produced in a year through multiple cropping. It could, therefore, be asked whether we have reached the ceiling to yield potential in our major food crops or whether there is scope for raising the ceiling to higher levels.

This scientific potential for improving food production and nutrition has been brought out in a series of excellent papers in *Science* wherein Revelle and Lakshminarayana (1975) describe some approaches towards making better use of one of Nature's greatest gifts to man, namely, the river Ganges and its tributaries, and the flat and fertile plains through which they flow. Similarly, the present and future possibilities for improving crops and animal productivity have been dealt with in a report published by the U.S. National Academy of Sciences in 1975. Such analyses indicate that there is still much scope for raising yield ceilings through maximising the utilisation of solar energy by both more scientific work and greater and more efficient use of different forms of cultural energy (i.e., all forms of energy which man has introduced into agriculture and animal husbandry for increasing yield).

The efficiency of high utilisation by plants can be computed as the ratio of calories of yield to calories of photosynthetically active sunlight absorbed by the plant. Although the theoretical quantum of efficiency of photosynthesis is 12 per cent, incomplete capture of sunlight by leaves throughout the growing season and wasteful respiration of CO_2 from photosynthetic product restrict the observed efficiency of most plants to the range of 0.1 per cent to 3 per cent. For example, the average maize crop captures only 1 per cent of the 10^{12} calories of photosynthetically active sunlight falling upon an acre of land during a 3-month growing season.

Various calculations have been made to estimate the theoretical and potential yield of crop plants. In such calculations it is assumed that light interception is full but that there are albedo and inactive absorption losses. Whatever be the absorption of light energy plant, its conservation is only about 26 per cent because of the conversion efficiency of quanta into chemical form. When losses for respiration are also accounted for,. one expects only 71 gm/day (CH_2O) production. There could be differences in such calculations.

CRUCIAL ROLE OF WATER

A major variable in calculations of this kind is the radiation received at any given place which varies considerably. Second, the calculations also assume that there is no shortage of inputs, such as water, adverse temperature, nutrients, pesticides, etc. If we consider only three factors, namely light duration (energy), water availability and temperature, the period of maximum insulation in tropical regions unfortunately coincides with low availability of water and high temperature. The latter would lead to high evapo-transpiration and consequently greater demand of water. In the absence of ground water or lack of its exploitation, water becomes the chief limiting factor in crop productivity. Thus, the period of potential maximum productivity unfortunately becomes in reality a period of minimum productivity. This fact is generally not recognised when scientists working in temperate regions estimate the potential for productivity in the tropics. In many countries of Europe and North America, the period of maximum day length fortunately coincides with periods of precipitation and temperatures conducive to growth. Hence, the conservation and efficient use of all available water resources should get the highest priority in our developmental and educational efforts. If there is water and nutrients, tropics and sub-tropics afford the possibility of growing several crops in a year through suitable multiple, relay and intercropping techniques. Also, full benefit can then be derived from the period of potential maximum productivity.

It has become increasingly clear that only by a suitable understanding of the basic aspects of biological productivity among the community as a whole and by co-operative management of certain farm operations by groups of farmers with small holdings that substantial and sustained progress can be achieved in agriculture. Increasingly, modern technology aims to introduce integrated approaches in farming. For example, now-a-days the term 'pest management' is replacing the old term 'pest control'. Pest management involves the development and introduction of integrated pest control systems such as the use of resistant varieties, adoption of crop sanitation and agronomic methods of pest avoidance, biological methods of control and finally, the use of chemicals to the extent necessary. In the area of manuring, integrated nutrient supply systems are being developed which involve the appropriate use of organic manures, biological nitrogen fixation and chemical fertilisers. Watershed management in drv-farming areas involves the capture of excess rain water and storing it in farm ponds for later use for a life-saving and yield-increasing irrigation when the rainfall stops. Successful mixed farming, multiple cropping and aquaculture systems also involve a considerable understanding of recycling principles and of the principles of synergy and harmony among different components of a farming system. This has been dealt with in some detail in an earlier article (Swaminathan, 1973). Therefore, it has become imperative that we develop appropriate methods of techniracy. Some of the approaches which the Indian Council of Agricultural Research (ICAR) is promoting in the area of adult education are mentioned here.

KRISHI VIGYAN KENDRAS (FARM SCIENCE CENTRES)

The first *Krishi Vigyan Kendra* on the concept of learning by doing according to this pattern was established at Pondicherry under the guidance of the Tamil Nadu Agricultural University. The basic aims of these *kendras* are to (i) identify the felt needs of the rural population in the area to be served by the *kendra* in terms of specific training programmes which can help them to derive the maximum benefit from the agro-ecological assets of the area, (ii) design courses in such a manner that literacy is not a prerequisite for admission to the *kendra*, (iii) develop training programmes which would help the trainees to acquire a mastery over the relevant technology, (iv) restrict the admission in the initial stages to practising farmers and in-service personnel so that the training imparted is effectively used, and (v) develop the *kendra* in such a way that existing facilities belonging to either government or voluntary or other organisations are used in the most profitable manner. In other words, the aim is not to invest money and time on brick and mortar jobs but to get for the community the full benefits from investments already made and from the available technical manpower.

A weakness in our earlier training programmes designed to bring about a scientific upgrading of farming has been the lower priority accorded to the training of farm women. It needs hardly any emphasis that several of the key agricultural operations, both in the production and post-harvest phases, are in the hands of women. Their contribution to agricultural operations, is even higher in the hill regions and neglected areas. Several problems of health are now known to arise from the improper storage of basic staples leading to the development of food toxins in them. Therefore, under the *Krishi Vigyan Kendra* Programme, special emphasis is being placed on the development of *kendras* for rural women.

Any such new programme should be supported by an effective trainers' training arrangement, which can help to update the technological skill of the teacher and introduce him or her to the purpose and philosophy of the project. Appropriate institutions have hence been identified for undertaking trainers' training programmes in agriculture, horticulture, fisheries, animal husbandry, and land and water management. Plans are being prepared for the establishment of two women's trainers' training centres—one in central India and the other in the north-eastern Himalaya. The ultimate success of these *kendras* will depend upon a combination of factors, such as the technical skill and mental attitude of the teachers, the relevance of the fields of training chosen, and the availability of mobile training teams and mass media support which can enable the *kendra* to become a radiating centre for a techniracy drive.

OPERATIONAL RESEARCH PROJECTS

The Indian Council of Agricultural Research has initiated through our agricultural universities and research institutes, and in a few cases, bilateral agencies, a series of whole village watershed projects which are designed to bring about more efficient land and water use patterns based on principles of ecology and economics. An issue of the *Indian Farming* (1975) contains several articles which describe the purpose and design of these projects. Such projects will provide considerable opportunities for the education of both school children and adults. In several cases, *krishi vigyan kendras* and operational research projects will be linked. Whole village projects, such as the rural aquaculture projects and the integrated pest control projects in rice and cotton can be used to help school children to learn science through work experience and to introduce adults into the world of biological balance, harmony and synergy.

FUNCTIONAL LITERACY FOR RURAL PEOPLE, BASED ON THEIR OCCUPATIONAL INTERESTS AND NEEDS

The literacy courses for farmers in use in several states, both as a correspondence course and as a direct literacy course, are undergoing continuous refinement. Such courses should obviously be based not only on interests and needs of farmers, but should also be so designed that they are closely related to the cycle of agricultural operations, so that an incentive for farmers to continue is built into them. A recent example of an innovative approach in this area is the work done in Rajasthan to develop functional literacy courses on the basis of clearly identified bottlenecks and solutions to the improvement of agricutural production by small and marginal farmers. Similar courses need to be prepared specifically for the use of farm women.

BY-PASSING THE REGULAR LITERACY ROUTE

To the extent that the mass media can succeed in transmitting the necessary information and demonstrating the necessary skills for daily living and successful farming, the question of formal literacy can be by-passed. Radio and films are already being used for this purpose, but there is considerable scope for refining the techniques of communication and spreading the message wider. This implies that the technical programmes should be still more specific in both content and time, geared to needs and frequently repeated. Also, the imparting of knowledge and information has to be synchronised with the availability of the inputs essential for utilising the knowledge. For example, there is no point in recommending a new crop variety or a pesticide or fertiliser, if these are not available in the block or the village. There is therefore need for effective co-ordination between agencies supplying knowledge and inputs.

Fortunately, we now have the assistance of regular television as well as a Satellite Instructional Television Programme in several parts of our country. If this medium is used intelligently it could become a powerful tool for transmitting timely and proper advice to farmers. In the audio-visual world of the future, extended formal literacy may be necessary only for those who are interested in pursuing education to higher levels. This is also likely to be true in a different way for nations which are already advanced in technology, since books imparting knowledge tend to get out of date quickly. Hence, if we make the transition from the pre-literary to the post-literary world in adult education without passing through the conventional intermediate steps, enormous resources and time can be saved. Emphasis therefore needs to be given to the planned expansion and improvement of appropriate mass media.

Agricultural growth is an organic and dynamic one involving continuous interaction between man, animals, plants, soil, water and weather. Unless we tailor educational and development projects to suit the organic nature of growth in this sector, we shall be consistently faced with disappointments. Adult education programmes will have to take cognisance of this requirement of agriculture. Mental resilience and humility are needed both to absorb, continuously, new knowledge, and to modify approaches to the transmission of knowledge according to changed needs and circumstances.

REFERENCES

Anonymous, Not form but content, *Indian Journal of adult education*, Vol. XXXV-8, (1974).

Government of India, Ministry of Education and Social Welfare, Directorate of Adult Education, *An Inventory of the Central Government's Programme with Relevance for Youth Work*, New Delhi, (1974).

Indian Farming, August 1975.

Husain, Zakir, Sardar Patel Memorial Lectures, All India Radio, New Delhi, 1958.

Mesarovic, M.; E. Pestel, *Mankind at the turning point*, The Second Report to the Club of Rome, 1974.

Agricultural Production Efficiency, Washington : U.S. National Academy of Sciences (1975).

Roger, Revelle; V. Lakshminarayana, The Ganges water machine, *Science*, Vol. 188, No. 4188 (1975).

Swaminathan, M. S., Agricultural transformation and opportunities for a learning revolution, *Dr. Zakir Husain Memorial Lectures*, U.G.C., Delhi, (1970).

Swaminathan, M. S., Agricultural evolution, productive employment and rural prosperity, *Princess Leelavathi Memorial Lectures*, Mysore University (1972).

Swaminathan, M. S., Our agricultural future, *Sardar Patel Memorial Lectures*, All India Radio, New Delhi (1973).

NON-MONETARY INPUTS IN EDUCATION

Their Role in Improving Quality and Relevance

8

WHAT IS 'quality of education' and how can we improve it ? It is difficult to define the term 'quality' in relation to education or any other field of human endeavour without reference to the ethos and aspirations of the society which the system is to serve. It is, however, commonly agreed that the primary purpose of education is to enable students to read and write, to do a certain amount of arithmetic, to understand enough science and history to interpret the world around them, to develop the seeing eye and understanding and questioning heart and above all, to learn enough civics to be aware of the rights and responsibilities as citizens. Education, according to this concept, is not meant merely to adapt pupils to their society, but also to equip them to alter it. Education should be looked upon as a key input into development and it should not be regarded merely as a social service activity. Since education helps to impart relevant skills and the ability to innovate and adapt, it becomes an essential input for the optimum utilisation of natural resources. Education is the foundation for the development of science and technology. One could thus assess the quality of the educational system operating in a country with reference to its impact on the creation of good citizens who place equal emphasis on rights and responsibilities. Yet another criterion of quality could be the extent of sensitisation the education system is able to create in students to the problems of poverty and destitution. Another yardstick could be its impact on sustainable development based upon opportunities for gainful employment and an awareness of the need for protecting basic life support systems. Before considering what can be done to find remedies to some of the maladies afflicting the system, it would be necessary to refer, briefly to the dimensions of our current educational effort and the dimensions of the problems of poverty and unemployment which the educational system will have to help to tackle.

Present educational scene

Despite a network of over 6.5 lakhs schools and colleges, the employment of over 3 million teachers and an annual budget of the order of Rs 3000 crores, it has not been possible so far for the education system to achieve the goal of universal education of all children up to the age of 14 years, as enshrined in the constitutional directive. The total enrolment in elementary education has increased from 223 lakhs in classes I—VIII in 1950-51 to around 904 lakhs during 1979 to 1980. Nevertheless, for every three children enrolled in primary and middle schools, one other eligible child is left behind. Over 80 per cent of the children not enrolled so far are confined to a dozen states who have not been in a position to allocate the necessary resources to achieve the goal of universalisation according to the present system of elementary education.

There are also socially disadvantaged groups, such as the economically poor, women, migrant labour and farmers, scheduled castes and scheduled tribes, whose children are on the periphery of the schooling system. About 58 per cent of the scheduled caste children (40 per cent of the boys and 74 per cent of the girls) and 63 per cent of the scheduled tribe children (48 per cent of the boys and 76 per cent of the girls) are yet to receive elementary education. As revealed by the Fourth Educational Survey, the non-availability of schools is not a major constraint in this regard. Socio-economic compulsions in families, particularly in rural areas and among the weaker sections, and curricular programmes unrelated to the needs of real life seem to be some of the more important factors contributing to the slow progress. Even the existing facilities for elementary education are not optimally utilised : overaged and underaged children account for around 20 per cent of the enrolment and nearly 64 per cent of the children who are enrolled in Class I, drop out by the time they complete Class V. This represents economic loss in resource utilisation, and stratification of elite-poor distinctions, not to mention the long-term social loss of the individual child and the family on account of the incomplete development of the former's educational career.

In the area of secondary and higher education, facilities have been expanded during the last three decades. Nonetheless, the reforms for qualitative improvement and system reorganisation, as envisaged in the National Policy on Education (1968), are yet to be completed effectively. This is particularly so for the integration of practical aspects in the educational programmes and for planned growth of programmes directed towards gainful employment to be implemented in close co-operation with all the developmental agencies. Intersectoral linkages are yet to be brought about and co-ordination established between work places, schools and development activities for fostering appropriate manpower development programmes.

Employment

The expansion of educational facilities in the country over the past three decades is considerable. As a result of this, the number of educated persons entering the labour market is on the increase from year to year. According to an estimate made by the Planning Commission, there were 3.7 million educated unemployed in the beginning of 1980, a bulk of whom (about two-thirds were matriculates. Employment Exchange statistics, however, puts their number on the higher side. According to this source, the number of educated job-seekers (matriculates and above) registered with the Employment Exchanges was 7.30 million in December 1979 of whom 4.00 million were matriculates, 1.9 million higher secondary school leavers and intermediates, 1.3 million graduates and 0.1 million post-graduates. The Planning Commission has estimated that about 8.1 million economically active educated people would be added during the Sixth Plan period. If unemployment among the educated has to be removed, efforts are required to be made to take care of about 12 million to 15 million educated persons during the Sixth Plan. As the bulk of the educated are matriculates, they will require special attention. The educated women job-seekers who are about 16 per cent of the total educated job-seekers, also need special attention.

Poverty

The percentage of population estimated to be below the poverty line in the rural and urban areas of different states in the country is given below :

Percentage of population below the poverty line by states separately for rural and urban areas in 1977-78

State	Rural	Urban	Combined
Andhra Pradesh	43.89	35.68	42.18
Assam	52.65	37.37	51.10
Bihar	58.91	46.07	57.49
Gujarat	43.20	29.02	39.04
Haryana	23.25	31.74	24.84
Himachal Pradesh	28.12	16.56	27.23
Jammu & Kashmir	32.75	39.33	34.06
Karnataka	49.88	43.97	48.34
Kerala	46.00	51.44	46.95
Madhya Pradesh	59.82	48.09	57.73
Maharashtra	55.85	31.62	47.71
Manipur	30.54	25.48	29.71
Meghalaya	53.87	18.16	48.03
Nagaland	N.A.	4.11	N.A.
Orissa	68.97	42.19	66.40
Punjab	11.87	24.66	15.13
Rajasthan	33.75	33.80	33.76
Tamil Nadu	55.68	44.79	52.12
Tripura	64.28	26.34	59.73
Uttar Pradesh	50.23	49.24	50.09
West Bengal	58 94	34.71	52.54
All Union Territories	34.32	17.96	21.69
All India (Weighted)	50.82	38.19	48.13

Note : The above estimates are derived by using the poverty line of Rs 65 per capita per month in 1977-78 prices corresponding to minimum daily calorie requirement of 2100 calories per person in rural areas and the requirement of 2100 calories in urban areas.

These results are based on the provisional and quick tabulation of the National Sample Survey on household consumer expenditure of 32nd round (July 1977 to June 1978).

The difference between the aggregate all-India private consumption expenditure estimate by the Central Statistical Organisation in their National Accounts Statistics and that derived from the NSSO data has been pro rata adjusted among the different States and Union Territories in the absence of any information to allocate this difference among the States and Union Territories.

A perusal of the above data would show that in States, such as Punjab and Haryana, where there has been considerable progress in improving rural income through agricultural and allied activities, the incidence of poverty is less in rural areas as compared to urban areas. Eminent economists and social scientists are agreed that poor nations remain poor mainly because they tend to under-value the human resource and over-value land, energy, steel, cement and other such resources. The global trends in development after the World War II also indicate that it is only countries where the human resource has had the requisite determination and dedication which could convert calamities of unprecedented dimensions into opportunities for accelerated scocio-economic evolution. In the human resource development programme of the Sixth Plan now under preparation, emphasis has been laid on the economic emancipation of families living below the poverty line through greater opportunities for (i) self, salaried and age employment, with particular attention being paid to women, (ii) education of children, which will become possible only if they can be made free for attending the school, and (iii) the voluntary adoption of the small family norm. Thus, education, employment, development and population stabilisation constitute the four major pillars of the movement for quality of life improvement. If the educational system is to respond to this challenge, it is essential that we improve its relevance in relation to the pedagogic as well as social objectives so far mentioned. It is in this context that an indepth examination of the role of non-monetary inputs becomes essential. Among the non-monetary inputs, the following five major groups of factors are important :

(a) Political will and university autonomy;
(b) management;
(c) academic ethos;
(d) learning by doing; and
(e) problems of first generation learners.

Political will and university autonomy

Professional skill is no substitute for political will and only a proper blend of political will, professional skill and peoples' action can help us to solve the many complex problems facing us. The question of university autonomy has been discussed in many forms. It is not relevant here to repeat the many issues relating to the need for an appropriate political climate for the flowering of academic institutions. Without this first step, which does not involve any financial outlay but only the observance of certain ground rules with reference to educational institutions, it may not be possible to make progress, however large the financial resource endowments of an institution may be.

Management

Management holds the key to getting the best out of available resources. Good management will promote harmony, team work and an ultimate end-result which far exceeds the sum of the individual inputs. Good management also involves the development of proper communication systems among faculty members, among students and between faculty members and students. Unfortunately, this feed-back relationship between the teacher and the taught is getting clogged, partly because of the numerical expansion in classes and partly because of attitudinal postures. Invariably those who are called upon to administer educational institutions are selected for the assignment because of their academic accomplishments. Management may, however, require new skills and appropriate temperament. It is, therefore, essential that those who manage educational systems are enabled to acquire these new skills through appropriate training procedures. There is no such thing as teaching (as is commonly understood); but there is only learning since a good teacher also learns all the time through contact with the young minds. Once teachers as well as the managers of teaching institutions recognise the fact that life is one long learning process, the needed mental humility for continuous self-analysis and improvement could be generated. It is high time that we gave careful attention to the management aspects of educational system.

Academic ethos

We all do as we learn. The example set by elders often becomes the norm of behaviour for the young. Of late we find that genuine pleasure and pride in teaching is tending to go down, probably because society itself has not placed sufficient stress on according due recognition to good teachers. A good teacher is one who is able to inspire the students as much by non-verbal communication as through verbal means. This is not to underrate the importance of clear articulation of ideas and thought while presenting them to young minds. Equal stress however, should be placed on factors, such as punctuality, not missing any class unless it is owing to unavoidable circumstances, not undertaking, during term time, numerous other assignments such as examinerships, participation in symposia, national and international conferences, etc. Above all, particular importance should be attached to stimulating students to question the teacher. Unfavourable teacher-student ratios often make it difficult to establish the kind of personal rapport which is desirable. However, there are a variety of ways by which the general academic ethos could be raised to a level that makes a distinct impact on the value system of the student community.

Learning by doing

A common reason given for our inability to promote learning through work experience is the absence of adequate facilities in educational institutions for vocational training. Mechanical work given in the educational institution in the name of vocationalisation is unlikely to kindle the learning spirit. In fact, such exercises degenerate into routine procedural requirements and thereby lose their educational value. The practical aspects should be emphasised. For example, the study of birds and flowers, identification of weeds, the detection of alkalinity, the harvesting of rainwater, and the prevention of damage by rats and pests both in the field and in the store rooms, would all have immense educational and practical value. The equipment needed for such studies is simple and inexpensive and requires mostly only a well-informed teacher, who does not curb the questioning mind and is not afraid of long walks.

Problems of first generation learners

The composition of the student population in our universities is fortunately shifting to a direction when more and more boys and girls, whose parents have not had the advantage of formal literacy, are joining institutions of higher learning. However, our system has never seriously tried to analyse and understand

and this process of recombination followed by segregation generates wide variability. Thus, in practice except for identical twins, no two individuals are exactly similar. Mutation, or heritable change, adds to the capacity to respond to changing selection pressures.

Another remarkable property of genes is the system of vertical and horizontal co-ordination to which they subject themselves. Thus, each gene performs its specific function and is able to replicate itself, to change and to work co-operatively and sometimes competitively with other genes. Integration of vertical and horizontal co-ordination has invested the heredity system with precision and power. If only everyone of us was aware of the way in which our own bodies function and applied the lessons learnt from it in our daily life, we might be more successful in achieving what individually and collectively we wish to accomplish.

What is it that we want to accomplish? In my view, the most important task to draw the greatest benefit from our existing human resource and to limit its further unplanned growth. Past experience suggests that human resource cannot be effectively used by traditional approaches to 'creating jobs', which often tend to degenerate into doles. What is needed is the growth of employment policies from an overall strategy of resource utilisation designed to convert sunlight, soil, water, mineral, plant, animal and other resources into wealth, meaningful to people. Instead of devoting undue attention to brains drained to other countries, we should pay serious attention to the utilisation of brains within the country. The starting point is, obviously, the village, which is where both untapped assets and native brains exist.

Eighty per cent of our population now live in rural areas. Some experts have calculated that this percentage will be 71 in A.D. 2000. Even if the percentage goes down, the rural population is expected to grow in number from 441 million in 1971 to 662 million by A.D. 2000. Of the existing rural population, nearly 50 per cent is believed to suffer from poverty. Rapid rural development based on the scientific utilisation of all our resources, both natural and human is, therefore, a must.

It is worth noting, that countries which have gone too far on the road of urbanisation are now repenting this choice.

Rapid urbanisation has generated a steep rise in the consumption of non-renewable forms of energy. For example, the transport needs of large cities have grown so vast that the number of motor vehicles in the world increased by 120 million during the 1960s, generating problems of atmospheric pollution and human temper. There is, today, a marked movement back to the countryside, but with the integration of some of the basic benefits of urban life with rural living. A planned re-clustering of jobs, services and amenities more widely throughout the country, in accordance with the agro-ecological potential and socio-economic needs of each area, will facilitate this movement.

RURAL-URBAN RELATIONSHIPS

Education in the past, particularly at the university level, unfortunately tended to promote the concept that rural jobs, which were mostly related to agriculture, required only brawn and not brain. The exodus of the educated caused neglect of the hinterland. Yet we now know that unless life in a rural community is made tolerable for all, the problem of poverty not only cannot be solved, but will get progressively worse. Therefore, a national policy of scientific rural-urban development as an integrated package is essential.

So far, we have generally tended to pay only lip service to the cause of rural development. People living in cities talk about the freshness and beauty of nature but would not like to go and enjoy them even after retirement. Similarly, public policies have tended to promote an interest in urban living. For example, today if a scientist or a public servant moves from a class 'A' city to a smaller place, he loses in his total emoluments. It is only in the case of the Defence Services that the principle of serving all parts of the country has been developed with appropriate provisions for non-family postings. Recently, the Indian Council of Agricultural Research has introduced the concept of compulsory service for a specific period in a tribal or neglected area by all members of the Agricultural Research Service. Compulsion alone cannot yield the desired results. What is important is to incorporate, in personnel policies, appropriate provisions for the education of children and for medical facilities to enable qualified scientists and technologists to work in areas where these facilities do not yet exist.

RURAL ASSETS AND LIABILIIIES

An important task for us is to review our rural assets and liabilities and the present state of the art of harnessing science to improve rural economy and living. On the basis of such a review, certain broad guidelines can be developed for using the tools of science to enhance the assets of rural life.

Though our assets are well-known, it is worth repeating them because they are so impressive (Swaminathan 1973). First, we have the second largest human population in the world, most of whom are young. Although a considerable proportion of the adult population is classified as illiterate in the formal sense, they have shown a great capacity to absorb, adapt and benefit from modern technology. There are abundant recent examples to justify this statement. The doubling of wheat production within a span of five years, the progress made in improving rice and wheat production in areas where they were unimportant before, the spread of maize, formerly regarded as a *kharif* crop, in the *rabi* season along the Indo-Gangetic plains, the spurt in long staple cotton production, the availability of apples everywhere in the country, the progress in the production of potato, tapioca and other tubers, the development of low-cost ground water exploitation technology such as bamboo tubewells, the spread of *gobar* gas plants, and the growing diversification of export products from the rural sector are all indices of rural capability. Striking changes are visible in several parts of our country in farming systems, and animal husbandry is beginning get more efficient. Our farmers have thus shown their readiness to adopt new technology provided it is economically viable and low risk in character and if appropriate packages of services and public policies help to ensure a reasonable return for their labour and investment.

Our animal wealth is also vast. We have over 16 per cent of the world's cattle population, 45 per cent of the buffalo population, over 69 million goats representing the largest population in the world, over 43 million sheep occupying the sixth position in the world, and rich populations of poultry and inland and coastal fisheries. We are also endowed with excellent wild life resources. Our soils are by and large robust and productive, although in some areas lack of care has led to considerable erosion and the development of salinity, alkalinity and other problems. Shifting cultivation is still the major source of living for nearly two million people in the north-eastern Himalayan region. This method of handling the soil was developed hundreds of years ago as the only then available answer to the law of the diminishing return from the soil. There is however no place for it now.

Our water resources are vast and varied, and the National Commission on Agriculture has calculated that the area under irrigation can almost be doubled during the next 25 years from the present 42 million hectares (in 1976). In the gross sown area of about 164 million hectares, regions with high (1150 mm and above), medium (750 to 1150 mm) and low (less than 750 mm) rainfall occur in almost equal proportion. Thus, over 45 per cent of the net sown area in the country has a reasonably assured water supply. Even in the arid zone of Rajasthan fortunately, there is a good underground water reserve. The water quality is by and large, good although there are areas where the groundwater is saline. An integrated strategy for the utilisation of ground and surface water and for harvesting all rain water in each ecological and topographic area will help to transform our agriculture and rural economy.

The high priority accorded to irrigation, command area development and groundwater exploitation in the Fifth Plan should help to make our agriculture self-reliant and provide considerable resilience in crop planning. If we consider only light duration (energy), water availability and temperature, which are three of the major factors regulating crop production potential, the period of maximum insolation in the tropics and sub-tropics unfortunately coincides with low availability of water and high temperature, the latter would lead to high evapo-transpiration and consequently greater demand for water. In the absence of irrigation, water becomes the chief limiting factor in crop productivity. Thus, the period of potential maximum yield unfortunately becomes in reality a period of minimum productivity. In contrast, in the temperate zone the period of maximum day length fortunately coincides with periods of precipitation and temperatures conducive to growth (see table). The high and stable yields obtained with irrigation during *boro* and summer seasons in our country with several crops have fortunately focussed attention on this problem.

Estimated yield potential and per cent achieved in four rice-growing countries*

Country	Approximate duration of effective grain-filling period (days)	Average sunlight (cal. cm^{-2} day^{-1})	Estimated yield potential	Average yield** (t/ha)
Spain	35	500	17.9	6.27
Australia	35	600	21.1	6.25
Japan	35	350	12.1	6.02
India (*kharif*)	25	300	7.3	1.85
(Andhra Pradesh) (*rabi*)	25	500	13.4	2.20

* Efficiency for solar energy utilisation is assumed to be 2.5 per cent.

** FAO Production Yearbook 1973.

Our plant resources are vast and we have nearly 20,000 plant species, a greater number than in countries with a much larger geographical area. This is yet another index of the varied agro-climatic conditions prevalent in our country which offer scope for a wide range of plant species to thrive.

Thus, if one draws an agricultural balance-sheet purely in quantitative terms, our assets are great. It is an irony, therefore, that we should still find it difficult to provide for the basic minimal needs of our population and that we should face problems of unemployment and underemployment both in rural and in urban areas. Since the population-food supply equation and the population-employment equation are equally important and interdependent, it would be worthwhile to dwell briefly on certain scientific aspects of these two equations.

FOOD REQUIREMENTS

According to the estimates of the National Commission on Agriculture, our population by 1981 may be about 668 million.

district of Visakhapatnam. The yields in this district were formerly poor, but by a correct varietal choice such as the variety Co. 997, and by extending the needed help to growers through co-operative societies which run all the sugarcane factories in the district, there has been a steady increase in sugar production. Similar co-operative endeavour in the supply of disease-free planting material, scientific nursery and planting practices, and pest management will have an immediate beneficial effect on sugarcane yield in Uttar Pradesh and Bihar.

SCIENTIFIC DISCOVERY, PRODUCTION ADVANCE AND PROSPERITY IMPROVEMENT

A few basic steps are needed if we want to convert the scientific breakthrough now taking place in most crops, farm animals and in inland and coastal aquaculture into increased production and increased production into improved prosperity for all sections of the rural community. First, all groups must accept the concept of productivity. For this purpose, minimum productivity targets will have to be fixed and a farmer who does not achieve the target continuously for a few years without valid reasons should stand every chance of losing his land. Minimum targets such as three tonnes per hectare per year from two crops on irrigated land and one tonne per hectare per year in areas with over 1000 mm rainfall are neither ambitious nor unrealistic if proper institutional arrangements are made for supporting farmers. Appropriate Agricultural Productivity Acts by our state governments could provide the social compulsion for co-operative efforts in areas, such as soil and moisture conservation and pest control. As an ingredient of such legislation, consideration deserves to be given to minimum limits to operational land holdings, below which the holding should not be fragmented as a unit of management, whatever be the ownership pattern.

The second need is to match the obligations of farmers under Agricultural Productivity Regulations with corresponding obligations on the part of state governments. For this purpose, the *gram sabhas* or *panchayats* may have to be restructured in such a manner that every member of the *panchayat* assumes specific responsibility to organise the social support necessary for the effective adoption of a technological innovation. Unless there is a link between those who move society and those who move science and technology, it will be difficult to achieve the ends we desire. Every prospering experiment in our country in rural transformation owes its impact to a combination of these two factors.

Unlike in industry, no depreciation can be allowed on the basic assets of agriculture. The land-man ratio has already reached critical limits in several parts of our country. The history of agricultural progress of the past century has shown that in many countries productivity has continuously risen through scientific farming without any harm to the long-term production potential of the soil. As productivity increases, the area under a specific crop can go down and more land could become available for energy plantations and silvi-pastoral systems, which are essential for meeting rural fuel and feed needs. In a few states, such as Karnataka, there is evidence that total production is going up in a few major crops side by side with a reduction in area. This trend should become national.

Need for accelerated research

The emphasis so far has been on the institutional and policy packages needed for increasing the feasibility and efficiency of adoption of new technology in our villages. This does not mean that all that needs to be done on the scientific front has been stated. On the contrary, every change produces several reactions, some favourable and some adverse. Scientific vigilance and vision will be needed to maximise the beneficial effects and minimise the negative consequences of new technology. Reference has already been made to the undesirable association between a high-yield environment for plants and a corresponding favourable atmosphere for pests. Unscientific multiple cropping and monoculture of the same genetic strain of a crop over large and contiguous areas compound the problems of pests, which are even otherwise serious in the tropics and sub-tropics. Not only annual crops but perennial crops such as citrus, mango, coconut and sandal wood are affected by serious disease problems which are still evading solution. Besides pest management, it would be useful to discuss a few more obvious areas where research work needs to be stepped up speedily.

Inventory of natural resources

Of the highest priority is more intensive work on the preparation of an integrated inventory of land, water, mineral and other natural resources, area by area, and the development of scientific land and water use plans. Such an inventory should indicate the steps needed to reclaim large areas now stricken by salinity, alkalinity and acidity, as well as to conserve water, soil fertility and germ plasm of plants and animals.

The effect of weather on crops and animal productivity

A more careful examination of weather in relation to crop and animal productivity is necessary. Fortunately, close coordination has of late been developed between meteorologists and agricultural research and extension workers. Day-to-day decisions by farmers require the correct interpretation of short-range weather outlook. We have a good mass-media network and we can easily develop the capability to convey accurate and timely advice to farmers. Meanwhile, research on soil-crop-weather correlations, weather modification, hail dispersal and efficient forms of utilising dew should go on.

Conversion of cultural energy into digestible energy

A critical study must be made of the efficiency of conversion of cultural energy (i.e. all forms of energy introduced by man after he domesticated plants and animals) into digestible energy. The most important components of cultural energy are implements and farm power, water and nutrients, particularly fertiliser. In the technology developed so far in the affluent countries, the ratio of conversion of cultural energy into digestible energy became less coincident with an increase in productivity. For example, Pimental and co-workers in an article (1975) point out that by the use of U.S. agricultural technology to feed a world population of 4 billion a high-protein calorie diet for one year would require the equivalent of 5000 billion litres of fuel. If petroleum were the only source of energy for food production and if we used all petroleum resources solely to produce food the estimated reserve of 66053 billion litres would last a mere 13 years.

The challenge, therefore, lies in developing techniques which will help to improve productivity continuously without a concurrent loss in the efficiency of conversion of cultural energy. This will need a stepping up of research on tillage, water use, integrated nutrient supply and recycling of recoverable sources of energy. Also, this needs support from well-defined public policies. For example, the conservation and use of all organic wastes would need the introduction of a rural fuel supply policy based on a combination of steps, such as raising energy plantations, organisation of community biogas plants, supply of coal or lignite at subsidised prices, and supply of electricity and other forms of energy at reasonable rates.

Control of pests, diseases and weeds

As mentioned already, research relating to the control of the menace posed to crops through the triple alliance of pests, diseases and weeds must be stepped up. It is obvious that for the foreseeable future chemical pesticides will continue to be used. For applying them with due care and caution, surveillance and early warning systems need to be developed more extensively, which will facilitate the timely application of the minimum quantity of pesticide needed. Simultaneously, work on genetic resistance through screening at hot-spot locations and through collaboration with international agricultural research centres needs to be intensified. Diverse genes for resistance will have to be identified since biotypes occur in many serious pathogens and insect pests, leading to the breakdown of host resistance.

Efficient use of solar energy

All aspects of production physiology aiming at the improved utilisation of solar energy and reduction of photo-respiratory losses by genetic or chemical means will have to receive greater attention.

Fixation of biological nitrogen

The whole area of biological nitrogen fixation both by symbiotic and non-symbiotic mechanisms requires more attention. Nitrogen fixation research and development centres might well be established at state level jointly by agricultural universities and state departments of agriculture. Here, collections of nitrogen-fixing micro-organisms, both symbiotic and free-living, could be maintained. Such centres could distribute pure cultures of recommended strains for further multiplication and also administer quality control programmes. Since considerable basic work involving sophisticated instruments is also needed, the establishment of a national nitrogen fixation research centre supported by all the major scientific agencies might be desirable.

Optimum fertiliser use

We need more work on fertiliser technology in order to prevent the loss of fertiliser taking place during the *kharif* season through leaching. Some work has been done on reducing losses through blending nitrogenous fertilisers, such as urea with neem and other oil cakes and by using shellac-coated urea and sulphur-coated urea. What we need is a low-cost method involving locally available material which could simultaneously help us to reduce leaching losses and provide the needed micronutrients. Fertiliser technologists should concentrate on local problems and local solutions. Fertiliser is the most effective as well as most expensive input, and our requirement will grow not only for crop production, but also for animal and fish production. A national grid of small, medium and large fertiliser plants and compost units and an expanded soil testing service will hence be needed for sustaining agricultural advancement. Since data on the fertiliser needed for specific yield targets are becoming available for major crops, fertiliser could be used as an effective trigger in any national policy of stabilising food production.

Development and exploitation of forest wealth

All aspects of forestry research, including the development of quick-yielding fuel and pulp trees, such as annual strains of bamboo, need more intensive attention.

Improvement in the breeding of farm animals and in fish culture

Finally, increasing the production of domestic animals, poultry and fish by breeding, reduction of infertility, better nutrition and health care requires much closer study. The exploitation of hybrid vigour in cattle and fish deserves more attention.

Disease problems of new genetic strains of cattle and sheep, and the harnessing of non-conventional sources of feed, particularly call for more scientific work. Recent research on fish culture in both inland and coastal waters has opened up new vistas of production. This will have to be supported by vastly expanded research on fish diseases and nutrition.

Genetic engineering

As for the future, genetic engineering involving the transfer of genes from one species to another is being increasingly regarded as a potential tool for achieving re-combination of favourable genes. Basic research in this area requires expensive facilities. A recent symposium on basic research as relevant to agriculture, organised by the Indian National Science Academy has stressed the advisability of creating such facilities.

Post-harvest technology

A serious lacuna in our present research and developmental efforts is the inadequate attention to problems of post-harvest technology. An uneven match between production and post-harvest technology has resulted from our relative neglect of the latter. Even in areas where rice is cultivated with improved varieties and fertiliser, the harvested crop has to be dried by small farmers most of the time on paved roads. The high moisture content of grains at the time of harvest and inadequate drying prior to storage, particularly during the *kharif* season, are resulting in increasing problems of food toxins. Studies by scientists of the Central Food Technological Research Institute at the Gurupur village in coastal Karnataka revealed a heavy fungal growth and high levels of aflatoxin in rice consumed by the population. Hepatitis outbreaks due to toxins in food have been reported by scientists (1975) of the National Institute of Nutrition. Thus, appropriate post-harvest technology is essential both for the farmer to get the maximum return for his labour and investment and the consumer to get food of good quality.

POPULATION GROWTH AND OPPORTUNITIES FOR GAINFUL EMPLOYMENT

The population-employment equation, will assume even greater importance in the coming years than the population-food supply equation. The obvious first step is a vast intensification of our research and developmental efforts in the area of population stabilisation. Recently opened areas of research, such as vaccination against fertility, male contraceptives and immunisation with specific placental proteins, need to be extended full support. The cultivation of improved strains of plants containing certain steroids is now part of our strategy for reducing the cost of oral contraceptives.

The Bhagwati Committee had estimated that total employment opportunities of the order of 22.52 million man-years would have to be created in rural areas in 1969, if full-time employment was to be provided to all the available labour force. Other calculations have shown that at least 10 million man-years of employment need to be provided immediately in the rural areas. If we measure unemployment by the criterion of productivity per person-day, the figure becomes very high, as several economists have pointed out. Ultimately, it is only productivity per person-day that can provide the basis for true prosperity. Thus, rural employment, productivity and prosperity are all interdependent. Nutrition, in turn, is related to this triangle.

The National Commission on Agriculture has calculated that to generate full employment, at least 30 per cent of the rural labour force may have to be employed in the non-agricultural rural sector, including processing, textiles and other village industries. The Commission has hence suggested both agricultural and non-agricultural programmes for generating the needed number of jobs. Rapid generation of non-agricultural, though agro-based, sources of employment is also essential if a minimum limit to operational holdings is to be introduced.

Among non-agricultural occupations in the rural sector, the development of infrastructure such as roads, housing, irrigation works, electrification and agro-service centres, has been important in the past. As agriculture advances, marketing trade, processing, storage, distribution and transportation will demand more labour as has already been observed in north-west India, where the rice-wheat rotation and mixed farming practices are making substantial progress. There has been much talk of the growth of village and small-scale industries and the planned allocation of labour-intensive industries to rural areas, but in practice it has been difficult to make such projects viable. The non-availability of improved management and marketing techniques has rendered sustained progress difficult. Thus, wherever sericulture or honey production or any other such occupation makes progress in a village, marketing problems soon become overwhelming and farmers are unable to sustain their interest in the new vocation. There are, of course, outstanding exceptions to this trend and these are usually associated with either well-organised cooperatives or exceptional selfless individuals who command the respect of the rural society and are able to organise the entire production system efficiently. Considering the fact that about 75 million people may have to be employed in the non-agricultural sector during the next two decades, we need to pay urgent attention to the development of self-replicating models of rural growth. All the calculations mentioned here take it for granted that children need not look for jobs and that they can be spared for schooling. Today, child and woman labour, much of it unpaid, constitutes a dominant component of the rural work force. While steps have been taken to ensure that women and men get equal wages, only economic progress can result in the child being freed for school.

Steps have been taken recently through the establishment of rural banks to channel more credit to rural areas. Similarly, rural agro-industrial complexes are being developed. In addition to the various pilot employment schemes in the central government, different state governments have initiated programmes to meet the objective of full employment. Thus, Maharashtra is operating an employment guarantee scheme and Gujarat a 'right to work' project. Other projects include the labour-cum-development banks of Kerala, organisation of a land army in Karnataka and mobilisation of labourers in the Rajasthan Canal Project area. The small farmers, marginal farmers and agricultural labourers development agencies aim to generate more opportunities for self-employment through a diversified farming structure. A weakness of some of these programmes is the lack of detailed scientific attention to resource use. Little benefit has generally been derived from the data available from different surveys including the recent rural engineering surveys. Scientists, technologists, educationists and rural communities have not been involved in an organised manner in such exercises. In the Maharashtra employment guarantee scheme, a nutritional dimension has been incorporated and this process of integrating scientific approaches with human resource use needs to be fostered.

EDUCATION FOR RURAL DEVELOPMENT

The ultimate success in achieving balanced rural-urban growth will depend much upon the nature of our educational system and its integration with other developmental inputs. Different countries have approached this problem in different ways and case studies from several countries compiled for the World Bank generally indicate that the greatest success by any criteria has been achieved where there is a clear and overpowering national ideology and strong leadership committed to this ideology. Also, success has been assured where education, formal or non-normal, has been developed as an ingredient in a package where economic initiatives are central. Two other points emerge :

1. Women as a group have been almost universally neglected, and so too the landless, since most of the agriculture-based education programmes benefit only those with ability to farm land.

2. The danger of internal stratification developing between formal education is very great. This could further strengthen undesirable urban-rural, elite-masses and educated-illiterate dichotomies.

Our country has been a leader in many areas of educational thought and endeavour. What are our assets? We have (i) a huge and by and large well-organised infrastructure of formal education which can be reoriented to new needs and objectives, (ii) a large reserve of educated manpower, especially at the high levels, though insufficient at the middle levels, and (iii) well-developed mass media which can be geared to educational purposes. Our major liability is that the imperial legacy has tended to withstand too well the encroachments of innovation.

In 1947 it was generally assumed that quantitative expansion of the formal system of education at all levels, with suitable diversification, and qualitative improvement would be sufficient to take care of the needs of both economic development and social transformation. A radical change of consciousness is today evident for it is now recognised that the vast mass of human beings outside the formal system of education constitutes and will continue to constitute the majority of our citizens for a considerable time to come. As a result, non-formal education is now seen as the major task for the future. The new role for formal education in this larger context will be to underpin, support and contribute to the development of non-formal education in a variety of ways. The blend of both approaches will depend upon local needs.

Our attempt to equalise educational opportunities for children of all strata of society has also not been fully successful. While incentives such as midday meals have been of some help, the main tool for equalisation has been the scholarship schemes. A drawback of these schemes is that the child who has dropped out is not considered, while selection by tests tends to leave out the very persons whom it should help. Unfortunately, culture-free tests to evaluate natural abilities by unconventional approaches in villages and urban slums are yet to be devised. We could enrich science with unusual talent and skills with effective talent-scouting.

Vocationalisation as a response to unemployment

The assumption behind vocational education has been that it will equip a person with certain technical knowledge and skills to enable him to make a livelihood through a vocation. The absence of a close linkage between the available avenues of employment on the one hand and the training on the other has invalidated this approach. For example, though agriculture, forestry and fisheries account for the employment of over 80 per cent of the labour force, the fewest number of vocational courses are available in these areas. There is a shortage of teachers who can effectively teach these subjects even if courses were offered, and there has been no serious effort to train teachers on a large scale in these skills. Agro-industries too have been neglected.

Another lacuna is training for self-employment. Very few courses are offered in the skills needed for self-employment on a small or medium scale at the middle levels of education. Only recently, the Indian Council of Agricultural Research has started establishing *krishi vigyan kendras* which will cater to the needs of practising farmers and fishermen. Nearly all non-formal educational programmes for women undertaken by welfare agencies in the last twenty-five years have concentrated on teaching skills like sewing, embroidery and tailoring. Women tailors however are notoriously few. More recently, non-formal education programmes for women have emphasised home-based skills related to health, nutrition, child care and kitchen gardening. Schemes for training women in skills related to agriculture, forestry and fisheries are still few, despite the fact that 50 per cent of the agricultural labour force are women, and 80 per cent of all women in employment are engaged in the production and post-harvest aspects of agriculture.

Expansion of higher and professional education

The pattern of higher education and professional training in the past has evolved from colonial models on the assumption that quantitative expansion and high 'quality' ('quality' being measured according to hypothetical 'world' standards rather than in relation to national needs or objectives) would automatically take care of our scientific manpower needs. It is now recognised that the 'brain drain' is in part an outcome of a lack of correlation between the type of specialised education offered and the types of employment available. In retrospect, it appears as though unconsciously we have trained our scientific manpower to meet the requirements of western industry, science, technology and society. That 'content' is an important ingredient in 'quality' is now being realised. The recent committee on the restructuring of medical education has made a breakthrough in the subject by beginning from the needs and goals of the country for medical care and analysing the ingredients of a medical education suited to meet them. Similar exercises are needed in other areas. Agricultural education has generally tended to remain close to the field. Such nearness to field problems has a pay-off in research, as is evident from the fact that we are the first nation to cultivate hybrid cotton on a commercial scale, using labour-intensive technologies. Agricultural universities which have not yet done so should develop experimental and demonstration farms which will inspire farmers and serve as windows into our agricultural future.

Social responsibility of science

Though lip service is often paid to the ideals of social commitment, our system of selection, training and evaluation of scientific personnel at all levels, or of the teaching profession, does not provide for it. For instance, selection and later promotion are mainly based on academic records and attainments and publication of papers. Job requirements rarely include such elements as participation in developmental activities. These could take a variety of forms, ranging from the writing of textbooks and preparation of kits, toys, games and educational materials to participation in mass media programmes, demonstration and extension campaigns for the papularisation of science, and work in teacher training and lower-level education and training programmes. Such elements could be built into the system if the relevant activities with 'social' value that a scientist could legitimately engage in were spelt out.

Criteria for a suitable infrastructure to relate science and education to rural development

We should, now, take a look at the directions in which the existing institutional and educational institutions need to move to become a force for the regeneration of our rural economy and life. A satisfactory system should incorporate the following:

1. Steps should be taken to enable the formal education system and all scientific laboratories to become instruments which can further the non-formal education of the masses. Ways can be found, but the first essential is that institutions accept the servicing of the non-formal sectors as one of their basic objectives.

2. It is necessary to encourage group effort and group development in contrast to the attempt to lift individuals from one level to another. Acharya Vinoba Bhave's concept of simultaneously fostering a spirit of cooperation and competition among students by making a 'group of students compete with their own past' has to be translated into curricular and extra-curricular procedures.

3. Vocational education and training should be related to

the job requirements of the present and the future through intensive local studies.

4. The goals of professional education at all levels—from paraprofessional through middle level to high level specialists—in terms of the objectives and needs of our country should be clearly enunciated.

5. The social responsibilities of scientists (in both research and education) and of academics in all disciplines in concrete terms of job requirements should be specified. People should be enabled to understand and fulfil their responsibilities to development through professional contributions and not merely by being associated in their leisure time with political, social welfare or educational organisations.

With these as guiding principles, the necessary mechanism o get the system moving may be briefly indicated.

1. Every institution of higher education (including univer-ity departments, colleges, research and training institutions, unior colleges and schools) should incorporate some form of evelopment activity into their regular teaching-learning pro-rammes. This could take the form of placements of students 1 projects as part of their field practical work, or as apprentices; ivolvement of the staff or the institution itself in 'action or perational research, and other possible studies. Such participa-on should be a condition for the receipt of financial assistance rom the Government. This involvement should not be thought f merely in terms of 'adopting a village', holiday work camps nd other sporadic activities, or different forms of 'Sunday ocial work' but should be a part and parcel of the regular rogramme of work and be regularly budgeted for. As an xample of what can be done, the ICAR had submitted to vice-hancellors of our universities a programme for student and aculty involvement in rodent and pest management, control of ioxious weeds like 'carrot grass', and tree planting. The res-ponse has so far not been encouraging, except from a few gricultural universities.

2. Projects taken up will have to be extremely localised in haracter so that in each case it would be possible to have some ind of co-ordination between the various agencies concerned.

3. Grant-giving agencies and government departments inding scholarship schemes should introduce more group

awards as recognition of contributions of interdisciplinary groups to society in any walk of life, and group scholarships to enable institutions to strengthen themselves and provide better education and services to a whole community.

4. Academies and research organisations should start honouring those who have done good work under difficult circumstances; for example in tribal and neglected areas.

5. Curriculum planning at high school level should incorporate a period of field work placement as an integral part of the course for both academic and non-academic streams. Several ways are possible, including :

(a) Employment for specific period in an appropriate development project in the area.
(b) Survey or field study.
(c) Apprenticeship in a working agency.

These may sound fairly small steps to be taken now. However, the task is enormous and requires intensive work in localised studies, planning, working out of details, field surveys, co-ordination of a number of agencies, and learning new ways of working together. The involvement of students in the planning exercise is vital, as unless they are convinced of the utility of such an approach for their future, the attempts are unlikely to prove successful. Yet, movements in this direction seem pitifully small in comparison to the magnitude of the effort needed.

SPREADING THE INNOVATIVE PROCEDURES

All over our country, there are hundreds of little programmes pursuing innovative approaches. We are not short of ideas or the men to carry them out. But to transform these myriad efforts into part of an organised plan and to involve the entire academic community in this effort is the task before us now. It is a task of an order of magnitude which is probably unprecedented in the history of our education or scientific endeavour. Time is short. We may have forestalled the prophets of doom who predicted a future of starvation for our country, but shall we be content to drag the spectacle of our misery into the next generation? How much longer shall we drift, making valiant unco-ordinated individual efforts here and there to hold back disaster but seemingly unable to gear up the total organism to the challenge? This is the question to which the scientific community must address itself.

We need to fully exploit our human ability to create rational patterns of collective activity. Such patterns will continue to be coloured by personalities, but the basic structure should lend itself to replication, like the DNA molecule. It is easy to state this principle but the pathways of achieving it are by no means within easy reach, since they encompass our entire working culture. Nevertheless, we should begin by applying ourselves to the question of the basic common requirements that would enable us to move in the right direction and evolving the appropriate legislation that would serve as a framework for action. Legislative measures for integrated rural and urban development designed to promote the symbiotic growth of the village and the city can take into consideration the following needs :

(a) The setting up of scientific and administrative consortia for each block and town which can help to develop and implement ecologically sound rural works and urban growth programmes (in the scientific consortium, all scientific and technical institutions in the area as well as colleges and schools should be involved, and in the administrative consortium appropriate representatives of all rural community, industry and input supply agencies will have to be members);
(b) minimum limits for land productivity and operational holdings for irrigated and unirrigated land in each area to provide the social compulsion for cooperative endeavour and proper use of land;
(c) reservation of specific industries, credit and energy for the rural sector;
(d) an employment guarantee scheme as an integral part of an overall resource utilisation strategy;
(e) reservation of unproductive land for non-agricultural use, such as brick-making, construction of buildings, etc. and banning the use of good soil for such purposes;
(f) a rural drinking water and fuel supply policy;

(g) a scientific plant-animal-man food-chain policy for each agro-ecological area based on long-term considerations of the fertiliser, feed, water and land requirements of each production system;
(h) soil and water conservation and tree plantation; and
(i) an integrated formal and non-formal educational system involving participation by students and teachers in appropriate rural or urban development programmes.

A beginning towards providing ecological guidelines for development has been made through the Water (Prevention and Control of Pollution) Act of 1974. Comprehensive legislation for integrated rural-urban development will be a continuation of this process. However, we should also guard against the tendency to feel that once a law has been enacted all that is necessary has been done. Good administration and implementation of policies alone can make the legislation worthwhile. Our collective future depends on how fast we act to bridge the gap between theory and practice.

REFERENCES

The National Institute of Nutrition, *Proceedings of the Nutrition Society of India*, 12, (1975).
Pimental, David; John Krummel and John Kutzmann, Energy and land constraints in food protein production, *Science* 190, (1975), pp. 754-61.
Swaminathan, M.S., *Our Agricultural Future*, Sardar Patel Memorial Lectures, New Delhi (1973).

EMERGING AGRICULTURAL DEVELOPMENT STRATEGY 10

THE LARGEST number of those going to bed hungry live in Asia. Hence the results of a review of the agricultural situation in the Asian and Pacific region carried out at the Regional Conference of the Food and Agricultural Organisation (FAO) held in New Delhi in March, 1980 are of interest. One of the items discussed was the agricultural scenario towards A.D. 2000. The major points during this meeting were:

During the 1970s there has been a deterioration in the food situation in several countries in this region. To arrest the adverse trend in food-population equation, cereal production would have to grow at 3.5 per cent per annum during 1980-90 as compared to the historical rate of 2.8 per cent.

The greatest opportunity for increasing production immediately occurs in the case of rice. To take advantage of the untapped production potential in rice, both irrigated rice and rain-fed rice will have to receive equal attention.

Since the export unit value per hectare of some of the crops, such as cocoa, coffee, tobacco and sugar are much higher than the import unit value per hectare of cereal crops, the allocation of resources between the production of food crops for home consumption and production of non-food crops for export assumes importance.

There is need for a higher growth rate in livestock production in order to assist small and marginal farmers to secure a better and more stable income.

Since an improved quality of life has to be achieved without adding to the already formidable problem of unemployment, labour diversification and not displacement should be the end-result of technological advances.

To achieve all this FAO has concluded that there is need to double the investment in the farm sector. For example, it has been estimated that the total annual investment in the agriculture sector will have to increase from about 22.1 billion US dollars in 1980 to about 40.9 billion dollars by A.D. 2000. The major components of investment for crop production are: land development, irrigation and water management, soil and water conservation, flood control, afforestation, horticulture and farm machinery. There was also stress at the conference on the establishment of strong national food security systems. India's efforts in building up grain reserves were commended in this context.

The lessons from this discussion are obvious for a country such as India. First, agricultural growth rate should be stepped up both to feed the fast-growing population and to take advantage of the expanding opportunities for trade in agricultural commodities. Second, accelerating growth rate in production alone will not be enough. It is equally important that consumption is stimulated by improving the purchasing power of the rural and urban poor. In order to inject more purchasing power among the low income households, there is need for social security measures on the one hand and generation of opportunities for gainful employment on the other. Social security in affluent nations has been the result of economic advance. In contrast, in poor nations social security measures in the areas of employment, nutrition, clean drinking water supply, health care and housing should be so designed that they become instruments of economic growth. We, therefore, need an integrated strategy for stimulating production, conservation, consumption and trade. Let us deal briefly with the basic approach towards these four areas of public policy.

INCREASING PRODUCTION

There is considerable scope for increasing production in almost all the major farming systems in the tropics and sub-tropics. Even in agriculturally advanced areas as the Punjab region in India, yield levels are lower than what can be achieved. Improvement in total production has to be achieved largely through higher productivity and greater intensity of cropping. In other words, we will have to work for higher average yields in both rain-fed and irrigated areas and for an increase in the intensity of cropping (i.e. the number of crops grown in the same field during a year) in irrigated areas. Land and water use patterns have to be carefully restructured in order to optimise production from the soil, water and sunlight endowments of each area. This will call for scientific land use patterns. Our efforts to help farmers to produce more will depend upon the rapid popularisation of economically viable technology backed up by appropriate services, and public policies. Since the best 'fertiliser' to farmers is assured and remunerative marketing, there has to be a proper match between production efforts and post-harvest operations including storage, transport and distribution.

There is also considerable scope in improving the productivity of farm animals. This will need greater attention to genetic improvement of local breeds, health care, nutrition and marketing. Mixed farming practices will have to be promoted by rendering assistance to farmers in animal nutrition and health care. Both inland and coastal fisheries also provide immense potential for advance. With an exclusive economic zone of 320 km from the coast, the sea surface available to India for commercial use is about 62 per cent of its soil surface. Therefore during this decade equal attention should be paid to agriculture and to aquaculture and to the problems of small farmers as well as small fishermen. At the same time, there is need for promoting a greater awareness as well as action in the field of afforestation, soil conservation and better on-farm management of water.

TABLE 1 : **Wheat production in India**

Year	Production (in million tonnes)	Additional production over base year (in million tonnes)	Cost of additional grain (in million rupees)
1964-65 (base year)	12.3	—	—
1969-70	20.1	7.8	5850
1971-72	26.4	14.1	10575
1975-76	28.8	16.5	17325
1978-79	34.9	22.4	25099

An enduring food security system can be built only on the foundation of ecological security which would ensure that basic agricultural assets such as soil, water, flora and fauna are conserved both for current use and for posterity.

IMPROVING POST-HARVEST CONSERVATION

There are various estimates of post-harvest food losses in India. Whatever may be the statistical data, it cannot be denied that efforts in the field of conservation of both foodgrains and perishable commodities need to be greatly intensified. The losses at the post-harvest phase estimated by some experts even exceed the losses caused by the severe drought of 1979. The Government of India has promoted programmes, such as 'Save Grain Campaign' and rodent control measures. These alone will not be able to do justice to the magnitude and diversity of the problems. Unless every producer and consumer becomes conservation conscious and takes measures to prevent both quantitative and qualitative losses to food, it may be difficult to make a significant dent in this problem. Improved conservation measures assume significance particularly when the volume of agricultural trade expands. This aspect of post-harvest technology is equally important in the case of animal husbandry. There have been reports of death of poultry chicks as a result of feed grains containing aflatoxin. Aflatoxin problems arise from inadequate drying of grains. In fact, as production goes up, grain drying is becoming a difficult problem particularly for small and marginal farmers, since for them the roofs of houses and paved roads have generally been the major drying yards. This is why in rural godown schemes there is need for providing funds for the establishment of community drying and threshing facilities. We should expand our work in the area of grain, fruit and vegetable preservation and storage. If this is not done soon, neither the producer nor the consumer will derive full benefit from expanded production efforts.

PROMOTING CONSUMPTION

As mentioned earlier, efforts in increasing agricultural growth rates will either succeed or fail depending upon success in improving the consumption of major food items within the country. Consumption can be promoted only by improving the purchasing power of the rural and urban poor. Improvement of purchasing power will involve providing greater opportunities for gainful employment. How can the pace of progress in food production and employment generation be improved simultaneously?

A look at the distribution of workers in India in several decennial censuses 1911-71 shows up the historically unique fact that in spite of an impressive development of the large scale manufacturing and infrastructure sector, the share of agriculture in the work force has been around 73 per cent and has thus not diminished at all. In almost all countries, economic development is associated with a significant decrease in this share. Even during the decade 1965-75, the share declined in 13 Asian countries. In India, however, a fairly rapid growth in the non-agricultural sectors during the last 25 years of planned development has not made a noticeable impact on the industrial distribution of the work force. For these six decades, the share of mining and manufacturing in the work force has stuck around 9-10 per cent and that of the tertiary sector around 16-18 per cent. The inference is clear. The employment growth in these sectors has been insufficient to absorb an increasing size of the labour force. It is also seen that between 1961-76, in the modern factory sector, investment increased by 139 per cent and output 161 per cent, but employment increased only 71 per cent. Therefore, employment per unit of gross output decreased by 34 per cent and employment per unit of capital declined by 28 per cent. On the basis of information available, in respect of recorded employment, it is seen that the same increased from 19 million in 1967-68 to 26.5 million in 1977-78, the average annual increase being 0.75 million during this period. This means that recorded employment had accounted for just about 12 per cent of the estimated increase in the labour force. In the manufacturing sector alone, rccorded employment increased from 4.7 million to 7.0 million during this period.

As for the perspective, it may be mentioned that out of a net addition to the labour force of 33.5 million during 1980-85, even if we assume the rate of industrial growth at 7 per cent per annum, the organised sector would at best absorb about 7 million during that period. The rest has to be accommodated mainly in agriculture and in the unorganised non-farm occupations in rural areas. This situation is likely to be similar in several other developing countries.

It is generally known that unemployment in India is predominantly rural, and while the unemployment rate may not be very high, the sheer magnitude of the problem is staggering. Also, an examination of the state-wise incidence of unemployment shows that about 3/4 of the total unemployment in the country is concentrated in 7 States--Andhra Pradesh, Bihar, Kerala, Maharashtra, Tamil Nadu, Uttar Pradesh and West Bengal. Most of these states do not fall in the arid zone. There are also interstate variations in the overall level as well as seasonal variations in the unemployment rates. While formulating employment programmes for different states, the qualitative features of the problem occurring therein have to be kept in view.

The task of enhancing the income of the unorganised rural sector is complex, because employment in these sectors can mean nothing more than dependence on a variety of low-income agricultural and non-agricultural activities carried on in households or small farms or workshops. This sector has not only a severe capital shortage, but is also starved of technical and managerial support. Yet it has to bear the brunt of a fast-rising work force. Also, over 60 per cent of the total working population in the unorganised sector of the economy are self-employed in farm and non-farm activities as owners and unpaid helpers. The problems of self-employed are different from those employed in the organised sector, where employment is comparatively secure, and improvement of economic conditions can be brought about through well-organised means.

During this decade, the agricultural and informal sectors would be the principal areas for siphoning off the additional labour force. Therefore, a solution to the problem of unemployment and under-employment has to be found within the rural sector itself. Within the unorganised sector, agriculture and allied activities account for nearly 77 per cent of total employment. This share has remained unchanged since 1961. Available empirical evidence shows that within the unorganised sector, since employment opportunities in the non-agricultural activities have not been expanding, the labour force growth continues to press on the already crowded agricultural sector. The employment strategy for tackling the situation obtaining in the economy would, therefore, have to derive basically from a high rate of economic growth which is based upon an appreciation of the organic link between agriculture and the rest of the economy. In this context, a carefully designed plan for rural infrastructure build-up based on scientific resource utilisation strategies should help to absorb labour in the rural areas and also increase agricultural productivity.

This apart, the available employment potential can be exploited through a programme of irrigation, multiple cropping and improved technology, and through the development of cropping patterns and agricultural practices which would make the best use of land and water resources.

As the pressure of population on the land increases, it becomes important that the available land and water resources are managed in a scientific manner. For this purpose, there is need for horizontal co-ordination among all the concerned departments, such as agriculture, animal husbandry, fisheries, forestry, revenue, irrigation, public works, etc. Most states in India have already established land use boards. It is desirable that these are activated and made to function as land and water use boards for the purpose of optimising the economic and social benefits from units of land and water. Such boards should assemble expertise which can help to promote land and water use practices based on considerations of (i) ecology, (ii) economics, (iii) energy consumption, and (iv) employment generation.

Since land is owned individually, the method adopted will have to assist in stimulating collective or group management of certain important farm operations like water harvesting and management, drainage, soil conservation, land levelling, plant protection and post-harvest technology without affecting the individuality of farm ownership. For this purpose, suitable packages of incentives and disincentives will have to be introduced. The effectiveness of economic stimuli will be clear from the rapid spread of soy-bean in land earlier grown with an uncertain crop of rain-fed rice. Assured procurement at Rs 175 (about 21 U.S. dollars) per quintal of soy-bean brought about this shift from rice to soy-bean in the State of Madhya Pradesh in India. Irrigation departments in particular have a very important role to play in achieving the desired shifts in land use.

The other major factor is a diversification of the allied activities of rural households such as animal husbandry, horticulture, dairy, forestry and fisheries, where scope for the expansion of employment is even higher than in crop production. By the very nature of things, the employment strategy for the country would have to focus on the creation of an increasing number of self-employment avenues in the rural and urban sectors. Skilled and qualified persons would need to be enabled to become entrepreneurs for the progressive development of specified rural areas. The self-employed must learn to tackle marketing, financial and technical production problems either on their own or through co-operation with others similarly situated. Substantial enhancement of their earnings can only accrue by improving productivity through better technical knowledge, better means of production and capacity to better satisfy demand by adaptation of products. Producer-oriented marketing will play a key role in determining the economic viability of the occupations undertaken.

While the aforesaid specific policy measures have to form elements of any employment strategy, it is equally important to understand the implications of these policy measures. For instance, irrigation which is necessary for increasing cropping intensity, is a multi-dimensional variable; while substantial investment in irrigation would increase the labour absorption in agriculture by enabling changes in the cropping pattern and cropping intensity, the nature of the institutional set-up required for ensuring a more efficient use of water has to be gone into. In general, factors such as concentration of ownership, insecurity of share cropping tenancy, absentee landlordism, fragmentation and sub-division of holdings and usurious terms on which credit may be available could inhibit the utilisation of the already created irrigation potential. Again, while efficient water management may become difficult on larger farms, there is a tendency for a pre-emptive use of water by the larger farms which is made possible by the uneven distribution of land holdings and the consequent 'power pattern' in the villages. Equity in the distribution of water can be ensured by introducing the rotational water distribution system. Further, it needs to be ensured that the labour absorption possibilities of multiple cropping systems are fully realised through proper marketing arrangements.

A model of rural development which can serve the twin objectives of raising the production levels as well as the earning capacities of the poorer sections of the rural sector through the generation of additional employment opportunities, would have to focus on marginal farmers, rural artisans, women, and landless labourers. In this context, given the fact that labour absorption is relatively higher on the smaller farms, and also that labour use in crop production generally depends on the very factors which influence productivity, it is necessary to remove the constraints on the adoption of new technology by these farms. There is also the question of small farms *vis-a-vis* landless labourers which might develop; for, while the extension of the production frontiers of these farms would enhance the demand for labour, this would have implications for the wage rate, depending upon the degree of open unemployment prevalent and the relative prices of different sources of energy in any given situation. Similar problems are developing in coastal fisheries leading to confrontation between small and traditional fishermen and those owning mechanised fishing boats.

While the implementation of a well-chartered growth strategy would itself imply absorption of labour in rural asset creation, and also generate increased employment opportunities through the operation of multiplier effects, the nature and dimension of the problem of unemployment in the economy is such that given the present demographic trends, growth alone would not suffice. And where the normal growth process cannot take care of the problem, it would have to be supplemented by special employment schemes to ensure minimum number of working days at a reasonable wage to the unemployed. This may happen in areas or regions of acute unemployment and/or for specific categories of the labour force such as wage labourers, in areas where work opportunities do not grow adequately.

It would be seen, therefore, that at least during the eighties, we need a twin approach to the problem, consisting of vigorous programme of economic growth, and a specific public policy package for placing adequate purchasing power in the hands of the target groups. The special works programmes in turn could generate the requisite effective demand for sustaining the high rate of growth. It is in this context that programmes such as the Food for Work Programme, the Employment Guarantee Scheme in Maharashtra, the Operation Flood II Dairy Development Programme, and the beneficiary-oriented programmes, such as the Small Farmers Development Programme, have a significant role to perform in tackling the serious problems of unemployment and underemployment prevailing in the unorganised sector. The extent to which a co-ordinated implementation of such programmes can make a dent in the twin problems of poverty and unemployment can be seen from the fact that as much as 1.4 million person-years of 273 days a year of additional employment had been created under the food for work programme during 1978-79 with a utilisation of 1.25 million tonnes of foodgrains. In fact, during 1979-80, the allocation of 3.0 million tonnes of foodgrains under this programme helped to generate additional employment to the tune of 5-5.5 million person-years.

Such special programmes of employment could help in speeding up arrangements for drinking water supply, raising of energy plantations, land reclamation projects, soil conservation, afforestation, desilting of rivers, and works relating to village infrastructure, such as link roads, irrigation channels, land levelling, drainage, deepening of wells, and similar activities. Besides these durable physical assets, the programmes can also include social infrastructure projects which would contribute to better sanitation and public hygiene, protected water supply and the like leading to better quality of life and hence, higher productivity of labour. The projects under the special employment programmes should be as far as possible non-competitive with the normal developmental activity, and should be such as would enhance the employability of the beneficiaries and result in continuing employment to the extent possible. They should help to stabilise prices of essential commodities and prevent the fall of wages below a minimum level.

EMERGING FARMING SYSTEMS

The decisions of farmers are influenced by the entire system of agriculture around which their day-to-day life revolves. Hence, attention to the farming system as a whole is essential. It is only through such an integrated approach that agriculture can become a potent instrument of generating more jobs and income in the villages, in addition to being a source of food. Some of the existing and emerging farming systems in the tropics, particularly in India have been described in detail earlier (Swaminathan 1979).

Kitchen gardening and home fish gardening

Kitchen gardening can be one of the most efficient systems of farming from the point of view of solar and cultural energy conversion. Vegetables rich in β carotene and iron need to be developed and popularised. If planned intelligently and scientifically, backyard gardens, roof gardens and other methods of growing vegetables and fruits from whatever space is available around mud huts as well as brick houses can make a substantial contribution to improved nutrition. Where small ponds are available in large numbers as in West Bengal and Kerala, home fish gardening can be an excellent method of supplementing nutrition and income.

AGRICULTURAL GROWTH WITH STABILITY OF PRODUCTION

Estimates by FAO, the International Food Policy Research Institute and other bodies have indicated that the gap between demand and supply will continue to grow with regard to foodgrains during the rest of this century. Therefore, steps to build global and national food security systems should receive the highest priority. While an International Food Security System is yet to emerge, each country should build its own food security system. Such a system will have to include the following four major components :

(a) Ecological security, that is, protecting the land, water, flora and fauna resources in such a manner that sustained agricultural advance is possible;

(b) technological security which can help to increase and stabilise production under varying agro-ecological conditions;

(c) public policy packages which can help to stimulate both production and consumption, particularly by the small and marginal farmers on the one hand and urban and rural consumers living below the poverty line on the other; and
(d) safe storage of grains and their effective distribution.

But for a substantial grain reserve of nearly 20 million tonnes, India could not have faced the widespread drought which occurred in large parts of the country during 1979 without food import. During drought years, obviously the highest priority in relief operations will have to be given to the most seriously affected areas (MSA areas). In the matter of increasing crop production, obviously, the highest priority will have to go to the most favourable areas (MFA). MFA are those which have either irrigation facilities or adequate soil moisture to enable germination and growth of crops. By stepping up relief measures in MSA areas and by intensifying production effort in MFA regions, we can minimise, to a great extent, both hardship to the human and animal population and loss to the national food budget.

The crop production stabilisation strategy under conditions of drought will consist of :

(a) Popularisation of water conservation and crop life saving techniques;
(b) development and introduction of alternative crop strategies based on photo-insensitive crop varieties to suit different weather probabilities; and
(c) compensatory production programmes in non-traditional seasons and in irrigated areas.

The introduction of this three-pronged strategy in India during 1979 was very helpful in minimising loss to food production.

POTENTIAL AND ACTUAL YIELDS

The food production potential of most developing countries is very high but the average yields today are low. The absolute maximum production potential in terms of grain equivalent

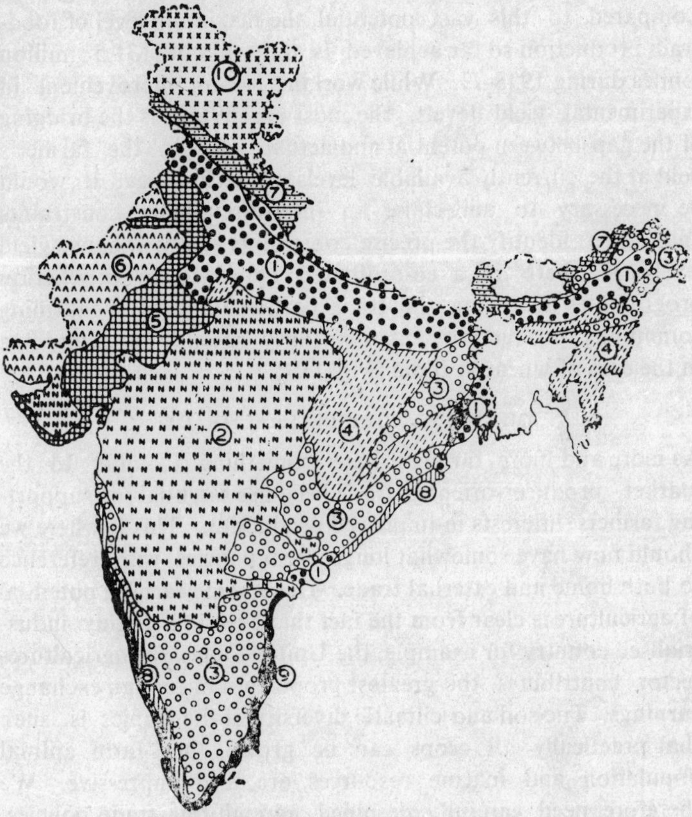

Fig. 1 : Absolute maximum production potential of different soil zones in India in terms of a grain equivalent

Maximum Production Potential million metric tonnes

Soil	
1. Alluvial	1536
2. Black Soil	1235
3. Red Soil	530
4. Red & Yellow Soil	669
5. Brown	115
6. Desert	23
7. Hill Soil	13
8. Laterite	29
9. Coastal including deltaic Alluvial	413

in different parts of India is indicated in Figure 1. Compared to this vast potential, the maximum level of food-grain production so far achieved is only about 131.5 million tonnes during 1978-79. While working for an improvement in experimental yield levels, the most urgent task is the bridging of the gap between potential and actual yields in the farmer's field at the currently available levels of technology. It would be necessary to undertake an inter-disciplinary constraints analysis to identify the precise constraints and to enhance yield levels. If there is a co-ordinated approach to production programmes involving the total participation of the farming community, production can go up fairly speedily as exemplified in the case of wheat in India (Fig. 1).

IMPROVING AGRICULTURAL TRADE

As more and more farmers have something to offer to the market, producer-oriented trade becomes essential for supporting farmers' interests in improved production. This is where we should now have somewhat longer term policies with reference to both home and external trade. The income earning potential of agriculture is clear from the fact that even in a highly industrialised country for example, the United States, the agriculture-sector contributes the greatest proportion of foreign exchange earnings. The soil and climatic diversity of the tropics is such that practically all crops can be grown. Our farm animal population and marine resources are also impressive. We therefore need carefully designed agricultural trade policies. Stability of supply, quality of produce, and competitiveness of price are the three major factors which will determine the demand for the farm products of developing countries.

Given appropriate government policies and greater resource allocation, it will be possible for Indian farmers to produce enough for our growing population and at the same time improve our entire economic well-being. During the 1970s we have changed the world's concept of India as a nation which leads a 'ship to mouth existence'. During the 1980s the task before India is to show that it has both the potential and the determination to become a major bread basket of the world. Given a right combination of political will, professional skill, and people's action, this need not remain a dream for India or indeed for most developing countries in the tropics and subtropics.

REFERENCE

Swaminathan, M.S., From begging bowl to bread-basket, *Foundation Day Lecture No. 11*, of the Administrative Staff College, Hyderabad, delivered on January 4, 1979.

DROUGHT MANAGEMENT 11

EFFECT OF THE 1965-66 DROUGHT ON FOOD PRODUCTION

ADDRESSING the Indian Society of Agricultural Statistics Sen (1967) pointed out that during the first three plan periods (1951-1966), there was a tendency for food production to show greater instability associated with an increase in the rate of its growth. Since this tendency is just the opposite of that witnessed in many of the developed nations, the reason obviously lies in the qualitative aspects of growth, namely, increased production arising from an extension in area rather than from an enhanced productivity per unit area. During the drought years of 1965-66, there was a 19 per cent drop in total food production, amounting to 17 million tonnes in quantitative terms. In spite of such a big drop, widespread famine was averted through a vigorous drive to mobilise food aid from many nations and more particularly through PL-480 food imports from the United States. During these two years the deficit from normal rainfall exceeded 50 per cent in many States. It has been postulated that a drought of this intensity and magnitude may occur only once in about 40 years. However, in relation to weather, statistics can only help to indicate trends from events which have already taken place and cannot help to foretell definitely what will happen.

OUR FOOD NEEDS AND GLOBAL TRENDS IN AGRICULTURAL PRODUCTION

In the 25th year (1972) after we became independent, we are justifiably happy that we need not beg other countries for our daily bread. Supposing a drought of the type of 1965-66 recurs in 1973-74, how shall we face it ? Will there be a drop again in food production of the order of 19 per cent and if so, what would be its impact in relation to the projected population size of 596 million and food needs of 129 million tonnes (Tables 1 and 2) ? After taking into account the government's buffer stock

TABLE 1 : **Projection of population and net domestic products**

(1967-68 prices=100)

	1967-68 (crores)	1973-74 (crores)
	Rs	Rs
Net domestic product at factor cost	282.0	384.7
Agricultural and allied services	149.7	190.0
Others	132.3	194.7
Net domestic expenditure	314.5	425.4
Net domestic product at market prices	306.7	422.4
Net imports of goods and services	7.8	3.0
	(millions)	
Population	514	596

Source : Fourth Five Year Plan 1969-74

TABLE 2 : **Required production of selected important items and projected imports and exports**

Item		Unit	Actual 1967-68	Projected 1973-74
Foodgrains		million tonnes	95.6	129.0
Cotton		million bales	6	8
Oilseeds		million tonnes	8.2	10.5
Sugar		thousand tonnes	2248	4700
High yielding varieties area covered		million hectares	8.5	24.5
Consumption of fertilisers :	N	thousand tonnes	1400	3700
	P	,, ,,	400	1800
	K	,, ,,	180	1100
Plant protection (area covered)		million hectares	54	80
Imports				
Fertilisers and their raw material		crores of rupees	212	360
Foodgrains		,, ,, ,,	518	nil
Total		,, ,, ,,	2059	2030
Exports				
Agricultural and allied products		,, ,, ,,	445	667
Cotton textiles and jute manufactures		,, ,, ,,	294	336
Total		,, ,, ,,	1199	1340

Source : Fourth Five Year Plan 1969-74 : Actual data for 1968-69.

operations, we would still need from other countries about 15 million tonnes of foodgrains, in case widespread drought again does the same damage to crop production as it did during 1965-66. Who will supply this 15 million tonnes?

The production trends in traditionally food surplus countries must be understood in relation to the fact that every nation tries to adjust its production policies in such a way that the output matches the needs of (i) the domestic market, (ii) export possibilities, and (iii) aid commitments. The trend to strictly limit production to immediate needs will grow rapidly in the developed nations from this year, since the forthcoming United Nations Conference on Environment is bound to underline the points made in recent publications, such as that of the Massachusetts Institute of Technology (MIT) team on *The limits to growth.* Using the system dynamics approach the authors (1972) of this book have pointed out that each doubling of yield from the land will be more expensive than the last one, a phenomenon referred to by them as the law of increasing costs. For example, assessing the cost of past agricultural gains, they point out that to achieve a 34 per cent increase in world food production from 1951 to 1966, agriculturists increased yearly expenditures on tractors by 63 per cent, annual investment in nitrate fertilisers by 146 per cent and annual use of pesticides by 300 per cent. The next 34 per cent increase will obviously require even greater inputs of capital and resources, if the same pathway of advance is followed. Based on a global computer model involving the five basic factors which determine growth, namely, population increase, agricultural production, non-renewable resource depletion, industrial output and pollution generation, the MIT team concludes that the earth's interlocking resources probably cannot support present rates of economic and population growth much beyond the year 2100, if that long, even with advanced technology. The point to be stressed is that the demand for zero growth rates will grow in the highly developed nations as a counter to the complex problems of the degradation of the environment, loss of faith in institutions, uncontrolled urban spread, insecurity of employment, alienation of youth, rejection of traditional values, and inflation and other monetary and economic disruptions. We may have to, therefore, depend largely on our own food production capacity if the 1965-66 weather descends on us again. How shall we feed 1/5 of humanity in a year of widespread drought? In order to deal with this question, perhaps we can start with Sen's analysis of the extent of instability in our production.

INSTABILITY IN FOOD OUTPUT

The periodicity of droughts in our country during this century has varied from region to region, the worst affected areas being Rajasthan, Gujarat, Uttar Pradesh and parts of the Deccan. Sen visualised that drought in high production areas, such as Bihar, Orissa, Madhya Pradesh, western Uttar Pradesh, coastal Andhra Pradesh or Tamil Nadu would have a much greater effect on total production than a similar drought in Rajasthan, Gujarat or the Rayalaseema areas of Andhra Pradesh. A detailed analysis of the production data during the period 1965-67 confirms Sen's conjecture. Classifying the country into four major categories with reference to instability in production, Sen suggested specific steps to reduce the instability in each category (Table 3). He urged greater attention to the category B area where instability and production are both high. A major component of the fall in food production during 1965-66 and 1966-67 was the drop in rice output by 5.3 and 6.8 million tonnes, respectively. The drop occurred during both the *kharif* and *rabi* seasons. The soil types of the areas of instability were terai, laterite, red and medium black soils in the case of rice and light and alluvial soils in the case of other crops during the *kharif* season (Table 4). The areas where the maximum reduction in food production took place are Bihar (67%), Madhya Pradesh (50%), Uttar Pradesh (40%), Maharashtra (39%), Orissa (27%) and Andhra Pradesh (25%). The States in which the reduction in yield per hectare was great were Gujarat, Madhya Pradesh, Maharashtra, Uttar Pradesh, Mysore and Orissa in 1956-66 and West Bengal and Uttar Pradesh in 1966-67. Both the autumn and winter crops suffered in Andhra Pradesh, a major rice producing area.

TABLE 3 : **Distribution of cropped area and food production over regions of instability**

	Category	Per cent contribution to cropped area	Per cent contribution to food production (1961-64)	Average yield (kg/ha)	Recommended measures
A	Stable and high yield	31	37	810	Maximise yield per unit area with intensive water use and management as in Intensive Agriculture Development Programme (IADP) and HYVP
B_1	Less stable and medium yield	27	28	700	Protective irrigation
B_2	Unstable and medium yield	15	14	630	Safe fertiliser dose and economic water use. Drought resistant and stable-yielding varieties.
C	Unstable and low yield	27	21	545	(a) Dry farming practices as moisture and soil conservation. (b) Optimum and stable economic returns per unit of water. (c) Change in cropping other than varietal pattern.

Source : S.R. Sen (1967).

TABLE 4 : **Regions of instability and predominant soil types for some principal crops of India**

Rice		Wheat		Sorghum		Bajra	
A	B	A	B	A	B	A	B
Bihar and adjacent Bengal	Alluvial, red and yellow	Bihar	Alluvial	Mysore	Light red, black	—	—
Madhya Pradesh	Red and yellow partly red and black	Madhya Pradesh	Medium to deep black	Madhya Pradesh	Light red (K) Black (R)	Tamil Nadu	Light (K) Heavy (R)
Maharashtra	Medium black	Maharashtra	Medium black	Maharashtra	Black	Maharashtra	Shallow black and brown
Andhra Pradesh	Alluvial, light red			Andhra Pradesh	Light red Heavy black	Andhra Pradesh	Red and light
Uttar Pradesh	Terai, alluvial	Uttar Pradesh	Alluvial	—	—	Uttar Pradesh	Alluvial
		Rajasthan	Red and yellow	Rajasthan	Red, sandy	Rajasthan	Red and yellow
		Punjab and Haryana	Alluvial	Gujarat	Black	Punjab and Haryana	Light, alluvial

Note : K=Kharif R=Rabi A=Region of instability B=Predominant soil type

Source : Annual Progress Reports of the All-India Co-ordinated Project on Agronomic Experiments and Simple Fertiliser Trials for 1969-71, and
Annual Progress Reports of the Co-ordinated Scheme for Investigations on Correlation of Soil Tests with Crop Responses for 1969-71.

TABLE 5 : **Percentage reduction in yield per hectare as compared to 1961-62 and the crop seasons where it occurs for some important crops**

State	Year	For some important crops								Wheat	Pulses
		Rice				Bajra	Jowar				
		Reduction (%)	Kharf	Rabi	Summer	Reduction (%) (Kharif)	Reduction (%)	Kharif	Rabi	Reduction % (Rabi)	Reduction (%) (kharif)
Andhra Pradesh	1965-66	5.2	yes	yes	.yes	17.3	23.6	yes	yes	not grown	14.3
Bihar	1965-66	6.1	nil	yes	nil	not grown	not grown			5.4	nil
Gujarat	1965-66	46.3	yes	nil	nil	nil	nil			nil	nil
Madhya Pradesh	1965-66	51.4	yes	nil	nil	nil	nil			19.3	11.3
Maharashtra	1965-66	39.1	yes	nil	nil	18 0	19.9	yes	yes	27.9	9.7
Mysore	1965-66	15.6	yes	yes	yes	nil	nil			15.0	5.3
Orissa	1965-66	15.6	yes	yes	nil	not grown	not grown			not grown	22.9
Uttar Pradesh	1965-66	30.5	yes	yes	nil	nil	nil			10.6	nil
	1966-67	43.4	nil	yes	nil	nil	nil			4.9	29.2
West Bengal	1965-66	3.1	yes	yes	nil	not grown	not grown			not grown	nil
	1966-67	4.4	nil	yes	nil	not grown	not grown			not grown	nil
Assam	1966-67	5.4	nil	yes	nil	not grown	not grown			N.A.	N.A.
Tamil Nadu	1965-66	5.6	yes	yes	nil	6.0	13.7	yes	yes	not grown	8.1

N.A. : Not available.

Source : Annual estimates of production in different crops.

A close examination of the regions and soil types given in Table 4 reveals that instability in production occurred in the alluvial and red soils of Bihar, Madhya Pradesh and Andhra Pradesh in the case of rice, alluvial, black and red soils of Bihar, Madhya Pradesh, Punjab and Maharashtra in wheat, black and red soils of Madhya Pradesh, Maharashtra and Andhra Pradesh in *jowar*, and black, red and alluvial soils of Andhra Pradesh, Uttar Pradesh, Punjab and Maharashtra in *bajra*. The reduction observed during different seasons is indicated in Table 5. While rice production was affected in many states, little or no reduction occurred in the production of millets and pulses.

The relationship between the deviation in rainfall and the fall in output of rice is indicated in Table 6. In Andhra Pradesh the reduction in production during 1965-66 was greater than what would be expected on the basis of the rainfall received. Other factors namely, pests and diseases may be involved. In general, in this state until recently the spread of high-yielding varieties of rice has been rather slow (Table 6).

MAJOR DEVELOPMENTS SINCE 1965-66

Spread of high-yielding varieties

The targets and the achievements of the High-Yielding Varieties Programme (HYVP) initiated in 1965-66 are given in Table 7. Mention is also made in Table 7 of the other developmental projects initiated during the fourth plan. The expected and actual increase in production and the extra income derived from the high-yielding varieties are given in Table 8. The increase in production is more or less in accordance with the expectations, in spite of severe drought in south India and other natural calamities such as flood and cyclone in Bihar, eastern India and the coastal regions. The impact of HYVP in reducing instability during 1960-70 has been the greatest for wheat in both areas of high and low productivity. In rice, the interaction between the levels of productivity and seasonal variation revealed that the stability in production is low even in areas of high yields and much lower in low-yielding areas, thereby underlining the role played by other factors such as the

TABLE 6 : **Changes in rice production in areas of maximum reduction during drought (1965-67)**

State	Periodicity of severe drought	Percentage reduction in total production over 1964-65		Percentage reduction in yield (kg/ha) over 1961-62		Percentage maximum deviation from normal rainfall or South-West monsoon		Percentage area under HYV
	Once in	1965-66	1966-67	1965-66	1966-67	1965-66	1966-67	1969-70
Andhra Pradesh	3-5 years	25	*	5.2	*	—10	—5	7.6
Bihar	5 years	13	67	6.1	56.5	—31	—38	10.1
Madhya Pradesh	5 years	50	5	51.4	43.0	—46	—31	3.4
Maharashtra	4-5 years	50	33	39.1	30.9	—32	—13	8.7
Orissa	5 years	27	16	15.6	5.0	—35	—31	3.8
Uttar Pradesh	3-4 years	33	40	30.5	43.4	—41	—41	22.8

* No reduction or marginal increase.

Source : S.R. Sen (1967).

TABLE 7 : **Targets envisaged in Fourth Five Year Plan for high-yielding varieties and some agricultural development programmes**

Crop	HYVP (million hectares)				Programme	Additional target in Fourth Plan (million hectares)
	End of Third and Annual Plan 1968-69	Additional target fourth Plan	Total	Coverage till 1970-71		
Paddy	2.5	6.6	9.1	4.5	Multiple cropping	9.0
Wheat	4.6	4.0	8.6	6.1	Soil conservation	5.6
Maize	0.4	1.0	1.4	0.6	Land reclamation	1.0
Jowar	0.7	2.2	2.9	1.2	Major and medium irrigation	4.2
Bajra	0.7	1.8	2.5	1.4	New area	3.2
Total	8.9	15.6	24.5	13.8	Replacement of depreciated area	2.4
					Total	27.0

Source : Fourth Five Year Plan 1969-74, Planning Commission.

TABLE 8 : **Area, production and extra return under high-yielding cereal varieties during 1970-71**

Crop	Area under HYV (million ha)	Percentage coverage by HYV	Percentage increase in production in 1970-71 over package period		Grain Price (Rs/q)	Extra gross income expected over (Rs in crores)	Extra cost involved (Rs in crores)	Net increase in income over package period (Rs in crores)	Percentage contribution to net increase in income totalled for all crops	Net increase in income/ha in area under HYV (Rs)
			Expected	Actual						
Paddy	4.45	11.81	7.83	6.22	45	325.4	137.0	188.4	12.2	423
Wheat	6.07	36.53	14.39	12.00*	75	1079.2	151.9	927.3	61.2	1527
Maize	0.61	10.37	1.86	2.88	55	102.3	9.5	92.8	6.1	157
Jowar	1.22	6.53	3.20	0.54**	50	160.0	12.1	147.9	9.8	1217
Bajra	1.42	11.34	3.16	4.02	55	173.8	14.1	159.7	10.5	1127
Total	13.8	15.08	29.84			1840.7	324.6	1516.1	100.0	

* Loss owing to logging and heavy rains.

** Reduction owing to severe drought in the Deccan.

Source : Annual Progress Report of IADP and High Yielding Varieties Programme, 1968-71.

TABLE 9 : **Benefits from major and medium irrigation schemes**

(*in million hectares*)

Source	Ultimate Potential	1950-51		1960-61		1968-69		1973-74
		Potential	Utilisation	Potential	Utilisation	Potential	Utilisation	Projected Potential
Surface water	60	16.1	16.1	21.0	19.7	26.7	25.1	32.0
Major and medium	45	9.7	9.7	14.4	13.1	18.6	17.0	23.3
Minor	15	6.4	6.4	6.6	6.6	8.1	8.1	8.7
Ground water (minor)	22	6.5	6.5	8.2	8.2	10.9	10.9	13.5
Total	82	22.6	22.6	29.2	27.9	37.6	36.0	45.5

Note : Percentage of irrigation: potential to the end of 1968-69=43.9
utilised to the end of 1973-74=53.4 (projected)

Source : Fourth Five Year Plan 1969-74.

incidence of pests and diseases in regulating rice output. In rainfed crops, for example, *jowar* and *bajra*, relative stability in yield level was achieved during 1960-70. The same is true of maize.

Infrastructure development

The drought of 1965-67 stimulated widespread interest in the exploitation of ground water and in the introduction of more efficient equipment for drilling. During 1970-71, one lakh private tubewells, 1,000 state tubewells and 1.7 lakh dug wells were developed and 2.65 lakh electrical pumpsets were installed. The benefits from major, medium and minor irrigation schemes have been steadily increasing (Table 9). There has also been greater attention to the qualitative aspects of water use, and data are now available for crops, such as wheat and rice, on the critical stages in the growth of the plant when water is needed most. Much work has also been done on the choice of crops to suit varying conditions of moisture availability, and the concept of income per 1,000 litres of water is slowly being introduced as a criterion in the development of cropping systems. Multiple cropping techniques are being developed for irrigated areas, which would help to maximise the benefits from the available irrigation facilities. The surface water resources indicate a utilisable surplus of 32 million hectare-metres of water, which could irrigate another 40 million hectares of land. The corresponding development programmes for ground water resources under the fourth plan can help to irrigate an additional 12 million hectares by better water management, conveyance and distribution (IARI 1972).*

Considerable progress has also been made since 1965-66 in improving the production and availability of fertilisers within the country. The targets for internal production during 1971-72 were 1.55 million tonnes of N, 0.45 million tonnes of P_2O_5 and 0.70 million tonnes of K_2O. There has been a steady improvement in the consumption of fertilisers, although the actual use is still far below the fourth plan target (Table 10). Slow but steady progress is also being made in the availability and use of pesticides.

* Towards Self-reliance in Agriculture, Indian Agricultural Research Institute, New Delhi. 1972, pp. 82.

TABLE 10 : **Progress of consumption of chemical fertilisers**

(*in million tonnes*)

Nutrient	1968-69 Achievement	1971-72 Achievement	Fourth Plan target (1973-74)
Nitrogen	1.15	1.78	3.20
Phosphorus	0.39	0.64	1.40
Potassium	0.16	0.34	0.90

Source : Planning Commission.

Programme development

Significant advances have been made since the last drought period in developing programmes which will help to identify and spread improved production technology speedily. In the field of research, 71 all-India co-ordinated research projects were initiated by the Indian Agricultural Research Institute (IARI) with the objective of achieving rapid advances in improving biological productivity through a critical study of complex problems by a national grid of multi-disciplinary research teams. In addition to the HYVP which started bearing results from 1967-68, special schemes for small and marginal farmers and agricultural labour, pilot projects for dry land farming and multiple cropping and programmes for the development of selected command areas have all been initiated during the fourth plan. These projects have provided considerable operational experience to our extension workers and administrators in the handling of developmental projects applicable to a wide spectrum of farming communities and cropping systems.

DIFFERENCES IN OUR TECHNOLOGICAL CAPABILITIES BETWEEN 1965-67 AND 1972-74

Besides the advantages gained in infrastructure and programme development, the most significant factors which provide room for optimism, that a drop in production of the magnitude witnessed during 1965-67 need not be permitted again even if the rainfall fails to the same or even greater extent, stem from recent scientific advances. The more important among these advances from the point of view of facing drought will now be discussed.

Development of relatively photo-insensitive crop varieties

The crop varieties used in traditional cropping systems are by and large season-bound or sensitive to factors such as the number of hours of sunlight and temperature with regard to the initiation of flowering and fruiting. We now have varieties which are relatively insensitive to photoperiod in a wide range of crops such as rice, wheat, maize, *bajra*, *jowar* and several pulses and oilseeds. Among oilseeds, sunflower is a striking example of a crop which can be grown in different seasons. The yield of wheat can be quite high even in sowings done in January in Punjab, Haryana and western Uttar Pradesh (Table 11). Hybrid maize gives better results in summer and in *rabi* seasons than during the *kharif* season, when it was traditionally cultivated (Table 12). Thus, there is now considerable scope for early or late sowing, sowing of crops in non-traditional seasons, and sowing quick-yielding strains.

TABLE 11 : **Effect of date of sowing on the yield of wheat varieties (1970-71) North-Western Plains Zone)**

(*in quintal per hectare*)

Date of sowing	Yield of variety		
	Kalyan Sona	Sonalika	Hira
9 November	57.6	58.6	63.7
29 November	51.0	56.5	51.4
19 December	43.1	46.3	43.4
8 January	39.5	43.8	40.9

Source : Annual Progress Report of the All-India Wheat Co-ordinated Project 1970-71.

Development of crop varieties which do well under moistur estress

A very fortunate characteristic of hybrids of *jowar* and *bajra* is their ability not only to give high yields under good management

TABLE 12 : **Yield of maize hybrids in different sowing seasons (Grain yield kg/ha at 15% moisture)**

Location :	Hyderabad		
Name of Hybrid :	Deccan		
Year	Kharif	Rabi	Gain in Rabi as % of Kharif
1965	5556(4)*	6719(8)	+ 20,9
1966	5796(10)	7046(9)	+ 21.5
1968	6032(7)	9776(3)	+ 62.1
Mean	5794	7847	+ 35.0
Location :	Pant Nagar		
Name of Hybrid :	Ganga 5		
Year	*Kharif*	*Summer***	Gain in *Summer* over *Kharif*
1968	5330(2)	6974(1)	+ 30.8
1969	5824(11)	8451(1)	+ 45.1
1970	4994(5)	6725(1)	+ 34.7
Mean	5382	7383	+ 37.0
Name of Hybrid :	Ganga 3		
1968	4656(3)	7779(1)	+ 67.0
1969	4905(2)	8235(1)	+ 67.9
1970	3286(2)	7232(1)	+120.1
Mean	4282	7748	+ 80.0

* Values in parentheses indicate number of trials on which mean values are based.

** Sown in February.

Source : Annual Progress Report of the All-India Co-ordinated Maize Improvement Project, 1965-71.

but also much higher yields than the earlier strains under conditions of low moisture availability. Several high-yielding varieties in some of the major cereals, millets and oilseeds do relatively well under rain-fed conditions (Table 13). They are medium to short in duration, are capable of attractive yields per day and respond very favourably to nitrogen fertilisation.

TABLE 13 : Yield and production per day of some high-yielding varieties under rain-fed conditions

Crop/Variety		Yield (kg/ha)	Duration (days)	Production per day per ha (kg)	Grain yield in kg* per kg N
Wheat	Kalyan Sona	3292	120	27	15 to 30
Bajra (Severe moisture stress)	23 A x J. 87	1133	82	14	40 to 120
	HB 3	3011	76	39	
	HB 4	2290	87	27	
	Local	641	85	8	
Jowar	CSH-1	2698	105	26	60 to 120
	Local	1685	101 to 12	13 to 17	
Rice	Jaya, Kaveri Krishna	3040	120 to 130	23 to 25	60 to 120
	Local	2332	120 to 130	18 to 19	
Castor	Aruna	1500	140	11	
	H.C. 6	450	240	2	

Source : Annual Progress Reports of the All-India Co-ordinated Projects on Rice, Wheat, Bajra, Jowar 1966-71, and A new Technology for Dryland Farming (1970).

Application of nutrients to irrigated and rain-fed crops

There have been considerable advances in recent years in the technology of nutrient supply to both irrigated and rain-fed crops. Deep placement and foliar feeding methods have yielded beneficial results in rain-fed crops (Tables 14 and 15). In the case of upland rice, the application of 50 kg N, 25 kg P and 25 kg K gave 50-100 per cent increase in yield when all the nitrogen was drilled at seeding, in Uttar Pradesh, Madhya Pradesh and Orissa. The red and yellow soils of Orissa and Madhya Pradesh, the terai region of Uttar Pradesh, the laterite soils of the west coast and the alluvial soils, in general, respond to the application of micro-nutrients such as manganese, zinc and boron during the *kharif* season. Because of the limited availability and high cost of fertiliser, the efficiency of its application should be improved. For example, a linear programming study has revealed that considerable savings can be made through an appropriate choice of fertiliser combinations (Table 16).

TABLE 14 : **Yield of dry land rice and wheat by aerial application of urea solution**

(in quintals per hectare)

Treatment	Rice		Wheat
	Bilaspur (M.P.) 44 cuts	Raipur (M.P.) 32 cuts	Kotah (Rajasthan) 24 cuts
Unsprayed	20.7	20.4	5.9
Sprayed	23.3	23.7	7.7
Percentage increase	12.5	15.4	31.0

Note :

Rice : 17.8 kg urea or 8.0 kg N in 89 litres of solution per hectare.

Wheat : 17.0 kg urea or 7.6 kg N in 73 litres of solution per hectare.

Source : R. De (1971).

Pest control and surveillance systems

Valuable data have been gathered in recent years on efficient methods of pest control. The emphasis is on integrated pest

TABLE 15 : **Grain yield (q/ha) of some crops under soil and foliar application of nitrogen**

Wheat				Rice		Hybrid Bajra		Mustard	
Rainfed		Irrigated							
Method of application (per/ha)	Yield	Method of application (per/ha)	Yield	Method of application (per/ha)	Yield	Method of application (per/ha)	Yield	Method of application (per/ha)	Yield
20 kg. N: Soil	23.7	24 kg. N: Soil	45.7	50 kg. N: 80% Basal +20% Top dressing	51.8	Foliar: 11.2 kg. N	8.2	Soil: 40 kg. N	11.1
$\frac{1}{2}$S+$\frac{1}{2}$F	30.3	Foliar	48.2	80% Basal + 20% Foliar	55.7	22.4 kg. N	10.3	60 kg. N	12.9
40 kg. N: Soil	31.3	36 kg. N: Soil	47.8	100 kg. N: 80% Basal	55.6	Soil: 22.4 kg N	8.2	40 kg. N: Soil + 40 kg N: Foliar	16.4
$\frac{1}{2}$S+$\frac{1}{2}$F	32.8	Foliar	60.8	80% Basal +20% Foliar	59.6	44.8 kg. N	10.3	60 kg. N: Soil+ 40 kg. N: Foliar	18.8
CD 5%=2.2				C.D. 5%=3.6				C.D. 5%=1.9	

Source : R. De (1971).

TABLE 16 : **Least cost combination for cereal crops based on a fertiliser cost minimising model**

Crop	Recom-mended dose N:P:K (kg/ha)	Common Practice							Minimum cost combination						
		N as ammonium sulphate (20.6% N) Rs 54/q		P as Super-phosphate (16% P) Rs 40/q		K as Muriate of Potash (50% K) Rs 55.40/q		Total cost	N as urea (46% N) Rs. 95/q		P as diammo-nium phosphate (18% N, 46% P) Rs 122/q		K as Muriate of Potash (50% K) Rs 55.40/q		Total cost
		Quan-tity reqd (q)	Value (Rs)	Quan-tity reqd (q)	Value (Rs)	Quan-tity reqd (q)	Value (Rs)		Quan-tity reqd (q)	Value (Rs)	Quan-tity reqd (q)	Value (Rs)	Quan-tity reqd (q)	Value (Rs)	
Wheat & maize	120:60.40	5.85	314.82	3.75	150.00	0.80	44.32	509.14	2.10	199.50	1.30	158.60	0.80	44.32	402
Paddy	100:60:30	4.35	261.90	3.75	150.00	0.60	33.24	445.14	1.66	157.70	1.30	158.60	0.60	33.24	349
Jowar & *Bajra*	100:40:20	4.85	261.90	2 50	100 00	0.40	22.16	384.06	1.83	173.85	0.87	106.14	0.40	22.16	302

Source : L.J. Singh and R.N. Pandey (1971).

TABLE 17 : Effect of plant protection on the yield levels in some major crops averaged over several locations and three seasons

	Jowar (CSH-1)		Bajra+		Maize		Mung (PS-7)		Gram		Mustard	
	Treated	Control	Treated	Control	Treated	Control	Treated	Control	Treated	Control	Treated	Control
Yield (Q/ha)	35.7	15.5	12.5	8.3	53.3	40.7	8.7	0.4	17.2	12.3	5.6	1.4
	62.6*	14.6*										
	80.4*	39.8**										
Chemical used	(a) Carbofuron 4 to 6 parts 100 parts of seed (b) Endosulphon 4% granules (3 applications)		Phorate or disulphoton		Endosulphon, cytrolane or carbofuron		Disyston 1.5 kg/ha		Endosulphon 0.07%		Lindane 0.1% spray twice after flowering	
Pest/ Disease	Shootfly stem borer and midge		Shootfly		Stem borer		All borer and sucking insects		Pod borer		Aphids	

* Integrated pest control using phorate, lindane and carboryl for shootfly, borer and midge respectively.

** Irrigated trial at Delhi, Udaipur, Poona and Parbhani.

+ Data at Coimbatore in 1970 under severe incidence.

Source : Annual Progress Reports of the All-India Co-ordinated Projects on Sorghum, Millets, Maize 1968-71, and Towards Self-Reliance in Agriculture (1972), IARI, New Delhi.

control involving an appropriate admixture of genetic, chemical, agronomic and biological methods of control. Dramatic increases in yield are obtained when appropriate pest control methods are adopted (Tables 17 and 18). Disease and pest warning systems are also under development for wheat and rice. An efficient disease surveillance system is already in operation in the case of wheat. The major difficulty in effective pest control has been the lack of co-operative effort on the part of the entire village community.

Multiple and relay cropping

Thanks to the development of relatively photo-insensitive crop varieties, the cultivation of three or four crops during a year has become possible in irrigated areas. Considerable data on the most profitable multiple cropping systems are being gathered under the National Demonstration Programme and the All-India Co-ordinated Agronomic Experiments Project. Yields ranging from 10 tonnes to 15 tonnes per hectare per year have been reported in these experiments (Table 19). The development of high-yielding varieties in tuber crops, namely potato and tapioca, has added a further dimension to the yield possibilities. The general approach has been the standardisation of various alternative rotation patterns, all of which are scientifically sound from the view-point of maintaining the long term productivity of the soil but from which the farmer can choose according to his capacity to mobilise inputs, market conditions and seasonal behaviour.

TABLE 18 : **Effect of carbofuron seed treatment (4% a.i.) on the yield (q/ha) of sorghum (Kharif 1970)**

Location	Yield of grain (q/ha)		Percent increase over control
	Untreated	Treated	
Delhi	36.5	54.6	49.6
Udaipur	8.8	44.1	401.3
Parbhani	15.7	34.9	122.3
Poona	12.3	36.4	195.9
Hyderabad	4.2	8.5	102.4
Average	15.5	35.7	130.3

a.i. = active ingredient.

Source : Annual Progress Report of All India Coordinated Sorghum Improvement Project 1970-71.

TABLE 19 : **Yields and total production of two- and three-crop annual sequence at various centres during 1970-71**

State	Centre/Soiltype	Crop sequence			Yield in kg/ha			Grain production per day kg/ha/day
		Kharif	Rabi	Summer	Kharif	Rabi	Summer	
Andhra Pradesh	Tirupati, Red Sandy	Rice (IR-8)	Rice (IR-8)	Rice (Hamsa)	4438	6410	3090	42.9
	Maruteru, Medium Black	Rice (IR-8)	Rice (IR-8)	Mung (P. Baisakhi)	4666	5583	910	34.1
		Rice (Pankaj)	Rice (Padma)	Rice (Kaveri)	4693	3871	2689	35.8
Uttar Pradesh	Banaras, Alluvial	Rice	Wheat	Rice	3732	5042	4309	39.4
Mysore	Mangalore, Laterite	Rice (MTU-20)	Rice (Padma)	Rice (Padma)	2450	1770	4570	34.3
Tamil Nadu	Bhavanisagar, Red loam	Rice (ADT-27)	Rice (IR-8)	Rice (CO-29)	3643	3908	5106	35.6
Orissa	Bhubaneswar, Laterite	Rice (Padma)	Rice (T-141)	Rice (Padma)	2648	1970	3127	28.8
		Jute (JRO-212)	Rice (T-141)	Rice (Padma)	1738	2055	4485	33.7

Source **: Annual Progress Reports of the All India Co-ordinated Agronomic Experiments, 1969-71.**

STEPS NEEDED TO CAPITALISE OUR TECHNOLOGICAL CAPABILITY TO FACE WIDESPREAD DROUGHT

The major differences between 1972-73 and 1965-66 can be summarised. First, we now have a larger area with assured irrigation both by virtue of several major and minor irrigation works becoming operational and the increased exploitation of ground water resources. Second, we have more fertiliser, pesticides and storage space. Third, we have non-season bound and quick-yielding varieties in the important cereals, millets, pulses and oilseeds and a better capability for rapid seed multiplication. Fourth, we have better methods of moisture conservation, nutrient supply, pest control and cropping patterns for the dry land farming areas. Fifth, multiple and relay cropping techniques capable of yielding more than 10 tonnes of foodgrains per hectare per year in the irrigated areas are now available. Lastly, we now possess considerably more operational experience in organising production and crop protection campaigns and in using the mass communication media, particularly the radio and national demonstrations, in what was recently termed as 'techniracy' (technical literacy) drives. The storage and warehousing facilities (including cold storage), are much better. All these developments have endowed us with the capacity to readjust our cropping programmes to suit emergency situations and to introduce midseason corrections in cropping systems in case of failure of monsoon. How can we take advantage of this power ?

The first requisite is the organisation of a National Crop Planning Board (NCPB) charged with the responsibility of developing alternative cropping strategies for every part of the country on the basis of different weather models. The board ought to have plans ready to meet crop failures arising from drought or floods, so as to ensure that not only does total crop production remain fairly normal under such conditions, but also, that the farmer has reasonable income and employment. It would not be adequate if the board just has paper plans, it should also make arrangements for implementing the drought-production strategies it develops. For example, we should not only have buffer stocks of grains but also buffer stocks of seeds of drought- or flood-avoiding and photo-insensitive and quick-yielding varieties of crops. Plans for the optimal use of water, fertiliser and pesticides during drought years should be developed. Seed and fertiliser reserves are as essential for crop security as grain reserves for food security.

In normal seasons, the NCPB can help in promoting rational land-use policies and in linking production with marketing possibilities so that prices can be maintained at levels which are reasonable to the consumer and remunerative to the producer. While planning at the national level is useful and necessary, the success of a plan would obviously depend upon execution at the field level. It should, therefore, be one of the essential tasks of the board to generate an awareness of the dynamics and economics of cropping systems under diverse agro-ecological conditions at the block level.

Above all, we should realise that there are limits to growth in our country also, although we are just in the infancy of the scientific upgrading of our agricultural production potential. The NCPB could also be the agency to ask and answer the following three questions suggested by the authors of *The limits to growth* before a new technology is introduced.

1. What will be the side-effects, both physical and social, if this development is introduced on a large scale ?

2. What social changes will be necessary before the new development can be implemented properly and how long will it take to achieve them ?

3. If the development is fully successful and removes some natural limit to growth, what limit will the growing system meet next ? Will society prefer its pressures to the ones this development is designed to remove ?

If we start thinking and acting on these lines, we may have every possibility of avoiding the environmental degradation of the developed nations on the one hand and the periodic recurrence of hunger from aberrant weather on the other.

EXPERIENCE OF 1979 DROUGHT

Evolution of government policies to meet natural calamities

It is but natural that a vast country such as India with variegated agroclimatic conditions should suffer periodically from different kinds of natural calamities including flood, cyclone or drought in some part or the other. There are references to famines in scriptures and other records of antiquity. But the famines in ancient and medieval India appear to have been localised, and relief was generally dependent on private charity rather than intervention by the state.

It was only in the late 19th century that a definite policy about the role of government in combating famines and scarcity conditions gradually evolved and ultimately culminated in the adoption of Famine Codes by different Provincial Governments.

The first beginnings can be traced to the investigations by Col. Baird Smith who was appointed by the Government of India to enquire into the causes of famine of 1860-61 in the North-West Province and suggest remedial measures. Col. Smith submitted three reports which, inter alia, recommended extension of the irrigation system, improvement of communications and remission of land revenue. Interestingly enough, he defined Indian famines as 'rather famines of work than of food; for, when work can be had and paid for, food is always forthcoming'.

However, the report of Col. Smith does not seem to have been utilised for meeting the situation created by the Orissa famine of 1865-67. This famine which was one of the worst in the 19th century led to the appointment of the Orissa Famine Commission under the Chairmanship of George Campbell. This commission also laid stress on improving the system of land tenure, construction of canals, streamlining of postal communications and compilation of correct figures of rainfall data and other agricultural statistics.

Although the Campbell Commission report was the first detailed and critical report of Indian famines, not much attention was paid to its recommendations. A landmark in the history of famine relief in India was, however, the appointment of the Famine Inquiry Commission under Gen. R. Strachey in May 1878.

The commission recognized 'the paramount duty of the State' to offer 'protection to the people of India from the effects of uncertainty of the seasons', and identified those areas of the country prone to drought as well as those relatively immune from it. The commission also traced the different famines from the year 1770 and listed 21 famines between 1770 and 1880 of which 8 were of great severity. The commission broadly laid down the following main principles of famine relief administration :

(a) a systematic collection and recording of agricultural and other statistics about failure of crops by a special department of the government;
(b) to provide employment opportunities to able bodied persons through relief works;
(c) to arrange gratuitous relief to destitutes through the village community;
(d) To organise a suitable system of village inspection and control;
(e) to relax the demand for land revenue by suspending or remitting it and to offer loans to small peasants who may be in need of such assistance.

One of the major recommendations of the commission related to the need for creating a separate department for the administration of famine relief and appointing a full-time Famine Commissioner to coordinate the relief activities at the time of actual scarcity. The commission also considered the question of decentralisation of financial responsibility but did not recommend such decentralization beyond the provincial level. A Provincial Famine Code was drawn up and recommended to the provinces. Arrangement and supervision of relief work at the field was entrusted to the District Collector.

Although the Famine Commission of 1880 laid down the general framework for famine relief administration, the Government of India and the provincial governments gained in experience from the subsequent commissions, notably the Indian Famine Commission of 1898 headed by Sir J.B. Lyall, the Famine Commission of 1901 headed by Mr Macdonnell and the Woodhead Commission of 1944 which enquired into the Bengal Famine of 1943. As a result of all these commissions, the Provisional Famine Code, which was first issued in 1883 for guiding the provinces, was updated and widened in scope to meet different kinds of natural calamities including drought.

After Independence, the system of financing of relief expenditure on account of natural calamities has been further streamlined and the relative responsibility between the centre and the state has been set periodically by the recommendation of the successive Finance Commissions. Steps have been initiated to prepare a Model Relief Manual for guidance of the states. Increasingly, the attention of the Government of India and the State Governments has also been drawn to the need for disaster preparedness programmes as distinct from post-disaster relief operations. Contingency plans drawn up by the State Governments and the Government of India in consultation with agricultural experts, irrigation engineers and the meteorologists are a recognition of the well-accepted principle that an ounce of preparedness is worth more than a pound of relief. At the level of the Government of India, the overall co-ordination of all drought relief and other disaster relief operations is done by the Department of Agriculture and Co-operation in the Ministry of Agriculture and Irrigation. Assistance is provided to State Governments on the basis of the guidelines given by the Seventh Finance Commission. A high level committee headed by a member, Planning Commission, determines the quantum and kinds of support to be provided by the centre. A Cabinet Committee on Drought headed by the Deputy Prime Minister takes policy decisions.

Drought of 1979

In an earlier paper compiled in September 1979, detailed information has been given on the behaviour of the south-west monsoon during 1979, yearly distribution of monsoon rainfall from 1875 to 1978 as well as the steps taken to provide relief to the affected areas. In this paper, further steps taken during October-November 1979 are summarised. The conceptual framework of the drought management strategy has been outlined in an address delivered on 14 November 1979 by the Minister for Agriculture and Irrigation at the Twentieth Session of the FAO Conference held in Rome. A detailed analysis of the south-west monsoon behaviour this year is provided in the note prepared by the India Meteorological Department. The rainfall budget relating to the south-west monsoon ends on 30 September. During the period 1 October to 21

November 1979, seasonal rainfall was in excess in Lakshadweep, Tamil Nadu, North Interior Karnataka, Gujarat, Rajasthan, Bihar Plains, sub-Himalayan West Bengal, Sikkim and Arunachal Pradesh; it was normal in Kerala, Coastal and South Interior Karnataka, Rayalaseema, Konkan and Goa, Jammu and Kashmir, Assam and Meghalaya and Andaman and Nicobar Islands. The seasonal rainfall was deficient over Telangana, coastal Andhra Pradesh, Marathwada, Madhya Maharashtra and West Madhya Pradesh. The rest of the country had scanty rainfall.

The action programme relates to mitigating hardship arising from scarcity of work, water and food associated with drought. In addition, scarcity of energy caused by reduction in hydel power generation as well as escalation in the cost of fossil fuels has added a new dimension to drought management problems. The global food and fertiliser situation emphasises the urgent need for stepping up national food production efforts by improving the efficiency of farm managements as reflected by the improved use of water and nutrients.

Early warning and timely action system

For this purpose, a crop-weather-watch group, a technology transfer group and an overall monitoring and co-ordination group have been set up in the Department of Agriculture and Co-operation of the Ministry of Agriculture and Irrigation. The drought and other calamity relief operations are co-ordinated by an Additional Secretary to the Government, who serves as the Relief Commissioner. The Relief Commissioner is also the Chairman of the Crop-Weather-Watch Group as well as the Inter-Departmental Co-ordination Task Force. Close liaison is maintained with the Director General and other staff of the India Meteorological Department who provide advice and guidance as well as information relating to the provision of applied climate services. The State Governments have been requested to set up similar monitoring and co-ordinating groups and also nominate a senior officer to work whole time as Relief Commissioner. All-party committees have been suggested at block, district and state levels to guide relief operations and assist in crop production programmes.

Food security

In the ultimate analysis, the food security of the nation can be assured only through :

(i) ecological security, that is, protecting the land, water, flora and fauna resources in such a manner that sustained agricultural advance is possible;
(ii) technological security which can help to increase and stabilise production under varying agro-ecological conditions;
(iii) public policy packages which can help to stimulate both production and consumption, particularly by the small and marginal farmers on the one hand, and urban and rural consumers living below the poverty line on the other; and
(iv) safe storage of grains and their effective distribution.

It is fortunate that the country has a reasonable grain reserve. Procurement efforts during 1979 have been maintained at satisfactory levels. Thus 8,008,207 tonnes of wheat were procured during this year. Also, as on 24 November 1979, 1,503,690 tonnes of rice have been procured. This compares with 5,468,833 tonnes of wheat procured in 1978 and 1,572,461 tonnes of rice procured up to 24 November 1978. It is essential that vigorous procurement is done in all areas which have had either assured irrigation facilities or favourable rainfall distribution. Only by maintaining reserves at a satisfactory level and by promoting scientific storage can we look forward with confidence to facing the present as well as similar situations in the future. In addition to staple grains, effective use should be made of all other sources of calories such as potato, sweet potato, tapioca and other tubers.

Insulating people in the drought affected areas from hunger

The twin approach to this problem has been the expansion of on-going 'Food for Work' programmes and the introduction of a 'Food for Nutrition' programme. It is possible that in single crop rain-fed areas, the special 'Food for Work' programme may have to be continued until September 1980. For this purpose, it is essential that a detailed portfolio of projects which can be implemented under this programme is prepared with the help of agricultural universities, institutes of technology, general universities, technical departments of State Governments and voluntary organizations. Voluntary and people's organisations can play a very important role in implementing the 'Food for Nutrition' programme in such a manner that all old and infirm persons, pregnant and nursing mothers and children are looked after properly. Women and children will need particular attention, since even under normal conditions, they may be more vulnerable to calorie deprivation.

Security of drinking water supply

Water scarcity deserves the greatest attention. In fact the crucial role of water in day-to-day life becomes apparent during a drought year and this awareness should be converted into an opportunity for strengthening on-going programmes in surface and ground water use. The 'Food for Work' programme should also be utilised for implementing minor irrigation programmes. A large number of dug wells and tube wells can be constructed in areas where the available data on ground water status indicate sufficient scope. As a long-term measure, there is both scope and need for establishing ground water sanctuaries. Steps are being taken for implementing this idea.

Energy management

Efficient management of the available resources of power, particularly electricity and diesel, will determine the size of the *rabi* crop. A detailed plan of optimising the return from the available sources of energy will have to be worked out at the block level.

Rabi production programmes

Several measures have been taken to assist farmers in the drought affected areas to get inputs at subsidised rates. Plan protection measures have been strengthened and an intensive extension drive for promoting scientific water management has been launched. The contingency plans will have to be put into effect depending upon when moisture becomes available. The immediate need is for mobile subsidy-cum-credit-cum-input supply vans which can ensure that all farmers are able to get the needed inputs on time.

Marketing and storage

Steps have been taken to ensure that farmers get the support price for soy-bean, rice and coarse grains. There is need for promoting the construction of rural godowns at a fast pace. This will help :

(i) to avoid distress sales by farmers with little or no holding capacity;
(ii) to avoid panic purchase; and
(iii) to restructure land use patterns on scientific lines.

In other words, the conservation and storage of water and foodgrains in all parts of the country have to be the most important aim of block level planning. Simultaneously, food losses of all kinds will have to be avoided. Ostentatious and conspicuous consumption will have to be curbed.

Animal saving programme

Detailed guidelines have already been issued for saving farm animals during scarcity periods through emergency feeding procedures. Cattle camps will have to be organised around sources of water, and special rations based on the fortification of available cellulosic material including wastes will have to be introduced. Enough technical expertise is available in the country for undertaking such programmes.

Priorities in action programmes

Obviously, the highest priority in relief operations will have to be given to the most seriously affected (MSA) areas. Details of the MSA districts are known to State Governments. In the matter of increasing crop production, obviously the highest priority will have to go to the most favourable areas (MFA). MFA areas are those which have either irrigation facilities or adequate soil moisture to enable germination and growth of *rabi* crops. By stepping up relief measures in MSA areas and by intensifying production efforts in MFA regions, we can minimise, to a great extent, both hardship to the human and animal population and loss to the national food budget.

REFERENCES

De, Rajat, *Fertilizer News*, 16 (1971), 72-81.

Directorate of Economic and Statistics, Ministry of Agriculture, *Annual estimates of Production in Different Crops*, (1961-70).

Meadows, D.H. ; D.L. Meadows; J. Renders; and W.H. Behrens, *The Limits to Growth*, Potomac Associates, Universe Books, New York (1972).

Saxena, P.N., *et al.*, *Indian J. Agron*, (1970-71).

Sen, S.R., Growth and Instability in Indian Agriculture, Technical Address at the 20th Annual meeting of Indian Society of Agricultural Statistics, Waltair, *Ind. J. Agri. State.*, 19. (1967), pp. 1-30.

Sen, S.R., op. cit., (1967).

Singh, L.J., R.N. Pandey, *Farm Extension Digest*, 3, (1971), pp. 214-19.

Swaminathan, M.S. ; B.R. Murty, *Production Trends in the Sixties* (1972).

Swaminathan, M.S., From begging bowl to bread basket, *Foundation Day Lecture Series*, No. 11, Administrative Staff College, Hyderabad, 4 January 1979.

SCIENTIFIC UTILISATION OF NATURAL RESOURCES The Key to Generating Opportunities for Gainful Employment

12

COUPLING SCIENCE AND TECHNOLOGY WITH NATURAL RESOURCES UTILISATION

THE MOST important among our resources are the large human population and abundant sunshine. We can find meaningful solutions to the problems of poverty, unemployment, regional imbalances and inflation only by coupling these two resources in a symbiotic interaction. This in turn, can be done if we learn to use photosynthesis in an effective way to help in solving problems in the fields of energy, income and employment generation. The photosynthetic pathway of development can help to convert the concept of 'production by masses', into reality, by enabling the members of every household to engage themselves in productive activities based on a wide range of occupations in agriculture and agro-based industries. Fortunately, this is also the pathway that can help to achieve accelerated economic development without harm to the basic life support systems and quality of environment. This can be illustrated in relation to the energy crisis facing us today.

ORGANISATION OF RENEWABLE ENERGY ASSOCIATIONS

Energy is a key input in all developmental activity. While we should intensify our efforts in oil exploration, coal utilisation and hydel and atomic power generation, the vast untapped sources of renewable energy can become our greatest strength. We need, therefore, to step up very considerably our research and development effort in the following areas.

Solar energy utilisation

For the effective utilisation of solar energy we shall require to:

(a) Increase phytomass production through extensive energy plantations consisting of fast-growing trees, particularly leguminous shrubs and trees which can provide fuel, fodder, feed and fertiliser (through biological nitrogen fixation);

(b) through the cultivation of economically viable hydrocarbon yielding plants, initiate the production of ethanol and methanol—ethanol from tapioca and methanol from wood distillation—along with charcoal;

(c) promote the more extensive use of solar-thermal devices;

(d) step up efforts both in material development and design engineering with regard to photo-voltaic applications; and

(e) capture as much solar energy as possible through the cultivation of green plants in all empty patches of land.

Animal energy and waste recycling

There are over 360 million domesticated animals consisting of cattle, buffaloes, sheep, goats etc. which are generally estimated as worth about Rs 25,000 crores. This is comparable to the investment in organised industry. This inestimable resource can play a greater part in solving our energy problems in two ways:

Biogas production from organic wastes

There is scope for a much wider use of both community and individual biogas plants for domestic purposes as well as for pumping water, lighting etc.

Direct use of animal energy

There are about 80 million work animals, most of them bullocks. They should make available, according to raliable estimates, 40 million horse power equivalent to 30,000 mega watts of electric power. There are also about 15 million animal-drawn vehicles. There is great scope for a better use of this vast source of energy both for farm operations and for transportation.

In particular, a decentralised public distribution network linked to a grid of rural godowns-cum-post harvest technology centres could be operated mainly with bullock or camel cart transportation.

Wind energy

We have hardly made a beginning to any considerable extent in the use of wind, which is particularly valuable in coastal, desert and hill areas.

Water and tidal energy

Apart from large and mini-hydel plants, simple water-wheels and other water-driven sources of power can meet, to a great extent, the domestic energy needs of people in the Himalayan region. Similarly, tidal energy could be tapped in several areas close to major river systems and oceans.

Geothermal energy

The scope for exploiting geothermal energy has been pointed out by the Geological Survey of India in several areas in the Himalaya and in the cold desert areas of Ladakh.

Thus, we have a wide array of possibilities. We should not be content with just listing them in lectures and articles. To take advantage of one or more of the above renewable energy sources, we need a blend of social and government action. People's participation and co-operation are vital to the success of these programmes. The organisation by the people in every town and block of 'renewable energy associations' could help in developing suitable energy harvesting and management strategies in each area. Detailed micro-level planning to meet the energy needs of the people for domestic, agricultural, industrial and community needs would then become possible. The needed energy could be supplied to the extent possible from renewable resources, the balance being met by fossil fuels. Such associations could also spearhead a movement for energy conservation.

PLANNING EMPLOYMENT GENERATION PROGRAMMES

On the basis of available information, the size of the labour force in India is placed at 286 million in 1980 (in the age group of 5 years and above)* and is likely to increase by about 35 million in 1985. More importantly, the youth in the age group 15-29 years constitute about 28 per cent of the population and 40 per cent of the labour force. This invaluable resource needs to be harnessed in productive activities. As against this, however, what we observe is an underutilisation and improper deployment of the human resource. As per the National Sample Survey results, the magnitude of average unemployment on daily status basis in 1977-78 for the age group 15-59 years has been estimated at 16.9 million of which 12.8 million are in the rural areas. As regards educated unemployed, tentative calculations indicate the backlog of 3 million unemployed persons in 1980 who are matriculates and above. While at one end of the spectrum, there exists the problem of providing employment to the hard core of the rural poor who are either totally unemployed or underemployed, there is at the other end an equally formidable issue of ensuring employment to the educated and the skilled manpower. To find feasible solutions, it is necessary to disaggregate the employment issue and evolve specific policies and programmes for different segments of population. The problem is not merely one of generating empioyment opportunities, but also that of providing more productive employment and more efficient utilisation of resources with a view to upgrading the production capabilities of those who have been left out of the process of economic regeneration.

Basically, employment generation and utilisation of human resources in an optimum manner would have to derive from a speedy rate of economic growth. The problem here is that employment opportunities and incomes of the weaker segments of the population would need to grow at a fairly fast rate if the sheer luck of purchasing power in their hands is not to retard the desired rate of growth of the economy. For example, in the farm sector, while a 4 per cent growth rate is technically feasible, it may not be possible to sustain it unless the capacity to purchase food is increased among the rural and urban poor.

* The size of the labour force in the age group 15-59 years is estimated to be about 251 million.

It is, therefore, necessary to view employment as an integral component of development and ensure that both in concept and implementation, employment and development become catalysts of each other. A systems approach is needed for generating self-propelling growth movements.

Ideally, only that activity should be regarded as employment which results in value added at least equal to the wage paid. In order to get rapid and feasible results, some departure from this strict criterion may be necessary in some areas. But. it would become highly dangerous if the value added does not come up to a substantial proportion of the wage paid. When assessing employment potential, account should be taken both of employment in terms of time and the value likely to be added by that employment.

Scientific mobilisation of human resources in fact means a very careful manpower and employment budgeting, sector by sector and even skill by skill. We only know the broad aspects of the problem. We have seen that despite the impressive growth of manufacturing and infrastructure sectors which has occurred in the last 30 years, the share of agriculture in the work force has not diminished. Some estimates also indicate that even with a 8-9 per cent rate of industrial growth, the organised sector would be able to absorb only a portion of the additions to the labour force. Hence, the bulk of these additions would need to be productively employed in the agricultural and allied sectors. In view of this, it seems clear that agriculture and informal sectors would be the mainstay for siphoning off the accretions to labour force for some years to come and that, therefore, the solution to the problem of unemployment or underemployment has to be found within the rural sector itself. The entire approach to economic development and employment promotion has to be based upon an appreciation of the organic links between agriculture and the rest of the economy and acceleration of the pace of agricultural and rural development.

However, as Dantwala (1978) has observed:

> There cannot be any unique relationship between the level of agricultural output or its growth rate on the one hand and employment on the other. Apart from the variations in

> basic agronomic (soil-climatic) conditions, the type of techniques and technology of agricultural production and its class bias would be important determinants of the employment effect. In simple language, what would matter is, where (apart from agronomic conditions), how and for whom the growth takes place. ...

On the question of what can be the employment strategy for those for whom agricultural development *per se* is not likely to benefit significantly, he stated:

> Apart from the chronically unemployed for whom some sort of public works would be needed, those who are unemployed for varying durations at sometime or the other do have some occupation which provides them livelihood, albeit much below the desired level. In such cases, the objectives of the employment policy should be to augment, to the extent possible, the duration of their employment in their existing occupations. . .

In this connection, he is also of the view that effective implementation of structural and institutional reforms, perhaps, has a greater employment generation potential than the so-called special programmes for the weaker sections.

If we define the hard core of the rural poor as consisting of the small farmers, rural artisans and the landless labourers, then the strategy should be to diversify the activity mix in respect of the small farmers and rural artisans and provide wage employment to the landless. In fact, the most affected group is landless labourers whose numbers may be expected to rise in the years ahead owing to demographic pressures on the available land. Agricultural labour constitutes about one-fifth of the rural work force and 50 per cent of the agricultural labour households are landless and have virtually no asset base. The landless labourers are the most underprivileged and malnourished sections of the population. Landless labourers suffer from a number of handicaps which include lack of assets, inability to mobilise credit or take risk and adverse effects of the existing power structure in the villages. For them, it is a compounded problem of unemployment and uncertain income and nutritional deficiencies; the problem is one of enabling them to attain higher and more stable incomes by enlarging the farm and non-farm job opportunities in the rural and non-rural sectors at socially acceptable wage levels. The question is one of identifying and transferring the right types of technology for them and evolving a policy which provides a blend of wage employment and self-employment avenues. What is required is a well-planned and integrated programme of family-centred poverty alleviation methodology with technology support, proper services and appropriate public policies as essential elements. The family or household approach to poverty alleviation should aim at:

(a) Economic emancipation of the family, with specific attention to women;
(b) education of children; and
(c) voluntary adoption of the small family norm.

It is proposed to initiate an all-India co-ordinated project for the development and transfer of technologies, which will help to augment the income of landless labour families through wage-cum-self-employment. This project will be jointly operated by all the major scientific agencies, Indian institutes of technology and universities.

The measures for generating employment opportunities in rural areas and mobilisation of human resources therein would have to be directed towards:

(a) A composite programme of irrigation, multiple cropping and appropriate technology and development of cropping patterns with specific emphasis on high-value, labour-intensive crops that would optimise the utilisation of land and water resources;
(b) diversification of activities of the rural households in terms of allied activities, such as animal husbandry, dairying, agro-forestry and fisheries, where the scope for extension in employment is often higher than in crop production;
(c) reorganising the credit delivery system for making

IMPROVED TECHNOLOGY AND THE POTENTIAL FOR ADDITIONAL EMPLOYMENT GENERATION IN THE FARM SECTOR

Irrigated areas

Both in irrigated and rain-fed areas, scientific land and water management practices can help to promote more avenues for employment. Thanks to the development of relatively photo-insensitive crop varieties, multiple and relay cropping will be possible in irrigated areas, if suitable crop rotations are devised. For example, some of the labour intensive crop rotations developed under the All-India Co-ordinated Agronomic Research Project of ICAR are given.

1. In the north-western region, the three-crop sequences, maize-potato-potato and rice-potato-potato, have labour requirements of 396 and 450 man-days, respectively. The four-crop sequence, maize-potato-potato-green gram (*moong*), had a labour requirement of 488 man-days at Ludhiana. This sequence yielded nearly 59 quintals of grain and 384 quintals of potato per hectare.

2. In the north-eastern region, the three-crop sequences, maize-potato-wheat, had the maximum labour requirement (341 man-days) among the various rotations tried. The four-crop sequence, maize-potato-wheat-cowpea (fodder) and rice-potato-wheat-cowpea (fodder), increased the labour requirement to 411 and 465 man-days, respectively.

3. In the eastern region, rice-potato-rice at Chiplima involved a labour requirement of 420 man-days.

Unirrigated areas

Research conducted under the All-India Co-ordinated Research Project for Dryland Agriculture of ICAR indicates that during the *kharif* season, new technology could raise employment of human labour by 19 per cent for cereals, 34 per cent for millets, 74 per cent for pulses and by about 2 per cent for oilseed crops. The recommended intercropping system provides additional employment for human labour to the extent of 52 per cent over the traditional intercropping system. The employment of bullock labour is also increased ranging between 10 per cent to 60 per cent for different crop enterprises. During the *rabi* season, the additional employment available for human labour is about 21 per cent for cereals, 29 per cent for pulses, and 31 per cent for oilseed crops. For bullock, more employment to the extent of 11 per cent for cereals, 8 per cent for pulses and about 10 per cent for oilseed crops is generated by the use of recommended practices.

Considering specific crops *jowar* amongst the cereals, *bajra* and *ragi* amongst the millets, red gram and *moong* amongst pulses and castor along with *til* and sunflower, etc. are the crops which provide significantly more employment to both human and bullock labour during the *kharif* season (Table 1).

TABLE 1. **Employment of human and bullock labour with recommended technology in dryland farming areas, crop-wise 1976—79**

(days/hectare)

Crop	No. of locations		Human labour	Bullock labour
(1)	(2)		(3)	(4)
KHARIF SEASON				
Cereals				
Jowar	7	R	70	18+0.04*
		T	56	15+0.02*
			(25)	
Maize	4	R	100	24
		T	89	23
			(12)	
Upland paddy	4	R	125	30
		T	110	27
			(14)	
Millets				
Bajra	12	R	57	17+0.60*
		T	41	11+0.01*
			(39)	
Setaria	1	R	27	9
		T	24	9
			(13)	
Ragi	2	R	114	32
		T	90	30
			(27)	(7)
Pulses				
Red gram	3	R	99	17
		T	38	10
			(161)	(70)

TABLE 2 : **Employment of human and bullock labour at different categories of farmer holdings dryland Areas**

(days/hectare)

Location	Year	Practices	Categories of farmers holding							
			Large farmers		Medium farmers		Small farmers		OVERALL	
			Human	Bullock	Human	Bullock	Human	Bullock	Human	Bullock
Hissar	1976-77	Recommended	84	14	103	8	104	8	90	12
		Traditional	58	10	101	7	97	8	72	9
		Per cent increase	45	40	2	14	7	0	25	33
Kovilpatti	1976-77	Recommended	7	1	15	3	26	6	11	2
		Traditional	5	1	15	3	17	6	9	2
		Per cent increase	40	0	0	0	53	0	22	0
Bangalore	1977-78	Recommended	NA	NA	140	26	151	40	144	31
		Traditional	NA	NA	137	26	75	30	116	27
		Per cent increase	—	—	2	0	101	33	24	15
Anantapur	1977-78	Recommended	94	26	76	24	44	18	82	24
		Traditional	79	25	61	20	34	13	67	22
		Per cent increase	19	4	25	20	29	38	22	9
Rahuri	1977-78	Recommended	15	5	229	27	61	16	83	13
		Traditional	10	4	214	23	14	3	68	9
		Per cent increase	50	25	7	17	336	433	22	44

Source: Data supplied by Dr. B. K. Rastogi, All-India Co-ordinated Dryland Farming Project, Hyderabad.

production. The application of science and technology, however, is not an end in itself but only the means to an end and even as a means, they are not always guaranteed. The tasks to be achieved are manifold. The productivity of artisans and craftsmen in rural areas has to be enhanced, by upgrading the existing processes, tools and techniques and improving their understanding of technological content often by introducing simple techniques of production for the purpose of rural adaptation. Optimal use has to be made of local natural resources including agricultural wastes, and agro-industries have to be developed. This may also entail non-conventional utilisation of local materials, such as pine needles, rice husks and the like, used as fuel in the rural areas today. Converting such wastes into brickets would enable more effective utilisation of these materials. As such, research and development efforts should be primarily directed against better utilisation of local resources through the mechanism of appropriate technology, which aims at evolving and introducing that technology which can be the most viable and the best suited under any given market input availability or given social conditions.

The mechanised units in the small scale sector suffer from a number of limitations, such as lack of resources, lack of marketing experience and know-how, paucity of funds, inadequate quality control and testing facilities. Even sales promotion and marketing research are very inadequate. These problems are further magnified if the needed or available technological improvements are not able to make the small scale units' products increasingly competitive and cost-effective. An integrated programme of supply of raw materials, improved designs, training, credit, marketing support, quality control and testing facilities is a must, if the units set up in the tiny sector are to make a significant impact on production, employment or exports.

Organisations, such as Khadi and Village Industries Commission (KVIC), Handicrafts and Handloom Boards, presently engaged in the research and development field have played a vital role which can neither be duplicated nor ignored. For this reason, sustained efforts are being made to bring these different organisations together, mobilise their support and effectively introduce appropriate technology in different areas.

Some of the areas where research and development effort is called for would be in the fields of hand-spinning, palm gur, biogas, leather, bee-keeping, non-edible oils, match manufacture, pottery and other related areas. Technological improvements in these spheres would yield far-reaching results. In the case of palm-gur and non-edible oils, immense scope for product diversification exists. Cottage match manufacture is pressed with the problem of finding effective alternatives for 'veneer' which is scarce and expensive. Product development is crucial in the case of fibre so as to tap the unexploited fibre available. Bee-keeping and the integration of aquaculture in all major farming systems merit attention. Since leather is becoming scarce on account of international demand, and a sizable number of people are engaged in this field, better methods of conserving and utilising animal skin should be devised. Special effort needs to be made to find effective alternatives to the use of scarce raw materials, such as steel and cement which are presently being used for manufacturing biogas plants.

Some of the organisations presently engaged in the task of technological improvements in rural areas are the Small Scale Industries Development Organisations (SSIDOs), Council for Scientific and Industrial Research (CSIR), Indian Council for Agricultural Research (ICAR), Khadi and Village Industries Commission (KVIC) and others. These organisations have already established a network of regional organisations capable of assisting rural and village industries. NRDC has the responsibility of commercialising various technologies developed at some of the CSIR laboratories. The SIET institute provides consultancy services besides entrepreneurial training facilities. The appropriate technology unit of the Ministry of Industry had identified various areas of industrial development which could be undertaken in rural regions in order to provide greater employment opportunities and augmentation of production in those areas. However, the task of identifying the technological needs of these different industries and mobilising and disseminating the existing technical know-how to satisfy such requirements is often beyond the competence of any one specialised organisation. Even several other related programmes, such as field testing, setting up of pilot projects, making comparative cost studies, evaluating the comparative advantages of available technologies and other such items of work require special organisational support.

The decentralised sector consisting of village and cottage industries, sericulture, coir, handlooms and handicrafts generally use traditional technology. Improvement in technology is vital in these industries if the productivity of the artisans is to be stepped up and the quality of the products made competitive in relation to the organised sector. For all these different industries, separate boards and commissions are engaged in the field of research and development.

The All-India Handloom Board runs 23 weavers service centres and 2 institutes of handloom technology. One more institute is being set up in the north-eastern region. The weavers service centres are engaged in evolving new designs and supplying them to weavers, and also in field servicing and in training. The institutes impart technological training. Technological improvement constitutes one of the requirements of the programmes of intensive handloom development projects and export production projects. As a result of the advanced technological innovations, improvements have been made to pitlooms; replacement by frame looms have taken place in some cases. Improved accessories and equipment might go a long way in effecting quality improvement.

The Handicrafts Board has set up design and technical development centres which undertake on a continuous basis technological improvement, design development, quality control, research, training and extension and organisation of artisan co-operatives. As designs form a critical input in the case of handicraft items and if the products are to find a wider and spontaneous acceptance in the world of changing tastes and requirements, the need for developing market research and consumer preference studies both in India and abroad is urgent.

There are three central research institutes under the umbrella of the Central Silk Board, one each at Mysore, Ranchi and Berhampur, 8 regional research stations and 29 extension centres. The institutes at Mysore and Berhampur cater to the needs of the mulberry silk industry while the Ranchi institute is engaged in research on tasar. Evolution of a few superior strains of mulberry, such as M-5 has been released for large scale propagation in the field needs mention. Other newly evolved mulberry strains, for example, S-35, S-54 etc. are presently under trial. Introduction of bivoltine rearing and the evolution of a number of high yielding multi-voltine breeds of silk worms and strains of mulberry are the other fields in which efforts have been made. Increased production of mulberry raw silk has been accompanied more by extension of area under food plants than improved per hectare productivity in the intensive sense. Improved practices should be evolved to more than double the present yields. In the case of both mulberry and tasar culture, a wide gap seems to exist between the results obtained at the Research Institute level and that in the field. Eri and muga culture are also beset by many technological problems both in the case of food plants and evolution of suitable high yielding races. Unless a technological breakthrough takes place, there is little chance of taking this up on a commercial scale. Further experiments should take into account the agroclimatic conditions of the country. Technological improvements by themselves hardly touch the fringe of the problem of poverty. Unless producer-oriented marketing is arranged, tribal silk producers are particularly subjected to considerable exploitation by middle men.

Technological improvement is one of the regular programmes of the Coir Board. The National Coir and Training and Design Centre at Kavaloor and the Technical Institute at Bangalore are already engaged in developing appropriate technology for improving the looms and other equipment in the coir industry. The application of technical improvements achieved so far should help to diversify the coir industry across a wider spatial horizon.

Rapid strides have been achieved by the Khadi and Village Industries Commission to promote appropriate technology in the khadi and village industries which provide a vast employment potential in the rural sector. The Jamnalal Bajaj Central Research Institute in Wardha has been engaged in creditable research activity since its establishment in 1955. Its activities have been further strengthened by the establishment of close links with the national laboratories. The Central Bee Keeping Research and Training Institute at Pune and the various pottery research organisations have also been making tremendous progress in their respective areas. The science and technology programme of the KVIC presently covers a wide range of village industries. The various research and development programmes carried on by the commission have culminated in enabling the KVIC to bring to the market new types of toilet soaps, matches, mini-power dehuskers, polishing and carding machines and utility leather articles. These qualitative improvements have already increased the productivity and earnings of the artisans and reduced their drudgery. But these improvements have merely touched the fringe of the problem of poverty to which the artisans are subjected. Considering the fact that about three million persons are currently engaged in activities within the purview of the KVIC, and its coverage extends to khadi and 25 village industries, the scope for ever widening the research work in these traditional, village and agro-based industries is tremendous. In the years to come, KVIC needs to play an increasingly important role in effecting technological improvements in the decentralised sector.

Realising the importance of the application of science and technology in the development of rural areas, the CSIR through its large number of well-equipped laboratories, institutes and other establishments, has been working on a number of research and development programmes of direct or indirect benefit to the rural population. Its experiment in the Karimnagar district and mobilising scientists for area development programmes had been novel approaches. These examples need to be multiplied speedily. Besides the CSIR, there are many other governmental and voluntary organisations already working in the field. What we actually need is a realistic appreciation of their working and identifying a focal point for coordinating the research activities of the different organisations engaged in these various sectors. There is vast scope for improving the management efficiency and productivity of the village industries through accelerated research and development effort.

REGIONAL VARIATIONS IN THE IMPROVEMENT OF PER-CAPITA INCOMES

An examination of state-wise incidence of daily status unemployment in 1972-73 shows that about 74 per cent of the total unemployment in the country was concentrated in seven states—Andhra Pradesh, Bihar, Kerala, Maharashtra, Tamil Nadu, Uttar Pradesh and West Bengal. Nearly the same proportion of urban unemployment was also concentrated in these 7 states. The position has, however, been improving in Andhra Pradesh, Karnataka, Kerala and Rajasthan. Punjab, Haryana, Gujarat, Maharashtra and Himachal Pradesh, however, have been able to show much better improvement, largely due to relatively better progress in the farm sector. A marked increase in agricultural employment generally leads to a significant growth in secondary and tertiary employment. The general position with regard to variation in per capita state incomes is indicated in Tables 3 and 4.

An analysis of the factors responsible for improvement shows that along with agricultural progress, diversified opportunities for employment grow. Karnataka and Rajasthan showed improvement in the relative position with respect to income from manufacturing and allied sectors.

TABLE 3 : **Coefficient of variation in per-capita state incomes**

(*in percentage*)

	1960-61	1975-76
Agriculture and allied sectors	14.6	25.8
Manufacturing and allied sectors	54.5	43.9
Services	39.3	36.2
Total	22.1	24.9

Source: Data from the draft Sixth Five Year Plan (1978-83).

THE FUTURE

So far, we have not been able to grapple successfully with the problems of unemployment and underutilisation of our rich

TABLE 4 : **Change in relative position of states with respect to per-capita income (1960-61 to 1975-76).**

	Position in 1960-61	
	At or above the average	Below the average
(a) Improved position in 1975-76	Gujarat, Maharashtra, Punjab, Haryana, Himachal Pradesh	Andhra Pradesh, Karnataka, Kerala, Rajasthan
(b) No change	Tamil Nadu	Bihar, Orissa
(c) Worsened position in 1975-76	Assam, Meghalaya, West Bengal	Jammu & Kashmir, Madhya Pradesh, Uttar Pradesh

Source: Data from the draft Sixth Five Year Plan (1978-83).

human resource. The growth in population has offset even the limited gains made in agriculture and industry. It is obvious that in a poor country, the only method of generating any significant level of additional employment is through the better use of locally available resources both through self-employment and public works. The National Rural Employment Project, if properly implemented, could help in ecological and economic development. The challenge lies in the preparation of a portfolio of useful projects in each block and in giving a new deal to the self-employed in the areas of technical training and support and marketing.

The challenge can be met if we can mobilise the skills of the staff and students of our universities and technical institutions for meaningful and mutually beneficial participation in regional and rural development. Over 150,000 qualified science and technology personnel are produced every year. The total stock of science and technology manpower exceeds 2.5 million, that is, nearly 5 per village. Can the task to be performed and the personnel we have trained be brought together ? Numerous isolated examples show that this can be done by promoting a symbiotic relationship between education, employment and development.